NEW SLAVERY

A Reference Handbook
Second Edition

Other Titles in ABC-CLIO's
CONTEMPORARY
WORLD ISSUES
Series

Books in the Contemporary World Issues series address vital issues in today's society such as genetic engineering, pollution, and biodiversity. Written by professional writers, scholars, and nonacademic experts, these books are authoritative, clearly written, up to date, and objective. They provide a good starting point for research by high school and college students, scholars, and general readers as well as by legislators, businesspeople, activists, and others.

Each book, carefully organized and easy to use, contains an overview of the subject, a detailed chronology, biographical sketches, facts and data and/or documents and other primary-source material, a directory of organizations and agencies, annotated lists of print and nonprint resources, and an index.

Readers of books in the Contemporary World Issues series will find the information they need in order to have a better understanding of the social, political, environmental, and economic issues facing the world today.

NEW SLAVERY

A Reference Handbook
Second Edition

Kevin Bales

**CONTEMPORARY
WORLD ISSUES**

A B C CLIO

Santa Barbara, California
Denver, Colorado
Oxford, England

Library of Congress Cataloging-in-Publication Data

Bales, Kevin.
   New slavery : a reference handbook / Kevin Bales. – 2nd ed.
      p.   cm.— (ABC-CLIO's contemporary world issues series)
   Includes bibliographical references and index.
   ISBN 1-85109-815-1 (hardback : alk. paper)
   ISBN 1-85109-816-X (ebook)
   1. Slavery—History—20th century. 2. Slavery—History. I. Title.
II. Series: Contemporary world issues.
HT867B37 2005
306.3'62'0904—dc22

                                                           2005015943

07   06   05   10 9 8 7 6 5 4 3 2 1

This book is also available on the World Wide Web as an eBook.
Visit abc-clio.com for details.

Production Team
   Acquisitions Editor: Mim Vasan
   Production Editor: Laura Esterman
   Editorial Assistant: Alisha Martinez
   Production Manager: Don Schmidt
   Manufacturing Coordinator: George Smyser

ABC-CLIO, Inc.
130 Cremona Drive, P.O. Box 1911
Santa Barbara, California 93116-1911

This book is printed on acid-free paper ∞.
Manufactured in the United States of America.

To Ernst Borinski

Contents

Preface

This book is about the newest forms of one of the oldest institutions on earth. Slavery has been part of human existence since the dawn of history. Slaves have tilled the soil, swept the floors, prepared the food, and worked and worked and worked in any number of ways from the very beginnings of civilization. In almost every culture and society there has been, at one time or another, slavery. In all of those societies, slavery has reflected the ideas, the economy, and the power relationships of the moment. At times slavery has been about legal ownership of one person by another. At other times it has been about controlling people, but not about owning them as property. Though it has taken many forms through history, slavery has always been a kind of relationship between people. It is a personal as well as a social relationship, and it is almost always an economic relationship, for slavery is about making a profit from the work of others. Sometimes it has also been a legal relationship. The important point is that slavery is dynamic, reflecting local customs and practices, but also changing over time.

We live in a world that is changing rapidly, and slavery is changing rapidly as well. For example, slavery has always been part of war. In the past, slaves might be taken on the battlefield or captured in raids. In the Crusades of the Middle Ages, enslaving the enemy was part of the strategy for victory, as well as a way to finance the war effort. In the twentieth century, mass slavery became part of the mass warfare of 1939–1945. The German war effort relied on millions of enslaved men, women, and children. Many of these slaves worked to construct the very weapons that would be used to enslave others. Since World War II, the pace of social and technological change has accelerated. As the twentieth century turned into the twenty-first, very rapid change was sweeping the world. Some of the most important changes have been the end of colonialism, the population explosion, and the end of the Cold War, followed quickly by the globalization of technology, culture, and the economy. These changes have also brought the evolution of new forms of slavery. The most important change concerns the price of slaves.

Today slaves are cheaper than they have ever been in human history. The population explosion has created a vast supply of potential workers, and the rapid economic changes of the past fifty years have ensured that many of these people are desperate and vulnerable and easily enslaved. Because they are so cheap, slaves today fulfill a new role in the economy. They are no longer thought of as major investments; they are used and disposed of according to the whims of their slaveholders. But the profits they generate are remarkably high even though they are normally used in only the most basic kinds of work. Today slavery is a very profitable business.

Slaves are found in almost every country. Altogether, there are millions of slaves in the world—concentrated in the developing countries, but exploited in the United States, Europe, and Japan as well. The rapid change in the way slavery operates means that governments, other organizations, and the public are still trying to understand today's slavery. In the United States, many people still think of slavery in terms of the slavery of the American South before the Civil War. The reality is much more fluid and more difficult to see. As part of the criminal economy, slavery is hidden from view. But as part of the global traffic in human beings and their exploitation, we know that it is growing. This book aims to illuminate the slavery of today and to show how it is changing.

It has to be recognized that there is still a great deal to learn about slavery. Since many people believe that slavery was abolished long ago, only a few people are researching it or campaigning against it. Governments and other organizations are only recently coming to grips with the volume and extent of slavery in the economy. So this book is just a beginning, a starting point for people who want to be part of the quest to understand slavery. Reading and using it should help to clarify what we now know (and what we still need to learn) about slavery. It points to the sources, organizations, and people that will carry the reader still further. The aim of this book is not to have all the answers but to be a tool that will help you find the answers to your own unique questions about slavery.

Chapter 1 defines slavery and gives examples of slavery today. It gives estimates of the number of slaves in the world and describes their conditions. The process of change that has created new forms of slavery is traced, and the key factors that comprise slavery are discussed. In order to clarify the nature of slavery, the slavery of the American South in 1850 is compared and contrasted to the slavery of today. Since the notion of "race" or ethnicity is much less important to an understanding of contemporary slavery, this shift from slavery based in racism to slavery centered on vulnerability is explained.

Chapter 2 looks at slavery around the world. Case studies provide examples of these forms. The process of globalization is linked to changes in the nature of slavery, and this process and those changes are examined. Once a picture of contemporary slavery has been drawn, this question is addressed: Who is responsible for global slavery? Since many people look to the United Nations to take the lead on the issue of slavery, the role of the UN and its work are examined. One of the areas that the UN is especially concerned with is the transport, and often enslavement, of illegal migrants. This is called human trafficking, and it is a growing problem.

Other groups and organizations are involved in the work against slavery. Examples of these organizations and descriptions of their work are given for the international, national, and local levels. Many of these groups are concerned with directly liberating slaves and then helping them through rehabilitation, and that process is examined. Chapter 2 concludes by considering the important question: What can we do?

Chapter 3 looks at slavery in America. Human trafficking brings people from all over the world to be slaves in the United States. They are trapped in sweatshops, worked in the fields, held as servants in the homes of the economically privileged, and forced into prostitution. It is a large and complex criminal enterprise and happens, often, right under our noses.

Chapter 4 presents a chronology of slavery worldwide, with emphasis on key events in the last fifty years; Chapter 5 contains a selection of biographical sketches of modern abolitionists and a few historical figures as well. Most of the individuals included in the biographical sketches will be unfamiliar to readers. The ones listed here are just a sample, some suggested by antislavery activists and some from my own experience of researching slavery around the world. Young antislavery workers have been singled out for inclusion. Of course, many people around the world work to combat slavery in near anonymity. In the developing world, as you will read in these sketches, working against slavery can be a dangerous business, and researchers and campaigners have been killed trying to free slaves. Those who work at the more dangerous grassroots level often prefer to keep their identities secret to protect their families. For that reason, the names of some real heroes in the struggle against slavery may never be known.

Chapter 6 presents facts, data, evidence, and firsthand testimony about modern slavery. After some basic statistics about slavery are identified, the key international laws and conventions on slavery are reviewed. Relevant excerpts from these laws and conventions are reproduced here with brief introductions. Most of Chapter 6 is given over to reports, evidence, and testimony about different forms of slavery. These may be press reports, radio transcripts, interviews, statements to the United Nations (UN), or the personal accounts of being a slave. Evidence is given for each of the following types of contemporary slavery: bonded labor, contract slavery, chattel slavery, war slavery, slavery linked to religious practice, forced labor, commercial sex slavery and trafficking, domestic slavery, and slavery linked to child labor.

Chapter 7 lists and describes those organizations concerned with fighting slavery. These include international, national, local, and overseas groups, but with a special emphasis on the key American antislavery organization, Free the Slaves. A special effort has been made to provide links, mostly through the Internet, with organizations in the developing world that are so often ignored in Western media. The information about all these organizations was current at the time of writing, but since these are fluid and dynamic collections of human beings, they are continually changing, reorganizing, restructuring, and expanding or contracting like all human groups.

Chapter 8 lists all sorts of resources. Slavery receives relatively little attention, and the number of printed works is not large. In an area concerned with a human rights violation like slavery, much of what is written is produced by campaigning groups rather than academics or professional writers, and consequently many of the listed works are briefing papers or reports. In many ways, the nonprint resources listed in Chapter 8 are more rich and varied than the print resources. Many filmmakers have worked to open the subject of slavery and have produced investigative programs exploring the issue and depicting the lives of slaves. These are listed along with other resources, such as exhibitions, posters, press kits, and digital images that can be downloaded from the Internet.

Preface to the Revised Edition

There has been great and rapid change since *New Slavery* was first published, change that seems to be growing in its momentum and reach. New laws have been passed, a new UN Convention has come into force, and, especially, a new awareness of slavery has grown in the American public. As this awareness of modern slavery expanded, other books, films, scripts, poems, articles, law reviews, photo essays, theses and dissertations, songs, even a dance program, expressed people's deeply felt desire both to understand and to end slavery. For me personally, the growth in interest led to hundreds of interviews on television, radio, and in magazines and newspapers. It is an explosion of concern that is being felt at the local, national, and international level.

One of the most exciting changes is the establishment of Free the Slaves, the first broadbased antislavery organization in modern America. Set up in late 2000, just after *New Slavery* was finished, Free the Slaves is based in Washington, DC, and has been joined by thousands of Americans who seek to end slavery. In its very short life, Free the Slaves has achieved breakthrough after breakthrough: forging an agreement with the chocolate companies to take slavery out of their product chain, playing an instrumental role in getting new antitrafficking laws passed at both the state and federal level, supporting the liberation of child slaves in India and West Africa, educating the public, and bringing together clubs, churches, schools, universities, and individuals to fight slavery. It works against human trafficking and slavery in the United States and across the globe. Sometimes it does so by advising governments, but most importantly by backing up those grassroots groups that are literally kicking in doors and bringing slaves to freedom. Imagine my joy when I get an e-mail like this one from India:

> We had a rescue operation and rescued seven children from a carpet loom in Allahabad. All seven children are aged between 10–12 years. Two of them are very sick, suffering from jaundice, and the others look malnour-

ished . . . after medical check ups they will be sent to Bal Vikas Ashram for rehabilitation. Their parents have been contacted.

Slave children in the carpet looms are often kidnapped at the age of seven or eight. Their desperate parents won't see them for years. Americans help bring these children out of slavery by joining and supporting Free the Slaves, which, in turn, helps fund rescue and rehabilitation in India and other countries. As a father and a son, my heart swells when I think about how these lost children are found and returned to their families.

I hope that this revised edition of *New Slavery* speaks to you. I've been helped by the many people who have read this book and talked to me about it. There are likely to still be errors, and these are all mine.

Kevin Bales
Oxford, Mississippi

Acknowledgments

This book benefited from the help, guidance, and hard work of a number of people. Foremost among these is Sally Ramsden, a London-based journalist well known for her work in development and human rights. She provided the research behind much of this book. Catherine Prior helped to construct the database used in Chapter 6. In the United States, Jenni Trovillion, Caroline Tendall, and Jacob Patton did a superlative job on Web-based searches and editing. The London-based organization Anti-Slavery International holds one of the best archives and information centers on contemporary slavery; without access to that resource, this book could not have been written. Mary Matheson, Mike Dottridge, David Ould, Becky Smaga, Jen Escher, Jeff Howarth, and Beth Herzfeld, all Anti-Slavery International staff, guided me through their library and checked my work to make sure I and my associates had not missed anything. Much of the work on the first edition of this book was done while I was on a sabbatical leave from my post at the School of Sociology and Social Policy at Roehampton University in London, England. The support of the Roehampton University, and especially Professor Graham Fennell, was very important. The writing was made much easier by the hospitality, support, and stimulating company provided by the Croft Institute for International Studies at the University of Mississippi and its director, Professor Michael Metcalf.

For the Revised Edition, Eden Hegwood was a most able and punctilious research assistant who deserves much credit for her excellent work. Lauren Welford, a student at the Croft Institute, provided essential help just as it was needed. The errors and omissions in this book, of course, all belong to the author. Gabriel Bales provided diversions, riddles, and jokes.

1

Background and History

Most of us think that slavery ended a long time ago—or that if it does exist, it only happens in poor countries far away. Maybe that is one reason why Hilda Dos Santos stayed in slavery for so long in the affluent suburbs outside Washington, DC. Hilda had worked as a domestic servant in her native Brazil for many years, and when her employers, Rene and Margarida Bonnetti, asked her to move with them to the United States in 1979, she agreed. Once in the United States, the Bonnettis stopped paying Hilda and locked her into a life of slavery. She cleaned the house, did the yardwork, cooked the meals, cared for the pets, and even shoveled snow without gloves, boots, or a coat. Her bed was a mattress in the basement, and she was not allowed to use the showers or bathtubs in the house. Her food was scraps and leftovers, and when Hilda made mistakes in her work, she was beaten. Mrs. Bonnetti once poured hot soup over her face and chest when she didn't like the way it tasted. When a cut on Hilda's leg became infected, the Bonnettis refused to provide medical care. A stomach tumor grew to the size of a soccer ball without any help from the Bonnettis; a neighbor finally took her to the hospital. It was there that social workers were alerted to her situation and the law stepped in. She had been in slavery for twenty years.

Hilda Dos Santos is typical of many slaves in the world today—poor, vulnerable people who are tricked into slavery. Her case demonstrates that slavery is alive and well. If her case was unique it would be shocking enough, but Hilda is one of thousands of slaves in the United Sates, and one of millions of slaves in the world. The slavery she suffered is much the same as the

1

old kinds of slavery we learn about in history. Slavery is still about one person controlling another, taking away an individual's free will and abusing and stealing his or her life and livelihood. But slavery today is also different, for slavery has evolved into new—and in some ways more destructive—forms that stretch through our global economy to touch us wherever we are.

What Makes a Slave?

Slavery has been with us since the beginning of human history. When the first Stone Age people begin to congregate in Mesopotamia and make the first towns around 6800 BC, they built strong external walls around their towns suggesting a situation of raiding and war. Drawings in clay that survive from 4000 BC show captives taken in battle being tied, whipped, and forced to work by ancient Sumerians. Papyrus records from 2100 BC record the ownership of slaves by private citizens in Egypt. Slavery has been with us so long that it came before both laws and money. After slavery had been around for about 2,000 years, we find the first record of the price of a slave: eleven silver shekels. Not long afterwards, slavery as a business enterprise takes off, and records show slave raiding expeditions from Egypt capturing 1,554 slaves in Syria. About one hundred years after that, around 1790 BC, the very first written laws introduced the legal status and worth of slaves. The basic idea in these Babylonian laws, that slaves are worth less than "real" people, is repeated off and on through human history for the next 4,000 years. The ancient Babylonian code is gruesomely clear: a physician making a fatal mistake on a patient, for example, is ordered to have his hands cut off, unless the patient is a slave, in which case he only has to replace the slave. For most of human history, the right to inflict violence on a slave was enshrined in law.

Unfortunately, when the legal ownership of slaves ended, as it did in the United States in 1865, many people thought that slavery ended as well. They were confusing *ownership* with *control*. This is not to diminish the great achievements of the abolitionists and the slaves who fought for their freedom—if there are thousands of slaves in the United States today, it is worth remembering that there were once millions. Even with legal abolition, slavery never stopped; and as it has done for thousands of years, control over slaves today means violence. But if people are not legally recorded as being slaves, how can we really call them slaves? A good place to start is to look at someone's life and ask, "Can this person walk away from the situation they are in without fear of violence?" If the answer is "no" or the reality is that if they try to leave they will be beaten, then you have the beginnings of slavery. You might also ask, "Are they paid nothing, or does their pay just keep them alive from one day to the next?" This is another good indicator of slavery. Look again at Hilda Dos Santos, her free will was taken from her, she couldn't leave under a threat of violence, she was paid nothing and was given only enough food to keep her alive, and she was economically exploited. She was a slave.

Slavery Defined

Since the abolition of legal slavery in the nineteenth century, the word "slavery" has been used to describe many different things: prostitution, prison labor, even the sale of human organs. More than 300 international slavery treaties have been signed since 1815, but they rarely used the same definition. Before we can define "slavery," we need to recognize the characteristics and conditions that make it what it is. Slavery is a relationship between two people. It is both a social and economic relationship and, like all relationships, it has certain characteristics and rules. The key characteristics of slavery are not about ownership but about how people are controlled. Throughout history, the core characteristic of slavery, whether it was legal or not, is *violence*. The slave master or slaveholder controls a slave by using or threatening violence. Slavery is about no choices at all, no control over your life, and a constant fear of violence. This is the key to slavery. Violence brings a person into slavery. Many people who become slaves are tricked into it. Many people, following a trail of lies, walk into enslavement, but what keeps them there is violence. Once enslaved, there are all sorts of ways that slaves are held in slavery—sometimes it is the way the slave gives up and gives in to slavery, sometimes it is about the personal relationships that develop between slaves and slaveholders—but the essential ingredient is violence.

The second key characteristic of slavery is *loss of free will;* slaves are under the complete control of someone else. There is no other person, authority, or government the slave can turn to for protection. Slaves must do as they are told or they will suffer. The third characteristic is that slavery is normally used to *exploit* someone in some kind of economic activity. No one enslaves another person just to be mean; people are enslaved to make a profit. Most slaveholders see themselves as normal businesspeople. They have little interest in hurting anyone, in being cruel, or torturing people; it is just part of the job. Slavery is about money. If we put these characteristics together we can define slavery in this way: *Slavery is a social and economic relationship in which a person is controlled through violence or its threat, paid nothing, and economically exploited.*

In some ways this is a narrow definition. It excludes many things that people have called "slavery" (like the selling of human organs), but it includes all those relationships that most people agree are slavery, and it is broad enough to include many kinds of slavery around the world.

A definition that works for many different types of slavery is important because slavery, like all human relationships, changes over time. The main characteristic of slavery is control through violence, but that can take many forms. In those few places where old styles of slavery are still practiced, like Mauritania, there are long-term, often lifelong relationships between slave and master. In most countries, slavery is more short term and dangerous.

How Many Slaves?

No one knows exactly how many slaves are in the world. Slavery is illegal in virtually every country, and that means it is usually hidden from view. But if we carefully review all the information available about slaves around the world, we can estimate that there are perhaps 27 million slaves alive today. Where are all these slaves? The biggest part of that 27 million, perhaps 15 to 20 million, is in India, Pakistan, and Nepal. Slavery is also concentrated in Southeast Asia, Northern and Western Africa, and parts of South America, but there are some slaves in almost every country in the world, including the United States, Japan, and many European countries. To put it in perspective, today's slave population is greater than the population of Canada and six times greater than the population of Israel.

Slaves tend to be used in simple, nontechnological, traditional work that feeds into local economies. The largest proportion works in agriculture. Other kinds of work include brick making, mining and quarrying, textiles, leather working, prostitution, gem working and jewelry making, cloth and carpet making, domestic service, forest clearing, charcoal making, and working in shops. Much of this work is aimed at local sale and consumption, but slave-made goods filter throughout the global economy. Carpets, fireworks, jewelry, metal goods, steel (made with slave-produced charcoal), and foods like grains, rice, cocoa, and sugar are imported directly to North America and Europe after being produced using slave labor.

The Nature of Contemporary Slavery

As a human relationship, slavery has changed over time. Of course, slavery remains the same in that one person has complete control of another person, but exactly how that can occur changes from time to time and place to place. Slavery today is different from slavery in the past in three important ways. First, slaves today are cheaper than they have ever been. The cost of slaves has fallen to a historical low, and they can be acquired in some parts of the world for as little as $10. Second, the length of time that slaves are held has also fallen. In the past, slavery was usually a lifelong condition; today it is often temporary, lasting just a few years or even months. Third, slavery is globalized. This means that the forms of slavery in different parts of the world are becoming more alike. The way slaves are used and the part they play in the world economy is increasingly similar wherever they are. These changes have come about very quickly, occurring, for the most part, in the past fifty years. What has made these new forms of slavery possible?

How Slavery Changed into Its Modern Form

There are three key factors in the emergence of this new kind of slavery. The first is the *dramatic increase in world population* since

World War II, which has increased the supply of potential slaves. In a classic example of supply and demand, the increase in population has also driven down their price. Since 1945, the world population has tripled from about 2 billion people to over 6 billion. The greatest part of that increase has been in those countries where slavery is most prevalent today. In some of these countries, over half the population is under the age of fifteen. In countries that were already poor, the sheer weight of numbers sometimes overwhelms resources. Especially in those parts of the world where slavery still existed or had been practiced in the past, the population explosion increased the number of people who could be enslaved.

The second key factor is *rapid social and economic change*. This has been caused in part by the population explosion that created global conditions that make new forms of slavery possible. In many developing countries, the postcolonial period brought immense wealth to the elite and continued or increased the poverty of the majority of the population. Throughout Africa, Asia, and much of South America, the past fifty years have been scarred by civil war and the wholesale looting of resources by dictators, who were often supported by the powerful nations of Europe and North America. Countries with little to sell on the world market have been put deeply into debt to pay for the weapons the dictators needed in order to hold on to power. Meanwhile, traditional ways of agricultural life and farming were sacrificed to concentrate on cash crops needed to pay off those foreign debts. As the world economy grew and became more global, it had a profound impact on people in the Global South and the small-scale farming that supported them. The shift from small-scale farming to cash-crop agriculture, the loss of common land shared by all the people in a village, and government policies that pushed down farm income in favor of cheap food for city workers have all helped to bankrupt millions of peasants and drive them from their land. All across the Global South, the slums and shantytowns that surround big cities hold millions of these displaced people. They come to the cities in search of jobs but find they are competing with thousands of other people. With little income and no job security, they are powerless and very vulnerable.

Some national and global policies and trends also threaten these vulnerable and displaced people. The United States government pays $19 billion annually to subsidize American farmers. For example, it hands over $4 billion each year to cotton farmers in return for a crop that is valued at only $3 billion. This hits cotton farmers in Benin, Mali, Burkina Faso, and Togo—all countries with high levels of slavery and human trafficking. The European countries also pump money into the pockets of their own farmers, creating an unfair advantage on the world market. All this money pushes down the price of crops, leaving the farmers in the Global South unable to compete and locked in poverty. Although economic modernization may have good effects as well, particularly in improvements to health care and education, many developing countries concentrate on economic growth rather than on sustainable livelihoods for their people. While the rich people of the Global South grow richer, the poor have fewer and fewer options, and in the disruption that comes with rapid social change, slavery can become one of those options.

The end of the Cold War and the ending of state control of the economy in the former Soviet Union also served to widen the opportunities for slavery. William Greider explained it well:

> One of the striking qualities of the post–Cold War globalization is how easily business and government in the capitalist democracies have abandoned the values they putatively espoused for forty years during the struggle against communism—individual liberties and political legitimacy based on free elections. Concern for human rights, including freedom of assembly for workers wishing to speak for themselves, has been pushed aside by commercial opportunity. Multinationals plunge confidently into new markets, from Vietnam to China, where governments routinely control and abuse their own citizens. (Greider 1997, 37)

Government corruption is the third key factor that supports this new form of slavery. Just having large numbers of vulnerable people doesn't automatically make them slaves. In order to turn vulnerable people into slaves on any scale, violence must be used. One of the basic ideas about democratic government is that it should have a monopoly on the means of violence. The military and the police are generally the only ones who can use weapons and commit violence legally, doing so to protect citizens from crime. But if anyone in a society can use violence for their own ends, without fear of being arrested and imprisoned, then they can force others into slavery. To do that on any scale requires government corruption, and especially police corruption. In some countries, the police act as slave catchers, pursuing and punishing escaped slaves. Often police require that people holding slaves pay them weekly for police "protection." For many slave-using businesspeople, payments to the police are just a normal part of making a living. When laws against kidnapping are not enforced, those who have the means of violence (often the police themselves) can harvest slaves.

Old and New Slavery Compared

The population explosion, the vulnerability of poor people in the Global South, and government corruption has led to new forms of slavery. For the first time in human history, there is an absolute glut of potential slaves. It is a dramatic example of supply and demand. There are so many possible slaves that their value has fallen and fallen. Slaves are now so cheap that they have become cost-effective in many new kinds of work. Their value is so low that it has dramatically changed the basic economic equation of slavery. Slaves are no longer major investments. This fact has changed the nature of the relationship between slaves and slaveholders. It has also increased the amount of profit to be made from a slave and decreased the length of time a person might be enslaved. And it has also made the question of legal ownership less important. When slaves were expensive, it was important to safeguard that investment by having clear and legally documented ownership. Slaves of the past were worth stealing and worth chasing down if they escaped. The fact that ownership of slaves is now illegal is not really a problem for slaveholders; slaves are disposable.

Disposability means that the new forms of slavery are less permanent. Across the world, the length of time a slave spends in bondage varies enormously. It is simply not profitable to keep slaves when they are not immediately useful. Although most are enslaved for years, some are held for only a few months. In countries where sugarcane is grown, for example, people are often enslaved for a single harvest. Since they are used only for a short time, there is no reason to invest heavily in their upkeep. There is also little reason to ensure that they survive their enslavement.

TABLE 1.1
Old and New Forms of Slavery Compared

Old Forms of Slavery	New Forms of Slavery
Legal ownership asserted	Legal ownership avoided
High purchase cost	Very low purchase cost
Low profits	Very high profits
Shortage of potential slaves	Surplus of potential slaves
Long-term relationship	Short-term relationship
Slaves maintained	Slaves disposable
Ethnic differences important	Ethnic differences less important

Although slaves in the American South in the nineteenth century were often horribly treated, there was still a strong incentive to keep them alive as long as possible. Slaves were like valuable livestock; the owner needed a return on his investment. There was also pressure to breed them and produce more slaves, since it was usually cheaper to raise new slaves than to buy adults. Today no slaveholder wants to spend money supporting useless infants.

Table 1.1 lists key differences between old and new forms of slavery. This makes more sense when we look at an example. Perhaps the best studied and understood form of old slavery was the system of slavery in the American South before 1860, particularly the use of slaves in cotton cultivation (see, for example, Ransom 1989). Slaves were at a premium. The demand for slaves was reflected in their price. By 1850, an average field laborer was selling for $1,000 to $1,200. This was three to six times the average yearly wage of an American worker at the time; in today's money it would equal around $40,000. Despite their high cost, slaves generated, on average, profits of only about 5 percent each year. If the cotton market went up, a plantation owner could make a very good profit on his slaves, but if the price of cotton fell, he might be forced to sell slaves to stay in business. Ownership was clearly demonstrated by bills of sale and titles of ownership, and slaves could be used as collateral for loans or to pay off debts. Slaves were often brutalized to keep them under control, but they were also maintained as befitted their sizable investment. And there was, of course, extreme racial differentiation between slaveholder and slave. The racist element was so strong that a very small genetic difference—being one-eighth "black" and seven-eighths "white"—could mean lifelong enslavement (Genovese 1976, 416, 420).

Now compare the old slavery of the American South with the agricultural slave in modern India. In India today, land rather than labor is at a premium; the country currently has three times the population of the United States in one-third the space. The glut of potential workers means that free labor must regularly compete with slave labor, and the resulting pressure on agricultural wages pushes free laborers toward bondage. When free farmers run out of money, when a crop fails or a member of the family becomes ill and needs medicine, they have few choices. In a perilous situation, they borrow enough money from a local landowner to meet the crisis but, having no other possessions, they have to use their own lives as collateral. The debt against which a person is bonded, that is, the price of a laborer, might be as high as 5,000 to 10,000 rupees (about $100 to $200), but it may be as low as 1,000 rupees (about $20). The bond is completely open-ended; the slave must work for the slaveholder until the slaveholder decides the debt is repaid. The debt might be carried into a second and third generation, growing under fraudulent accounting by the slaveholder, who may also seize and sell the children of the bonded laborer against the debt. The functional reality is one of slavery.

Agricultural debt bondage in India still has some characteristics of older forms of slavery, such as slaves being held for long periods of time. A better example of new forms of slavery is the young women put to work in prostitution in Thailand. A population explosion in Thailand has resulted in a surplus of potential slaves. Rapid economic change has led to new poverty and desperation. Young Thai women and girls are often initially lured from rural areas with the promise of work in restaurants or factories. There is little ethnic difference; if anything, the key difference is rural (slaves) versus urban (slaveholders). The girls might be sold by their parents to a broker or be tricked by an agent. Away from their homes, they are brutalized and enslaved and sold to a brothel owner. The brothel owners place the girls in debt bondage and tell them they must pay back their purchase price plus interest through prostitution. The calculation of the debt and the interest is, of course, completely in the hands of the brothel owners. Manipulating the figures to their advantage, they can keep the girls as long as they want, and they don't need to show any legal ownership. The brothels do have to feed the girls and keep them presentable, but if they become ill or injured or too old, they are disposed of. In Thailand today, this often happens when a girl tests positive for HIV. This form of "contract" debt bondage is extremely profitable. A girl aged twelve to fifteen can be purchased for $800 to $2,000, and the costs of running a brothel and feeding the girls are relatively low. The profit is often as high as 800 percent a year. This kind of return can be made on a girl for five to ten years. After that, especially if she becomes ill or HIV positive, the girl will be dumped.

The Question of Race

In the new forms of slavery, race means little. In the past, ethnic and racial differences were used to explain and excuse slavery. These differences allowed slaveholders to invent reasons why slavery was not only acceptable, it even benefited the slaves. The *otherness* of the slaves made it easier to use the violence and the cruelty necessary for total control. This otherness could be defined in almost any way—a different religion, tribe, skin color, language, customs, or economic class. Any of these could be used to separate the slaves from the slaveholders. Maintaining these differences required tremendous investment in some very irrational ideas, and the crazier the justifying idea, the more strongly it was insisted upon. The "Founding Fathers" of the United States of America had to go through moral, linguistic, and political contortions to explain why the "land of the free" only applied to white people (Quarles 1975). Many of them knew they were lying, that they were betraying their most cherished ideals. They were driven to it because slavery was worth a lot of money to a lot of people in Colonial America. They still went to the trouble of legal and political justification because, at that time, they felt they had to make moral excuses for their economic decisions.

Today the morality of money overrides most others. Most slaveholders feel no need to explain or defend their choice to use slavery. Slavery is a very profitable business, and a good profit is reason enough. Freed of ideas that restrict the status of slave to "other" and of ideas that say you can't enslave your own people, modern slaveholders use other criteria to choose slaves. When you can enslave people from your own country, your costs are low. Slaves in the American South were very expensive, in part because the first generation of them had to be shipped thousands of miles from Africa. When you can go to the next town or region for slaves, transport costs fall to a minimum. The question isn't "Are they the right color to be slaves?" but "Are they vulnerable enough to be enslaved?" The criteria of enslavement are not about color, tribe, or religion; it is about weakness, gullibility, and vulnerability.

It is true that in some countries there are ethnic or religious differences between slaves and slaveholders. In Pakistan, for example, many enslaved brick makers are Christians, and the slaveholders are Muslim. In India, slave and slaveholder may be of different castes. In Thailand, they might come from different regions of the country. But in Pakistan, there are Christians who are not slaves, and in India some members of a caste are free while others are enslaved. Their caste or religion simply reflects their vulnerability to enslavement; it doesn't cause it. Only in one country, Mauritania, does the racism of old slavery persist. There, black slaves are held by Arab slaveholders and race is a key division, but this is the last and fading survival of old slavery. Of course, some cultures are more divisive than others. Cultural ideas in Japan strongly separate Japanese people from everyone else, and so enslaved prostitutes in Japan are more likely to be Thai or Philippine women, though they may also be Japanese. The key difference is that Japanese women are not nearly so vulnerable and desperate as Thais or Filipinas. And the Thai women are available for shipment to Japan because Thais are enslaving Thais. The same pattern occurs in the oil-rich states of Saudi Arabia and Kuwait, where Muslim Arabs might enslave Sri Lankan Hindus, Filipino Christians, or Nigerian Muslims. The common denominator is poverty, not color. Behind every assertion of ethnic difference is the reality of economic disparity. If every left-handed person in the world were made destitute tomorrow, there would soon be slaveholders arguing that slavery was perhaps the best thing for them. Modern slaveholders are color blind, but they are predators acutely perceptive to weakness. Although slavery has been around for thousands of years, these predators are rapidly adapting it to the new global economy.

Cheap to buy, easy to dispose of, extremely profitable— these are the attributes of the modern slave. If the emergence of the global market has helped to develop new forms of slavery, what does this mean for the slaves themselves and for our lives? In the next chapter we explore how slavery touches the life of almost every person on Earth, and what the United Nations, governments, and people just like you are doing about it.

References

Davis, David Brion. *The Problem of Slavery in the Age of Revolution 1770–1823*. Oxford: Oxford University Press, 1975.

Genovese, Eugene. *Roll, Jordan, Roll: The World the Slaves Made*. New York: Vintage, 1976.

Greider, William. *One World Ready or Not: The Manic Logic of Global Capitalism*. New York: Simon and Schuster, 1997.

Quarles, Benjamin. *The Negro in the American Revolution*. Chapel Hill: University of North Carolina Press, 1961, reprint edition 1996.

Ransom, Roger L. *Conflict and Compromise: The Political Economy of Slavery, Emancipation, and the American Civil War*. Cambridge: Cambridge University Press, 1989.

Note

Parts of this chapter have been adapted or excerpted from my book *Disposable People: New Slavery in the Global Economy* (Berkeley: University of California Press, 1999) by permission of the publisher.

2

Problems, Controversies, and Solutions

To best understand the problem of contemporary slavery, it is necessary to look at the forms it takes and real examples of the suffering it causes. Then, it is important to take up some of the controversies that are linked to slavery. It may seem hard to imagine that anything could be controversial about slavery—after all, isn't almost everyone opposed to it? But while virtually everyone agrees that slavery must end, there are strong disagreements over *how* to end slavery. In particular, there is vigorous debate about how slavery and prostitution fit together, and another controversy about whether is it right to buy slaves their freedom, also known as *redemption*. Finally, this chapter will introduce groups that are working to fight slavery and explore how we can solve this global problem. Here there is some good news: even though 27 million people are in slavery, this is a problem that can be solved.

The Forms of Contemporary Slavery

Slavery has never existed in a single form. In some ways, every relationship of slavery that links two people might be unique, but there are patterns in these relationships. There are several forms of slavery common enough to have their own names. The three main types given here are not an exhaustive list, but they do represent the experience of most modern slaves:

15

Chattel slavery is the form closest to old slavery. A person is captured, born, or sold into permanent servitude, and ownership is sometimes asserted. The slave's children are normally treated as property as well and can be sold by the slaveholder. Occasionally, these slaves are kept as items of conspicuous consumption. This form is most often found in Northern and Western Africa and in some Arab countries, but it represents a small proportion of slaves in the modern world.

Debt bondage is the most common form of slavery in the world. A person pledges him/herself against a loan of money, but the length and nature of the service is not defined, nor does his or her labor diminish the original debt. The debt can be passed down to subsequent generations, thus enslaving offspring, or "defaulting," can be punished by seizing or selling children into further debt bonds. Ownership is not normally asserted, but there is complete physical control of the bonded laborer. Debt bondage is most common in South Asia.

There are, in fact, two distinct forms of debt bondage. In many cases of debt bondage, the slaves' work (and indeed their very lives) becomes *collateral* for the debt. This means that all of their work belongs to the moneylender until the debt is repaid. This establishes the trap of bondage—since all their work is the property of the lender until the debt is repaid, debtors are unable to ever earn enough to repay the debt by their own labor. This arrangement is the most common form of debt bondage in India. In other places, the work of the debtor may, supposedly, be used to pay off the debt, but through false accounting or charging very high interest, repayment remains forever out of reach. In the first form, the agreement that changes the debtor and all his or her work into collateral essentially means the debtor will never be able to repay his or her debt. In the second form, it is a violation of the loan agreement when the value of the work is not really used to pay off the loan that traps the debtor.

Contract slavery shows how new forms of slavery are hidden. Contracts are offered that guarantee employment, perhaps in a workshop or factory, but when workers are taken to their place of work, they find they are enslaved. The contract is used as an enticement to trick persons into slavery; it is also a way to make the slavery look legitimate if necessary. Ownership is not asserted, and if legal questions are raised the contract is produced, but the slave is under threat of violence, has no freedom of movement, and is paid nothing. This is the most rapidly growing form of slavery, and it is probably the second largest form today. Contract slavery is most often found in Southeast Asia, Brazil, some Arab states, and some parts of the Indian subcontinent.

These types are not mutually exclusive. Contracts may be issued to chattel slaves in order to conceal their enslavement. Girls trapped into prostitution by debt bondage will sometimes have contracts that specify their obligations, but not always. The important thing to remember is that *people are enslaved by violence and held against their wills for exploitation.* The labels we apply to the types of slavery are useful to help us keep track of the patterns of enslavement and for what they might suggest about how slavery might be attacked. The labels reflect the nature of the relationship between the slave and the slaveholder, but these relationships are fluid and changeable.

In addition to these three main types of slavery, several other kinds account for a small part of the total number of slaves. Most of these tend to be restricted to specific geographical regions or political situations. A good example of slavery linked to politics is what is often called *war slavery,* and includes government-sponsored slavery. In Burma (also known as Myanmar) today there is widespread capture and enslavement of civilians by the government and the army. Tens of thousands of men, women, and children are used as laborers or bearers in military campaigns against indigenous peoples or on government construction projects. The Burmese military dictatorship doesn't suggest that they own the people they have enslaved—in fact, they deny that they enslave anyone—but the International Labor Organization (ILO), U.S. State Department, and human rights organizations confirm that violence is used to hold a large number of Burmese people in bondage. War slavery was also a feature of the recent civil war in Sudan, as well as the ongoing civil war in Uganda, where children are enslaved and forced to be soldiers.

In some parts of the Caribbean and in Western Africa, children are given or sold into domestic service. They are sometimes called *restavecs.* Ownership is not asserted, but strict control, enforced by violence, is maintained over the child. The financial return on the enslaved child is not in terms of profits generated but in the domestic services provided. It is sometimes seen as a culturally approved way of dealing with "extra" children, and some are treated well, but for most of these children it is a kind of slavery that lasts until adulthood.

Slavery can also be linked to religion, as with the *devadasi* women in India, or the children who are ritual "Trokosi" slaves in Ghana (Australian Anti-Slavery Society 1996). Each year, several thousand girls and young women are given by their families as slaves to local fetish priests in southeastern Ghana, Togo, Benin, and southwestern Nigeria. The girls are given to the priests in order to atone for sins committed by members of their families, often rape. The girls may, in fact, be the products of rape, and their slavery is seen as a way of appeasing the gods for the crimes committed by their male relatives. The girls are given to a local priest as a slave when they are about ten years old, and it is required that they be virgins. The girl then stays with the priest, cooking and cleaning, farming, and being sexually exploited by the priest until he frees her, usually after she has borne several children. At that point, the slave's family must provide another young girl to replace her. Ghana's Constitution forbids slavery, and a law was recently passed banning Trokosi, but the practice is justified by villagers and priests as a religious requirement.

As can be seen by the preceding cases, slavery comes in many forms and can be found in virtually all countries. A recent investigation found hundreds of men and women enslaved as agricultural workers in Florida (Bowe 2003). Enslaved domestic workers have been found and freed in Washington, DC (Castaneda 2003). In the United States, textile workers have been found locked inside a factory and working under armed guards. Enslaved Mexican, Thai, and Philippine women have been freed from brothels in New York, Seattle, Los Angeles, and many other cities (Landesman 2004). This list could go on and on. Almost all of the countries where slavery "cannot" exist have slaves inside their borders. Altogether, slaves constitute a vast workforce that supports the world economy we all share.

Examples of Contemporary Slavery

Lives Up in Smoke

In a recent survey, around a third of all American high school students said that they used tobacco at least once in the last month. That students should be doing something so stupid is alarming, but what is even worse is that many of them were supporting slavery as they smoked. Thousands of students said that they had been smoking *beedis*—small, flavored cigarettes from India. Would they have done so if they knew that most beedis are made by slave children?

In the southern Indian state of Tamil Nadu, outside the big city of Madras, are small towns where millions of beedis are made. On the outskirts of one of these towns lives an eleven-year-old boy named Vikram. He and many of the other children in his town are slaves. When Vikram was nine, his younger brother became very ill. His family is very poor, and the only way his parents could buy medicine was to borrow money from a local man. This man controls the production of beedis in their village. This moneylender used the loan as a way to take Vikram into debt bondage. Since Vikram's parents had nothing else to give as collateral, the moneylender said they must pledge Vikram against the debt. His parents' choice was a terrible one: to save the life of their youngest son, they must put their oldest son into bondage. For the moneylender, it was business as usual, and he had obtained another slave for just a few dollars. Today none of the work that Vikram does pays off the debt. He is basically the property of the moneylender until his parents can find the money for repayment. Two years after it was first made, the debt has grown with extra charges to about $65.

Vikram works from six in the morning until nine at night, with breaks for breakfast and lunch. Each day he rolls about 1,500 beedi cigarettes by hand. Each beedi is smaller than a normal cigarette, and instead of paper, the tobacco is wrapped in a leaf from the kendu tree. Since no glue is used, each beedi must be tied shut with a thread and a tiny knot. Sitting cross-legged on the floor with a tray of tobacco and kendu leaves on his lap, Vikram's hands fly through the motions of wrapping, rolling, and tying the beedis. He has to work very quickly, like a machine, if he is to make the number required of him everyday. If he is sick, he still has to work, and if he fails to deliver the full number, his debt will be increased. He can watch the world, or a very small piece of it, from the porch where he sits rolling the beedis, but he cannot be part of it. Some of the local children go off to school in the mornings; he sees them go as he rolls beedi. In the afternoon, other children play around the village, and Vikram watches but cannot join in. His childhood has been taken by the moneylender to provide virtually free labor and high profits.

In some ways, Vikram's slavery could be worse. At night he is allowed to go home for supper and to sleep with his family. Of course, this is very clever of the moneylender, since it means that he doesn't have to provide food or lodging for his slave. Vikram, like so many modern slaves, was very cheap to buy and is also very cheap to maintain. Until recently, a boy in Vikram's position would have little to look forward to except years spent rolling beedis. Many children have had their whole childhood taken by beedi rolling. When they become young adults the moneylender will often turn them to other kinds of work, since their larger hands are not as nimble for rolling beedis. When they finally stop rolling beedis, they are young men with no education and little experience of the world. Their job prospects, if they can get away from the moneylender, are dismal.

Slavery in the City of Lights

In France I interviewed an animated twenty-two-year-old woman who told me of her life as a slave in Paris:

> I was raised by my grandmother in Mali, and when I was still a little girl a woman my family knew came and asked her if she could take me to Paris to care for her children. She told my grandmother that she would put me in school and that I would learn French. But when I came to Paris I was not sent to school, I had to work every day. In their house I did all the work, I cleaned the house, cooked the meals, cared for the children, and washed and fed the baby. Every day I started work before 7 AM and finished about 11 PM; I never had a day off. My mistress did nothing—she slept late and then watched television or went out.
>
> One day I told her that I wanted to go to school. She replied that she had not brought me to France to go to school but to take care of her children. I was so tired and run down. I had problems with my teeth; sometimes my cheek would swell and the pain would be terrible. Sometimes I had stomachaches, but when I was ill I still had to work. Sometimes when I was in pain I would cry, but my mistress would shout at me.
>
> I slept on the floor in one of the children's bedrooms; my food was their leftovers. I was not allowed to take food from the refrigerator like the children. If I took food she would beat me. She often beat me. She would

slap me all the time. She beat me with the broom, with kitchen tools, or whipped me with an electric cable. Sometimes I would bleed. I still have marks on my body.

Once in 1992 I was late going to get the children from school. My mistress and her husband were furious with me and beat and then threw me out on the street. I had nowhere to go, I didn't understand anything, and I wandered on the streets. After some time her husband found me and took me back to their house. Then they beat me again with a wire attached to a broomstick until I lost consciousness.

Sometime later one of the children came and untied me. I lay on the floor where they had left me for several days. The pain was terrible but no one treated my wounds. When I was able to stand I had to start work again, but after this I was always locked in the apartment. They continued to beat me.

Seba was finally freed when a neighbor, after hearing the sounds of abuse and beating, managed to talk to her. Seeing her scars and wounds, the neighbor called the police and the French Committee Against Modern Slavery (CCEM), which brought a case against Seba's abusers and took Seba into care. Medical examinations confirmed that she had been tortured. Today Seba is well cared for, living with a volunteer family. She is receiving counseling and learning to read and write. Recovery will take years, but she is a remarkably strong young woman. What amazed me was how far Seba still needs to go. As we talked, I realized that though she was twenty-two and intelligent, her understanding of the world was less developed than that of an average five-year-old. For example, until she was freed, she had little understanding of time—no knowledge of weeks, months, or years. For Seba, there was only the endless round of work and sleep. She knew that there were hot days and cold days, but she never learned that the seasons follow a pattern. If she had once known her birthday she had since forgotten it, and she did not know her age. She is baffled by the idea of "choice." Her volunteer family tries to help her make choices, but she still can't grasp the concept. I asked Seba to draw the best picture of a person she could. She told me it was the first time she had ever tried to draw a person, and this is the result:

If Seba's case were unique it would be shocking enough, but Seba is one of perhaps three thousand household slaves in Paris. Nor is this slavery unique to Paris. In London, New York, Zurich, Los Angeles, and across the world children are brutalized as household slaves. And they are just one small group of the world's slaves. We are beginning to understand the extent of slavery around the world and the suffering it causes. Interestingly, while slaveholders commit this horrible crime, they may not be the biggest challenge that we face in bringing an end to slavery. The problem is that slaveholders are able to enslave their victims without being noticed; there is a basic lack of awareness of the problem. While it is true that awareness is growing, most people in most countries still find it hard to understand that slavery is around them. In part, this is due to the fact that while 27 million slaves is the largest number of slaves in human history, it is the smallest *proportion* of the world's population to ever be in slavery due to the growth in the world's population. When slavery grew rapidly after World War II, it did so behind the curtain of crime, and few people noticed. Following from that lack of awareness is a lack of resources devoted to ending slavery. If you take all the money spent to fight slavery around the world and add it together, it is about the cost of a bomber, certainly less than an aircraft carrier, and a tiny fraction of the money spent on the "war on drugs." Awareness drives the public to push the politicians to spend money on problems the public is worried about. Not enough of the public is aware of slavery, so politicians don't make it a high priority. A well-resourced global campaign could end slavery, but for the time being, we are still trying to figure out the best ways to fight it with few resources and less experience. It is not always clear how best to combat slavery, and given that any mistake or confusion can lead to greater suffering, there are strong debates about the best way to bring slaves to freedom.

Controversies

Controversy 1—Are We All Responsible for Global Slavery?

The people who enslaved Vikram and Seba are clearly criminals, but if responsibility for slaveholding is extended to those who profit from it, we have to confront a shocking ethical problem. Those who profit from slavery might include you or me or anyone. Pension funds or mutual funds may be buying stock (which is, after all, part-ownership) in companies that own companies that subcontract slave labor. Some key questions are: How many links have to stand between a slave and an "owner" for them to be held responsible? Is ignorance an excuse? If your job were to depend on the availability of slave-produced raw materials, where would you stand? There are, in fact, several layers of responsibility. But how much responsibility does the average person carry for the eradication of slavery? William Greider points out that:

> The deepest meaning of the global industrial revolution is that people no longer have free choice in the matter of identity. Ready or not, they are already of the world. As

producers or consumers, as workers or merchants or investors, they are now bound to distant others through the complex strands of commerce and finance reorganising the globe as a unified marketplace. The prosperity of South Carolina or Scotland is deeply linked to Stuttgart's or Kuala Lumpur's. The true social values of Californians or Swedes will be determined by what is tolerated in the factories of Thailand or Bangladesh. (Greider 1997, 333)

If people do not participate in slavery through investment, they almost certainly do through consumption. Slave-produced goods and services flow into the global market, making up a tiny but significant part of what we buy. But the sheer volume of our consumption overwhelms our ability to make responsible choices. We don't have time to research the living conditions of the people who produced everything we buy. And if we *could* ask these questions, how would we go about it? Is it the responsibility of the local supermarket to investigate labor relations around the world, or is it to get you the best food at the lowest price? We also have to think about what happens when we get answers we don't like. For example, Haitian men, women, and children have been enslaved to harvest sugarcane in the Dominican Republic—sugar exported to the United States and other countries. Is the average consumer ready to pay $5 for a candy bar if that is what it takes to ensure that the producers are not enslaved and that they receive a decent wage? When enough research reveals where and how slave-made goods enter our lives, there will be an even bigger question to face: How much is the average person willing to pay to end slavery? Meanwhile, most people assume that the problem should be dealt with by governments and the United Nations, yet the power of the UN turns out to be less than that of consumers.

Controversy 2—Is It Right to Buy Slaves?

In Southern Sudan, a western charity pays $50 per person to free Dinka people. They have been enslaved after their villages were raided by militia linked to the Sudanese government. In Northern India, a group of women band together to form a small credit union; over a period of months they save enough to repay the debt that holds one of their members in bondage, then they begin to save to buy another woman's freedom. Today, with 27 million slaves in the world, redemption (making a payment to free a slave) can and does happen anywhere. But why is this happening? Is this the right way to free slaves?

While there has been controversy over slave redemption in the United States in the past few years, it actually has an extensive history. Long before there was slavery in the United States, slaves were being redeemed. In Greece, Rome, and other ancient societies, slaves were sometimes purchased from their owners and freed. During the Crusades, enslavement and ransom were central components of war finances and strategy. The first organizations that can be thought of as charities were set up in the Middle Ages in order to purchase the freedom of Europeans captured and enslaved by North African and Middle Eastern pirates and slave raiders. Indeed, one verse in the U.S. *Marine's Hymn*— "to the shores of Tripoli"—refers to an early nineteenth-century raid on these Barbary pirates to stop their slave raiding and ransoming of Europeans and Americans. Frederick Douglass, the famous nineteenth-century abolitionist and escaped slave, was himself redeemed after supporters of slavery had mounted a series of attempts to kidnap him.

The simple economic exchange of money for the freedom of a slave that is redemption has to be seen within its cultural context. Before slavery was illegal in most countries, redemption was an act of charity, in itself perfectly legal. Many cultures have a tradition of redemption, including those in Northern African countries such as Sudan. Today, however, within the context of the general illegality of slavery, the buying of slaves, even in order to free them, is seen by many people as complicity in a crime. The complexity of the civil war and the preexisting role of slave trading in Sudanese society are often overlooked. Redemption is presented as a moral imperative by some, while others see it as fuel to the fire of further enslavement.

While redemption can go on around the world wherever slavery exists, it came to the attention of most Americans when groups like Christian Solidarity International began to buy back slaves in Sudan. Slave raiding in Sudan was part of the government's strategy to destroy the resistance of the Southern groups that are fighting for independence. While slavery existed for hundreds of years in Sudan, it almost disappeared in the twentieth century but was reestablished as an act of terror in the civil war there. Controversy arose when European and American groups began to buy back slaves in 1995. Some international agencies expressed the criticism that buying back slaves would create an expanding market for slaves, feed resources to the slaveholders, lead to fraud in the process, and would not ultimately end slavery.

Not long after these criticisms emerged, I spoke with a man from Southern Sudan who answered them in this way: "Of course we understand that the money paid to buy back our relatives may go to buy arms to be used against us in the future, but when it is your family, your children at stake, you pay." Likewise, a man involved in redemption pointed out to me that there may have been fraud (the "buying back" of people who had never been enslaved), but he asserted that "it is better to buy back some people who have never been slaves, than to fail to rescue the many who are suffering in slavery." On the question of whether redemption in Sudan has brought a greater risk of slave raids, there is insufficient evidence to make a clear judgment.

The process of redemption must also be seen in its cultural context. The civil war has been marked by recurrent truces between the Dinka and the Baggara tribesmen who comprise the majority of the militia, truces that have provided the opportunity to recover, usually at a price, family members as well as livestock. Equally, the Nuer and Dinka tribes of Southern Sudan, while now allied against the Muslim North, have long been in a conflict that includes raiding between the two tribes. In early October 1999, their leaders met to discuss "the return of women, children, and cattle captured in raids or abducted during the years of hostility between the tribes" (*Sudan Democratic Gazette* 1999). The fact that the victims of slave raiding have themselves raided other tribes has rarely been mentioned in the Western press.

If there is good news about the controversy over redemption in Sudan, it is that the civil war there has entered a new stage and fewer raids are taking place while peace talks continue. The U.S. government has become involved and has exerted significant pressure on the Northern government to end the raids and come to an agreement with the Southern provisional government. However, the hoped-for ending of the need for redemption in Sudan will not resolve the questions that surround redemption. On the other hand, this change may allow us to enlarge the discussion to include how redemption fits into antislavery work around the world.

In India, for example, redemption is actually illegal. The law against debt bondage forbids that "debts" are repaid to bring slaves into freedom. The reason is that, since these debts were offered and manipulated illegally in the first place, they have no standing. Further, there is a resistance to "rewarding" any slaveholder. Since slavery itself is universally illegal, slaveholders should no more be recompensed for giving up slaves than a burglar should be paid to return the television he stole from your house. That said, in India there are situations where, primarily because the police are slow to respond to the crime of slavery, redemption is the only immediate and effective way to remove a person from danger.

The lesson to be drawn from these examples is this: redeeming slaves has a role in the antislavery movement, but only when other actions have failed or are impossible. In one way, it is the lesser of several evils. The greatest evil is enslavement. Paying a slaveholder or a middleman to free a slave is a regrettable, lesser evil since freedom is a basic human right and shouldn't need to be purchased. Yet, when the authorities will not take action, where the opportunity for freedom is available only through redemption, and where enslaved people are suffering and threatened, then redemption may be the only immediate answer. A good case can be made both for and against redemption; a key criterion has to be that it be used *only* when it won't make things worse. It is a tactic in an overall movement against slavery, one to be used when other actions won't serve. Sadly, the controversy over redemption has been bitter, and some groups and organizations have stated that they will not work with anyone who disagrees with their view on redemption. Ultimately, it is the slaves that suffer when the abolitionists fight. The same waste of energy and suffering has been caused by another controversy as well—the fight over prostitution.

Controversy 3—Is Prostitution Slavery?

There is no doubt that women around the world are enslaved and forced to be prostitutes. What is more controversial is how many prostitutes should be considered slaves and what should be done about it. On the one hand, there are those who believe that all prostitution is a form of slavery and that the exploitation of individuals through prostitution should be eliminated and the perpetrators punished (Barry 1995). On the other is the view that only forced or nonconsensual prostitution should be prevented by international standards and criminal law (CSEH 1998). Advocates of the first view argue that all prostitution is forced, explaining that women are "forced" to become prostitutes through violence or because of lack of money or other financial pressures. This point of view widens the meaning of "forced" beyond the threats of violence, intimidation, or coercion normally linked to slavery—although it is clear that the threat of starvation is a powerful coercion, especially when a society systematically denies opportunity to women. It was proposed by the Council of Europe that "forced prostitution" be defined as the "act, for financial gain, of inducing a person by any form of constraint to supply sexual services to another person" (Hirsch 1996). Constraint would include the more obvious forms of violence, such as beatings, rape, torture, and threats. It was suggested, however, that "any form of constraint" should be interpreted more widely to include the act of obtaining sexual services from a person "by taking advantage of his/her vulnerability resulting either from his/her precarious or illegal situation, or of his/her position of economic dependence." If this definition is used, practically every prostitute in the world could be considered "forced," and therefore enslaved.

On the other side of the argument are those who feel that prostitutes have an "outcast status" that "denies them whatever international, national or customary protection from abuse is available to others as citizens, women or workers. This social exclusion renders the prostitute vulnerable to exploitation" (Bindman 1997). They admit that prostitution can occur in situations of terrible exploitation, even slavery, but that it can also occur in situations where the prostitutes have some control over their lives and "work." This viewpoint argues that if prostitution is illegal, then the human rights of prostitutes will never be respected, and the cycle of their outcast status and exploitation will continue.

This controversy intensifies when solutions are being debated. Essentially, if all prostitution is slavery, then all prostitution should be illegal and the people (usually men) who use or exploit prostitutes should be punished. On the other hand, if women are stigmatized and marginalized because prostitution is illegal, then their "sex work" should be made legal and given health and safety protections. Also, if prostitution is illegal, then, in many countries, the women themselves will be the main target for prosecution and harassment by police. For example, a group based in Calcutta, India, has found that, on average, approximately nine out of ten arrests made under the "Immoral Traffic Protection Act" were of women caught in prostitution. There were few arrests and fewer penalties for traffickers or the men that used prostitutes (U.S. State Department 2002). On both sides of the issue people agree that organized crime gets involved in prostitution, even when it is legalized, and criminals have little interest in caring for their "workers."

Meanwhile, Swedish lawmakers have taken a novel approach. In 1999, Sweden passed a law that criminalized the purchase, but not the sale, of sex. According to the Swedish law, the economic and social relationship between a woman selling sex and a man buying sex is not a relationship that even approaches equality. The rationale behind the law is that as long as society remains male dominated, women selling sex will be in a more vulnerable position than men buying sex. Men's ability to buy women's bodies is seen as a form of male dominance to be resisted and controlled. This law leaves the *sale* of sex as legal; it is the *purchase* that is made illegal, thus attempting to redress the imbalance of power between men and women. An official report by the Swedish government concerning the law explained:

> The proposal by the Prostitution Report to criminalize both buyer and seller has been subjected to extensive criticism by almost all referral bodies. The government also deems that, even if prostitution in itself is not a desirable social activity, it is not reasonable to prosecute the party that, at least in most cases, is the weaker party, exploited by others to satisfy their sexual drive. This is also important if prostitutes are to be encouraged to get help to leave prostitution and can feel they will not have to worry about the consequences of having been prostitutes. (Boethius 1999)

This approach is unique and runs counter to recent laws in Germany and Holland that attempt to reduce prostitution by legalizing and inspecting brothels. Sweden is trying to extinguish demand for prostitution at the point of consumption. Which of these approaches work? At this point, no one knows for certain. Criticism has been leveled at the Swedish law that it has simply pushed prostitution underground, but no evidence has been forthcoming. Likewise, the government has stated that the law is reducing the number of women exploited in prostitution, but again, little evidence is available. In another country, the legalizing of brothels in one state in Australia has been interpreted as both decreasing trafficking by some commentators and increasing it by others.

It is important to remember that this debate is taking place in the midst of a world AIDS epidemic. The fear of AIDS means that some men are demanding younger and younger children as prostitutes in the belief that they are unlikely to catch HIV from a child. We need to understand how poverty and the lack of other opportunities make people vulnerable to prostitution. Given that demand for prostitution is often answered with women (and children) who have been trafficked and enslaved, it is critical that detailed and unbiased research is carried out as quickly as possible. Such research should focus on the constraints and force used to put women into prostitution, and to look for what they need to get out of prostitution. For example, research carried out by Supriya Awasthi, the Regional Coordinator in India of the Free the Slaves organization, found that if prostitutes could achieve an alternate income of 2,500 rupees a month (about $55) in work that didn't put them in contact with people that would try to exploit or stigmatize them, then they would leave prostitution for good.

Solutions

The Role of the State and the UN: International Law and Slavery

When the now-defunct League of Nations was set up after World War I, one of its first major statements was a convention against slavery (a convention is an agreement made between countries that is less formal than a treaty). Commonly known as the 1926 Slavery Convention, it called upon every country that signed (and most countries have done so) to "prevent and suppress the slave trade; and to bring about . . . the complete abolition of slavery in all its forms." When the Universal Declaration of Human Rights was published in 1948 by the newly formed United Nations, freedom from slavery was seen as one of the most fundamental of human rights. Article 4 reads, "No one shall be held in slavery or servitude; slavery and the slave trade shall be prohibited in all their forms." In 1956, a Supplementary Convention was added to the UN's definition of slavery that included debt bondage, serfdom, and unfree forms of marriage.

It is important to remember that only one arm of the UN, the Security Council, has the power to punish countries or mobilize armed forces. It is the Security Council that decided, for example, to send troops into Kuwait, East Timor, and Kosovo. And even the Security Council has to rely upon voluntary support from member countries. Most of the other UN organizations are primarily "talking shops." They investigate, review, discuss, present resolutions and conventions, but they cannot require any country to act in a certain way. Slavery is an important concern within the UN, but it must compete with many other concerns. The UN is a large bureaucracy; slavery comes under a number of its different divisions, particularly the Economic and Social Council. Within the Economic and Social Council is the Commission on Human Rights, and within that commission is the Subcommission on Prevention of Discrimination and Protection of Minorities. The commission and subcommission meet every year to consider human rights issues. Prior to these meetings, a number of working groups get together to focus on particular issues; one of these is the Working Group on Contemporary Forms of Slavery. It calls for reports from groups like Anti-Slavery International on slavery around the world, and it passes resolutions calling on countries to enforce their own laws and the treaties they have signed. But like other parts of the UN, the working group cannot require or force countries to take action against slavery. Sometimes the Commission on Human Rights also appoints people to be special reporters or investigators on particular issues, like torture or the rights of women. In 2004, the Commission agreed to appoint a Special Rapporteur (Reporter) on human trafficking, a very important step in bringing the issue to the fore.

Other parts of the UN are also very concerned with slavery, especially the International Labor Organization. The ILO, for example, runs the International Program on the Elimination of Child Labor (IPEC), which is responsible for raising awareness and combating child labor. IPEC focuses on preventing child labor and searching for alternative solutions such as decent employment for the parents of child workers, and rehabilitation, education, or vocational training for children.

Child labor has emerged as one of the most important global issues of our time, and international cooperation on the issue has been strengthened over the past few years. Children who are enslaved, perhaps through debt bondage, are a special concern in the fight against child labor. One nongovernmental organization, the Global March Against Child Labor, with key support from IPEC, has developed a worldwide network of political leaders and activists in many countries, raising the awareness and understanding of the issue. When child laborers from around the world marched on the UN in Geneva in 1998, their voices and example pushed politicians to enact much stronger rules in the new Worst Forms of Child Labor Convention, which includes child slavery.

Another UN body that confronts slavery is the International Organization for Migration (IOM). For years, trafficking rings have thrived on the exploitation of women from developing countries. Recently, countries of the former Soviet Union have become their latest targets. In Ukraine, women have become more economically vulnerable, and trafficking in women has become a dangerously booming "business." Lured by false promises and misled by false information on migration regulations, many women fall prey to unscrupulous traffickers, allowing their dream for a better life to be exploited. To stem the rising tide of trafficking in women, the IOM set up an information campaign that educated and warned women about the truth of trafficking. The result was a significant reduction in the number of women tricked in this way.

Groups and Strategies Working against Slavery

Examples at the International Level

A number of organizations around the world are working to stop the trafficking in people and to bring slaves to freedom. The most important of these are Anti-Slavery International and Free the Slaves. Founded in 1839, Anti-Slavery International is the oldest human rights organization in the world. It grew from an organization led by Thomas Clarkson (read more about him in

Chapter 5) that campaigned for the abolition of the slave trade in the British Empire in 1807. Free the Slaves is the American sister-organization of Anti-Slavery International. Together these organizations campaign, research, work with governments, raise awareness, and work with people in countries around the world who are fighting slavery.

In the United States, Free the Slaves has five main parts to its work:

- Working with partner organizations—this involves assisting groups around the world that are liberating slaves and helping them to build new lives.
- Raising awareness—one of the biggest challenges in the fight against slavery is that the public doesn't even know it exists, so a great deal of effort goes into working with television, magazines, public events, and anything that gets the message out. On its website is a "get active" section for students.
- Promoting slave-free trade—slave-made goods are in our homes, so Free the Slaves works with businesses and other organizations to eradicate slavery from product supply chains and build a consumer movement that chooses slave-free goods.
- Educating policymakers—this consists of working with governments to enforce effective antislavery and anti-trafficking laws and, where necessary, to draft new legislation.
- Researching slavery—modern slavery is taking new forms and presenting new challenges, all of which needs to be understood if effective action is to be made.

In the past few years, Free the Slaves has investigated the enslavement of children in West Africa and the plight of young men and women enslaved in agricultural work in the United States. It helped to get an important antitrafficking law through Congress in 2000, and helped build a coalition of businesses, government, and human rights groups that is taking slavery out of cocoa production. Most importantly, it has supported the freeing of many enslaved people, especially children, in India. Many of these children were enslaved to make carpets, and their rescue is also the aim of Rugmark, a key national organization.

An Example at the National Level: Rugmark

One of the worst industries in India for the abuse of child slaves has been rug and carpet making. If you have an oriental rug on your floor right now, there is a good chance it was woven by slave children. For many years, campaigners in India tried to free and rehabilitate these child slaves, with only partial success. But a few years ago, the Rugmark campaign set out to put the pressure not on the makers but on the buyers of carpets. Working from a tiny office with very little funding, Rugmark organizers proposed that people should look for a special tag on handmade rugs that guaranteed that they were not made by slaves. To earn this "Rugmark," producers had to agree to only three things: not to exploit children, to cooperate with independent monitoring, and to turn over one percent of the carpet price to a welfare fund for child workers. Special effort was put into building up a sophisticated monitoring team that can detect fake labels, that knows carpet making inside and out, and can't be corrupted. Today the German, Canadian, and U.S. governments recognize the Rugmark. The biggest mail-order company in the world as well as major retailers in the United States, Germany, and the Netherlands now import only Rugmark carpets. In the United States, you can find the stores selling Rugmark rugs on the organization's website, www.rugmark.org.

The most important aspect of the Rugmark campaign is its impact on the lives of enslaved children. Since 1995, the one-percent contribution from producers has provided an education to more than 2,300 children freed from the looms. They have also built six schools and a vocational training center in India, three schools in Nepal, and three schools in Pakistan.

An Example at the Local Level: The Break the Chain Campaign in Washington, DC

This book began with the story of Hilda Dos Santos, a woman held against her will and forced to work as a servant for a family near Washington, DC. Unfortunately, her story is not unique. Other women, from Cameroon, Ghana, and many other parts of the developing world are being brought into the U.S. capital on permits (called A-3 or G-5 visas) that allow foreigners to bring their servants with them to the United States. Some of these workers are then enslaved, and several legal cases have been brought by the government against the employers. Few of these cases would have ever come about, however, except for the work of the staff and volunteers of the Break the Chain campaign. The campaign is a coalition of legal and social service agencies, ethnically based organizations, social action groups, and individuals devoted to protecting the rights of migrant domestic workers. Specifically, they focus on those domestic workers carrying A-3 or G-5 visas. The most common countries of origin currently include the Philippines, Indonesia, Peru, India, Brazil, Sri Lanka, Mexico, Morocco, Chile, and Colombia.

Social service professionals and religious leaders have encountered numerous cases of abuse and exploitation of these domestic workers within the Washington, DC, area, and estimate that the problem is widespread. Abuse and exploitation range from wage abuse and contract violation to physical and even sexual abuse. Incredibly, though it is an organization fighting slavery in the nation's capital, the campaign has to run on a shoestring budget. Joy Zarembka, the young woman who coordinates the campaign, explained:

> Most Americans want to believe that slavery no longer exists, that it is just a racist vestige of the past. But, slavery is both colorblind and current. Americans need to be more vigilant and that is especially easier for young people who, by and large, are more observant and have better access to information. Before I began working on this issue, my own younger brother discovered a situation of domestic worker abuse right down the street from us and I didn't even know it was occurring. We need to learn to question situations that don't seem quite right: Is there someone in your neighborhood that you have seen go into a house and never come back out? Have you seen cleaning ladies and maids that don't seem to be allowed to go outside? Some people should even question themselves and ask if they treat their own housekeeper with dignity and respect.

The campaign has been able to serve over 150 clients and has coordinated public education events, media coverage, legal and training workshops, strategy meetings, and research on domestic workers. A roster of pro bono lawyers provide legal advice and research for the campaign, while others handle individual civil and criminal cases involving domestic worker abuse, exploitation, slavery, or trafficking.

What Can We Do?

Around the world, people—especially young people—are fighting against slavery. Many of these people have to invent the strategies and actions that they will take because the modern abolitionist movement is only just beginning. We have wonderful examples, such as Free the Children, where a group of twelve-year-olds has built a powerful international organization (see Craig Kielburger's story in Chapter 5). Even more inspiring are the lives of children liberated from slavery, children who have suffered terrible abuse and are not only rebuilding their lives, but also becoming leaders in the fight against slavery.

One of the things we know about slavery today is that it spans the globe and reaches into our lives. Whether we like it or not, we are now global people. We have to ask ourselves: Are we willing to live in a world with slaves? If not, we have to work to understand the links that tie us to slavery and then take action to break those links. If we don't do that, we are puppets, subject to forces we can't or won't control. If we don't take action, we are just surrendering and letting other people jerk the strings that tie us to slavery. Of course, there are many kinds of exploitation in the world, many kinds of injustice and violence to be concerned about. But slavery is important because it is exploitation, violence, and injustice all rolled together. There is no more potent combination of these three crimes. If there is one fundamental violation of our humanity we cannot allow, it is slavery. If there is one basic truth that virtually every human being can agree on, it is that slavery must end. What good is all our economic and political power if we can't use it to free slaves? If we can't stop slavery, how can we really say we are free?

One of the best ways to take action is to contact one or more of the organizations listed in this book to learn more about contemporary slavery and how you might contribute to eradicating it. Student groups and local organizations all across the United States are emerging that educate, lobby, raise funds, and campaign on slavery. All of them need volunteers.

References

Australian Anti-Slavery Society. *The Forgotten Slaves: Report on a Mission to Investigate the Girl-Child Slaves of West Africa*, 1996. Also see French, Howard W., "The Ritual Slaves of Ghana: Young and Female." *New York Times* January 20, 1997, pp. A1, A5.

Barry, Kathleen. *The Prostitution of Sexuality.* New York: New York University Press, 1995.

Bindman, Jo. *Redefining Prostitution as Sex Work.* London: Network of Sex Work Projects, 1997.

Boethius, Maria-Pia. "The End of Prostitution in Sweden?" Swedish Institute, October 1999, http://www.sweden.se/templates/Article_2295.asp.

Bona Malwal, Editorial, *Sudan Democratic Gazette,* N. 114, November 1999: 2 (published in London, UK). Bowe, John. "Slavery in America." *New Yorker* April 21, 2003, pp. 106–133.

Castaneda, Ruben. "Ghanaian Woman Tells of Life of Unpaid Labor: Takoma Park Couple Accused of Enslaving Her." *Washington Post* May 24, 2003, p. B07.

Center on Speech, Equality and Harm, University of Minnesota Law School. *Creating an International Framework for Legislation to Protect Women and Children from Commercial Sexual Exploitation.* Preliminary Report, January 1998.

Greider, William. *One World Ready or Not: The Manic Logic of Global Capitalism.* New York: Simon and Schuster, 1997.

Hirsch, Michele. *Plan of Action against Women and Forced Prostitution.* Council of Europe EG(96), April 9, 1996, p. 23.

Landesman, Peter. "Sex Slaves on Main Street." *New York Times*, January 25, 2004, pp. 30–39, 66, 67, 72, 75.

U.S. State Department. *Human Rights Report 2002*, Washington DC.

3

Slavery in America

The size of the modern slave trade is very difficult to measure. The victims of human trafficking are mixed with smuggled illegal immigrants, forced migration, and criminal networks. The United Nations estimates that, around the world, 600,000 to 800,000 people are trafficked against their will into some form of slavery or servitude each year. In the Global South, many people and families are poor and desperate and will do almost anything to improve their life. "Recruiters" take advantage of them, promising transportation and jobs in a new country. Once the recruiters have lured people away from their homes, they then use violence to take control of their lives. The U.S. State Department estimates that as many as 17,500 people are trafficked into the United States each year to be forced into agricultural work, prostitution, domestic service, or as bonded labor in factories and sweatshops.

The following recent cases show the nature of the trade (*Hidden Slaves* 2004):

> *The Case against Lakireddy Bali Reddy: Sexual Exploitation in California*
>
> Lakireddy Bali Reddy, a local businessman, sexually exploited several young girls from his native village in India. Uncovered in January 2000, his sex and labor exploitation ring spanned fifteen years and operated in India and California. He repeatedly raped and sexually abused his victims and forced them to work in his businesses in Berkeley, California, including a well-established Indian restaurant. Reddy pleaded guilty to

criminal charges related to immigration fraud and illegal sexual activity and agreed to pay US $2 million in restitution to several of his victims.

The Case against R&A Harvesting: Forced Farm Labor in Florida

Florida citrus pickers endured abuse by R&A Harvesting, a farm labor contractor, between January 2000 and June 2001. The company used threats of violence to force as many as seven hundred Mexican and Guatemalan workers to labor for little or no pay. After R&A Harvesting employees attacked a van driver suspected of assisting the workers, the Coalition of Immokalee Workers (see Chapter 7 for their Web site), a local community organization, pressured prosecutors to investigate the allegations of forced labor. The owners of R&A Harvesting, the three Ramos brothers and a cousin, were tried and convicted of forced labor charges in 2002.

The Case against the Cadena Family: Forced Prostitution in Florida and South Carolina

Based in Mexico, the Cadena family members lured young girls and women to come to the United States ostensibly to work as waitresses and domestic workers. Between August 1996 and February 1998, the Cadena family brought between twenty-five and forty unsuspecting victims to Florida and South Carolina and forced them to work as prostitutes to service primarily Mexican migrant farm workers. In March 1998 several Cadena family members and their associates were brought to justice, receiving criminal sentences ranging from two to fifteen years imprisonment.

The Case against Supawan Veerapool: Enslavement of a Domestic Service Worker in California

In 1989 a Thai woman by the name of Supawan Veerapool, the common law wife of Thailand's ambassador to Sweden, brought a domestic worker to Los Angeles to provide household support in her home. On arrival in the United States the domestic worker's passport was confiscated and she was then forced to work twenty-hour days, six days a week until she escaped in 1998. Convicted on criminal charges in 1999, Veerapool was sentenced to eight years in prison.

The Case against the Satia Family: Forced Domestic Servitude in Washington, DC

The Satias, two Cameroonian sisters and their husbands, recruited young Cameroonian girls, aged fourteen and seventeen, to work as domestics in their Washington, DC, homes. The girls were recruited with the promise of studying in the U.S. in exchange for providing childcare and domestic help. Once in the U.S., the domestic servants were confined to the Satias' homes, working in excess of fourteen hours a day without remuneration and under threat of violence and deportation. The younger survivor escaped in 1999 after two years of captivity. A year later the older survivor fled, after having been exploited for five years. In 2001, the Satia sisters and their husbands were charged with forced labor. Found guilty, they received criminal sentences ranging from five to nine years and were ordered to pay their victims over $100,000 in restitution.

Slavery exists in the United States because factors in the U.S. economy, legal system, and immigration policy support it. Human trafficking and enslavement are problems that are driven by a growing "informal economy" in the United States. The International Labor Organization defines an informal economy as "all remunerative work—both self employed and wage employment—that is not recognized, regulated, or protected by existing legal or regulatory frameworks and non-remunerative work undertaken in an income-producing enterprise" (ILO 2002, 12). Slavery exists in both legal and illegal industries that are poorly regulated and fail to comply with U.S. labor laws. "Employers" in such industries are often criminal entrepreneurs for whom forced labor may be one of a number of illegal activities. Over time, such employers have found that forced labor can be a lucrative business made possible through the ready availability of free labor, better and more varied transport, new methods of secure communications, and the increased permeability of borders.

Slavery is most prevalent in five sectors of the U.S. economy: prostitution and sex services, domestic service, agriculture, sweatshop/factory work, and restaurant and hotel work, though it can be found in many other types of work. This type of forced labor persists in these sectors because of low wages, lack of regulation and monitoring of working conditions, and a high demand for cheap labor. These conditions enable unscrupulous employers and criminal networks to gain virtually complete control over workers' lives. It is not clear what part slavery plays in our national economy, though the total is likely to be small. This is because slaves tend to be used on the lower end of the economic ladder—in manual labor such as fruit picking—not in high value manufacturing. However, using slave labor can mean very large profits for criminals.

While promises of good jobs with high wages are used to lure the poor into forced labor, in part due to a lack of legal possibilities for people to emigrate for work, it is not sufficient to blame external economic factors for human trafficking into the United States. Demand for trafficked labor exists in the American economy. There are citizens and others in the United States who are willing to exploit other human beings in this way. Also, it has not been the practice of most U.S. businesses to ask questions about the labor conditions of the companies that supply their raw materials or do their piece-work. Given the large and relatively unregulated informal sectors of the economy, this lack of questioning helps to create a context in which trafficked people can be exploited. This, in addition to an overt willingness to exploit by some criminals and informal sector businesses, results in a growing demand for trafficked workers.

It is also important to understand that those who supply workers for forced labor and the "employers" and "consumers" of forced labor are not necessarily the same individuals. The suppliers are the recruiters and transporters who entrap and move people into the human trafficking streams. They convert free people into victims of forced labor by taking control of their lives, brutalizing them, taking their passports and documents, and restricting their movement. There are certain attributes they seek in the "product" they will sell to those "employers" who use slave labor: gullibility, physical health, and, the most important attribute, profitability. Profitability, in turn, is determined by the demand the "employer" of enslaved labor has for certain skills and attributes in the people they will exploit. These attributes vary according to the jobs or economic sectors in which the "employer" intends to use slaves. Different attributes will be needed for prostitution or agricultural work or domestic service, though there will be overlap as well.

Most importantly, the suppliers and users of forced labor are themselves meeting a demand within the overall economy. American citizens are using the products and services of trafficked workers. In the case of prostitution, they are personally exploiting the women and children who are trafficking victims. Whether American consumers who benefit from trafficking know they are doing so, or whether they are ignorant of the suffering that supports their purchases, they are still driving the demand that supports human trafficking.

Victims of slavery in America come from numerous ethnic and racial groups. Recent research showed people trafficked from thirty-five or more countries and, through force, fraud, or coercion, were laboring against their will in the United States (*Hidden Slaves* 2004). This study found that the largest number of victims are Chinese people, followed by Mexicans and Vietnamese. Some of these victims are born and raised in the United States and find themselves pressed into servitude by fraudulent or deceptive means. Between 1999 and 2004, documented slavery cases have been reported in at least ninety U.S. cities. The criminal operations using slave labor tend to thrive in states with large populations and sizable immigrant communities such as California, Florida, New York, and Texas—all of which are transit routes for international travelers.

Those who survive slavery in the United States are at significant risk of developing health-related problems. Most survivors come from impoverished areas of the world where access to adequate health care is limited or nonexistent. Because slavery victims are rarely given the formal medical screenings for migrants, many arrive in the United States without proper immunizations and bearing communicable diseases. Once trafficked people reach their destination in the United States, they continue to face a variety of health risks as they begin working in dangerous and unregulated work environments. Those who work in the sex trade are especially at risk of contracting AIDS or other sexually transmitted diseases. Criminals using slave labor frequently use violence or the withholding of food as a means of "breaking," controlling, and punishing their workers.

Victims of forced labor often suffer psychological assaults designed to keep them submissive. Cut off from contact with the outside world, they can lose their sense of personal efficacy and control, attributes that mental health professionals have long considered essential to good mental and physical health. In such situations, many victims of slavery become increasingly dependent on their captors, if merely to survive. While little is known about the psychological impact of slavery, survivors often report feelings of depression, reoccurring nightmares, and panic attacks.

What Do We Know about Human Trafficking in the United States?

Human trafficking into the United States is only beginning to be understood. Major studies of this crime were only completed in 2003 and 2004. One study was commissioned by the National Institute of Justice (NIJ), the research arm of the Department of Justice, the agency with responsibility for prosecuting trafficking cases at the federal level. Since human trafficking and slavery are hidden crimes, our knowledge is still piecemeal, but certain themes are emerging. The NIJ-supported study noted these key facts from an in-depth study of trafficking cases (Bales and Lize 2004):

- Trafficking victims are most likely to be young and reasonably healthy people from poor, but not necessarily the poorest, backgrounds. Often, trafficking victims have a level of education that is inversely proportional to the likelihood of their enslavement. That is, case studies have found that those with the least education were most easily manipulated. Both the lack of, and desire for, education is also a strong predictor of susceptibility to being trafficked.
- Recruitment is particularly effective when traffickers rely on victims whom they have turned into loyal enforcers or recruiters. Recruitment is also effective when the potential victim's family members are involved.
- One-third of our case studies involved foreign-national victims who were recruited *within* the United States.
- In half of the cases, the trafficking operations were simple links between *single individuals or agencies* providing a single service—smuggling migrants across a border in order to exploit them in the destination country. One quarter of

the cases were *segmented businesses* involving a criminal network and a legitimate transportation or labor recruitment company. The final quarter of the cases were relatively *sophisticated and complex networks* spanning both long periods of time and large geographical distances.

- The principal methods traffickers use to control victims include taking away victims' travel and identity documents; repeatedly telling victims local police or immigration authorities will arrest, brutalize, or even kill them if they are found; sexual abuse; physical violence; threats of physical violence or death; isolation; and debt bondage. In cases with groups of victims, traffickers used victims as enforcers to intimidate and control the victims.

- The types of work that trafficking victims were forced to do in our case studies were prostitution, domestic service, agricultural work, entertainment, factory work, restaurant service, and street peddling. In every case, the period of exploitation lasted much longer than that of being trafficked. The length of captivity ranged from one month to five-and-a-half years. Once in their situation of forced labor, none of the victims in the case studies were sold on to different exploiters or forced into different types of work.

- Human trafficking operations in the United States are carefully planned and orchestrated to *make* victims vulnerable and *maintain* their vulnerability and dependence. Systematic isolation and disorientation of victims occurred in every case. Threats of violence or the use of actual violence were used to create a climate of fear. The premeditation and organization needed suggests that most instances of human trafficking and forced labor should be considered *organized crime,* not simply the opportunistic exploitation or coincidental negligence of an employer.

- In one-third of cases, the trafficking victims came to freedom on their own initiative by escaping their exploiters. In one-third of our case studies, private citizen interveners (sometimes called "good Samaritans") took an interest and helped secure liberation of the trafficking victim.

- Trafficking victims often have contact with local law enforcement authorities. But because they lack sufficient training, local law enforcement agents failed to notice the victims and take appropriate action to bring them to safety. Law enforcement played a role in the exposure and discovery of trafficking victims in only one of the cases studied.

- Not every federal arrest and search warrant execution was successful in the cases studied. Case study analysis showed that local nongovernmental organizations (NGOs) and service providers have a role to play in mounting successful arrests of traffickers. NGOs may provide needed intelligence facilitating the arrest. They also provide assistance in stabilizing victims to be able to cooperate with law enforcement.
- Fear of reprisals against themselves, and against their families in the origin countries, prevents many trafficking victims from effectively participating in prosecutions.
- The wide diversity of social, cultural, and linguistic backgrounds of victims of trafficking are a significant challenge to both gaining their cooperation and building successful cases.
- Commercial and other records are the "Achilles' heel" of traffickers and exploiters of forced labor; this is especially the case with those involved in trafficking into forced prostitution.
- Even though trafficked persons who cooperate with federal law enforcement agencies are eligible for benefits and protection, some cooperative trafficking victim-witnesses have not received the support to which they are entitled.
- Human traffickers are engaged in a wide range of crimes both against their victims (including rape, assault, extortion, homicide, and forced abortion) and against the state (for example, money laundering, tax evasion, document fraud, and corruption of officials).
- It is the nature of trafficking as a crime that when different official and civil society agencies work together, they are most likely to achieve successful interventions and prosecutions—the reverse is also true.

The themes emerging from new research tell us that the United States faces a great challenge in ridding itself of slavery. A key obstacle is the relative ignorance of the general public, which means they fail to realize or perceive slavery in their communities. In fact, young American women have been enslaved in their own communities; see the case of the teenage prostitution ring in Detroit given in Chapter 6.

Stopping Slavery in America

Legal slavery was ended in America at a terrible cost. The death toll of the Civil War, the devastation of the South, and then the botched emancipation of the slaves continue to haunt the United States today. Dumping 4 million slaves into the economy in 1865 without any recompense for the lives stolen from them, without giving them a chance at education, real citizenship, or the tools to build new lives, meant that subsequent generations were blighted by slavery's impact. Today the number of slaves in the United States is much smaller, probably around 50,000, but they are much more difficult to find and free because they are hidden away and exploited by criminals.

An example demonstrates the difficulty of measuring this hidden criminal economic activity. The State Department estimates that around 17,500 people a year are trafficked into the United States (U.S. Dept. of State 2004, 23); in 2003 federal prosecutions of this crime had increased 50 percent from the year before, to 111. The discrepancy between these two figures is what criminologists sometimes call the *dark figure* of crime statistics— that is, the difference between the actual number of crimes and the number of crimes that are reported to the authorities. The *rule of dark figures* is that the gap between actual crimes and reported crimes decreases as the severity of the crime increases. Normally, the crime with the smallest dark figure is murder (almost every murder gets reported); bicycle theft, on the other hand, has one of the largest dark figures (people just don't bother to report a stolen bike). What is sobering is that slavery and human trafficking are crimes of extreme severity, but they have the large dark figures normally associated with lesser crimes. The more reliable measures of criminal activity are the representative population sample victim surveys that are regularly carried out in the United States and Europe. These have proven to be the best way to achieve estimates of the dark figures of crime. But even in the United States, slaves are normally invisible, unreachable, unsurveyable victims, hidden away because the criminal has total control over them.

The realization of the growth of human trafficking and slavery in the United States has brought about a significant increase in effort at all levels. The U.S. government has been a leader in recognizing and combating slavery worldwide, and has been rapidly expanding its work inside the United States, though there is a long way to go. The 2000 Trafficking Victims Protection Act (see Chapter 6 for excerpts and a description of this law) embodies an aggressive, proactive approach to the problem of human trafficking and forced labor. It

- *Criminalizes* procuring and subjecting another human being to peonage, involuntary sex trafficking, slavery, involuntary servitude, or forced labor
- Provides social services and legal *benefits* to survivors of these crimes, including authorization to remain in the country
- Provides funding to support *protection programs* for survivors in the United States as well as abroad
- Includes provisions to *monitor and eliminate* trafficking in countries outside the United States

Despite these considerable advancements, the Trafficking Victims Protection Act has some shortcomings. The law only allows help with immigration and social services if a foreigner rescued from slavery in the United States cooperates with law enforcement in prosecuting traffickers. This creates the perception that survivors of slavery are primarily instruments of law enforcement rather than individuals who are, in and of themselves, deserving of protection and restoration of their human rights. Furthermore, much more action is needed to train law enforcement officers, particularly at the local level, to identify victims and slavery operations; improve cooperation and information sharing on trafficking and slavery between federal and state agencies; improve procedures for the handling of survivors; and provide survivors with protection, benefits, and compensation.

Many victims of slavery in the United States are reluctant to report their situation to law enforcement because they fear retribution from their traffickers. Often, victims have an inherent fear of police based on their past experience with corrupt authorities in their home countries. To overcome these obstacles there is an urgent need to train law enforcement personnel at all levels to recognize and assist trafficking victims. Trafficking is defined almost exclusively as a federal crime to be handled by federal authorities. This limited mandate has hindered coordination between federal and state law enforcement agencies that, in turn, has allowed perpetrators of slavery to go undetected. Moreover, federal law enforcement personnel are often unable to protect survivors and their families from traffickers because authorities lack the necessary legal tools, assistance, and funds to provide them with secure and safe refuge. Taken together, these obstacles can impede a survivor's willingness to cooperate in criminal investigations.

The Trafficking Victims Protection Act greatly amplified the federal government's role in investigating and prosecuting slavery cases in the United States, but the job of providing basic social and legal services to survivors has fallen squarely on the shoulders of NGOs and social service agencies. Yet fewer than half of these agencies are able to meet these needs. Social service agencies, such as shelters for the homeless or women suffering domestic violence, report that finding appropriate housing for survivors has been one of their greatest challenges. Housing that is safe and secure can protect survivors from their former captors. Yet housing of any kind can be costly for social service agencies. Much would be gained if these agencies were provided with greater financial support so that they can provide survivors of forced labor with safe and adequate housing and other basic legal and social services.

What Can Be Done?

Ignorance of the crime, lack of sensitivity to victims, lack of training and familiarity with the crime on the part of law enforcement, and the demand by the public for cheap goods and services all contribute to the continuation of trafficking and forced labor in the United States. This is an ongoing, underground, and brutal exploitation of men, women, and children. It is a hidden crime that preys on the most vulnerable—the poor, the uneducated, children, and especially the impoverished immigrant seeking a better life. It is a profound violation of human rights being perpetrated in the cities, suburbs, and rural areas of the United States. Yet for all its severity and breadth, trafficking can be stopped. The criminal enterprises that exploit forced labor are small and fragmented. The general public, when they understand the problem of human trafficking, are outraged and willing to see resources devoted to its eradication. Demand for forced labor in many sectors can be extinguished by increasing the cost of its use, in part by increasing both the likelihood and severity of penalties for this crime. The likelihood of apprehension can also be increased if all levels of law enforcement are trained and brought to bear on the problem. These actions can be taken within the United States and, if they are combined with raising public awareness in countries of origin, enabling safe and legal immigration, and the improvement of economic opportunities in the developing world, the supply of people vulnerable to human trafficking can be reduced as well. The United States does not suffer from the internal corruption and lack of resources faced by many countries that are fighting trafficking. With commitment and resources, trafficking and forced labor in the United States could be eradicated.

Increasing Law Enforcement

One of the greatest barriers to the eradication of human trafficking and forced labor in the United States is the lack of criminal intelligence on trafficking. While the routes and flows of illegal drugs have been studied, the emergence of the traffic in human beings is requiring a new effort in information gathering. While it is known that many of the same criminals traffic in drugs, guns, and people, law enforcement personnel have found it more difficult to identify a trafficked person when they are found. "If I find a bag of cocaine, I know what to do," one law enforcement official explained, "but if I open the back of a truck and find ten people, are they smuggled? Are they trafficked? Which one is the perpetrator and which are the victims? And the chances are that they will speak a language that I don't know, and the important first minutes of investigation will be blocked" (Bales and Lize 2004, 137). Often, cases of trafficking come to law enforcement from social service agencies, but these two groups may have differing, even opposing, goals for the forced labor survivors. There is a tension between encouraging law enforcement to crack down and prosecute and punish perpetrators and at the same time asking for an increased concentration on the appropriate treatment for victims and survivors. While law enforcement needs witnesses to clearly recount their victimization, social service agencies seek to help the survivor recover and move on from their experience. Likewise, social service providers sometimes feel that law enforcement takes over control of the victim in order to best serve the prosecution of perpetrators, but not always in the best interest of the survivor. This contrast in organizational goals and approaches to the survivor points to the need for increased collaboration.

Supporting the Victims and Survivors of Trafficking and Slavery

Across the United States, social service providers are trying to meet the needs of trafficked and enslaved people. For the most part, these are agencies that were established to serve another client base, such as survivors of domestic violence. Because their services were not designed to serve survivors of trafficking or forced labor, they are addressing this group without specific procedures or expertise. This is due, in part, to a lack of training and information about trafficking and slavery. Without such information and training, several problems occur. One is an inability to identify slavery and trafficking cases when they are met. A second difficulty, based on a low understanding of the issue, is a possible lack of sensitivity to victims and survivors, both to their unique cultural backgrounds and to their shared experiences of forced labor.

Cases are often complex, adding to the burden of supporting survivors. The crime of trafficking and slavery normally encompasses a host of other crimes, from falsifying documents and immigration violations, to crimes of extreme violence such as torture and rape. Each of these crimes has a set of needed responses—some minor, others that will be intensive and long lasting. Mental health issues, physical health concerns, legal problems and challenges, cultural differences, the basic requirements of food, clothing, and shelter, and the ongoing threat of violence, sometimes to the survivor and sometimes to their loved ones in the country of origin, must all be balanced and coordinated in the way that best serves the survivor.

Creating a context in which the survivor of trafficking and slavery can be reintegrated successfully into society is a significant challenge. It is not unusual for a trafficking victim to escape with nothing but the clothes on his or her back. Their immediate needs for medical care, safety, food, clothing, housing, and other forms of support are acute. Once acute needs are met, the requirements of participating in prosecution, as well as the need to reconstruct a coherent, autonomous life, are extremely demanding. These demands can be intensified because of the barriers of culture and language that often exist. Despite this challenge, proper response and care is crucial in preventing revictimization.

In addition to the actual trafficking victims themselves, the people who helped them escape and bring the traffickers to justice can face threats in the United States or abroad from criminals. Trafficking victims' families can also face considerable threat in their home countries, where U.S. law enforcement has no jurisdiction and where the traffickers or their associates can reach them. Repatriation to the country of origin is a path chosen by some survivors, or it is chosen for them by official agencies. Creating further problems through the "solution" of repatriation must be avoided. In their country of origin, the forced labor survivor can face stigmatization, rejection by their community, the threat of revictimization, physical assault, continued suffering of post-traumatic stress, lack of needed medical care, and the threat of violence to their families.

Public Awareness

A critical need within the United States is for an increase in public awareness of the crime of trafficking and slavery. This is especially true given the hidden nature of this crime. Since many law enforcement personnel have difficulty identifying slavery, it is not surprising that the general public also fails to recognize it. That said, private citizens have identified many cases of forced labor and reported them to the authorities. Often, this identification has not been precise; it has not been a realization that human trafficking and slavery is occurring, simply that a private citizen feels "something is not right" and reports his or her concern. Given the propensity of the American public to participate in crime reduction schemes like "Neighborhood Watch," helping the public to recognize forced labor could only increase the number of cases uncovered.

Public awareness work has commenced in the United States, but in a fairly uncoordinated manner. The issue has been addressed in newspapers and magazines as both news reports on individual cases and as feature articles. In 2003, several national wide-circulation magazines took up the issue (some of the best of these articles are listed in Chapter 8). Additionally, as a topic, human trafficking and slavery has been explored in a number of radio and television programs. It has been presented both within factual, discussion-format programs as well as included in the plots of fictional drama programs. Shorter, informational materials have also been aired, primarily in the form of public service announcements. Within the total volume of media information flow within the United States, however, the amount of programming and coverage linked to forced labor has been negligible. The "noise-to-content ratio" of American media is so large that, unless there is a very well-resourced, long-term, and coordinated public awareness campaign, the issue of forced labor will remain outside of public consideration. While existing public awareness efforts have helped raise a general public understanding of the issue, there has been no research to determine how far and how deeply such ideas have reached into the public consciousness.

Whether American consumers who benefit from forced labor know they are doing so or are ignorant of the suffering that supports their purchases, they are still driving the demand for forced labor. However, when educated through effective public awareness campaigns, consumers and consumer advocacy groups can play a role in reducing or even eliminating forced labor from the production and supply chains of the products they consume. The role of American consumers in eliminating forced labor cannot be underestimated. Consumers can pressure companies and industries to take responsibility for the treatment of workers in the production of components or ingredients in the products they sell in the United States. Consumers can also join and support antislavery and antitrafficking organizations that are working to end forced labor in the United States and abroad. American consumers can play an influential role in ending forced labor in the United States, but they have yet to be mobilized by public awareness.

If you are interested in knowing more about human trafficking in the United States, a good place to start is the Trafficking in Persons section of the U.S. Department of Justice (www.usdoj.gov/trafficking.htm), which includes fact sheets, a hotline number, and other resources.

References

Bales, Kevin, and Steven Lize. "Trafficking in Persons in the United States: A Report to the National Institute of Justice." Croft Institute for International Studies, University of Mississippi, 2004.

Hidden Slaves: Forced Labor in the United States. Berkeley, CA: Free the Slaves and the Human Rights Center, September 2004.

International Labor Organization, Employment Sector. *Women and Men in the Informal Economy: A Statistical Picture.* Geneva, 2002.

Richard, Amy O'Neill. "International Trafficking in Women to the United States: A Contemporary Manifestation of Slavery and Organized Crime." Center for the Study of Intelligence, Central Intelligence Agency, November 1999. Available at usinfo.state.gov/topical/global/traffic/report/homepage.htm.

U.S. Department of State. *Trafficking in Persons Report, June 2004.* Washington, DC: U.S. Department of State Publication 11150, 2004.

Note

Parts of this chapter are adapted from *Hidden Slaves: Forced Labor in the United States* (Berkeley, CA: Free the Slaves and the Human Rights Center, September 2004).

4

Chronology

Although this chronology concentrates on the past century, it begins with the ancient world in order to illustrate the age-old nature of slavery.

c. 6800 BC   The world's first city grows in Mesopotamia. With the ownership of land and the beginnings of technology comes warfare in which enemies are captured and forced to work: slavery.

c. 2575 BC   Egyptians send expeditions down the Nile River to capture slaves. Temple art celebrates the capture of slaves in battle.

c. 550 BC   The mighty Greek city-state of Athens uses up to 30,000 slaves in the silver mines it controls.

c. 120   Slaves are taken by the thousands in Roman military campaigns; some estimates put the slave population of Rome at more than half of the total population.

c. 500   In England, the native Britons are enslaved after invasion by Anglo-Saxons.

c. 1000   Slavery is normal practice in England's rural economy, as destitute agricultural workers place themselves and their families in a form of debt bondage to landowners.

c. 1250   The trans-Saharan slave trade carries between 5,000 and 25,000 slaves each year from West Africa to the Mediterranean. From there, they are sold into Europe and the Middle East.

c. 1380   In the aftermath of the Black Plague, Europe's slave trade revives in response to the labor shortage. The slaves come from all over Europe, the Middle East, and North Africa.

c. 1444   Portuguese traders bring the first cargo of slaves from West Africa to Europe by sea, thus beginning the Atlantic slave trade. With the "discovery" of the Americas, it will greatly expand; by the time it ends around 1870, some 13 million slaves will have been taken from Africa.

c. 1550   Renaissance art is peopled with slaves displayed as objects of conspicuous consumption.

1619   A Dutch ship delivers twenty Africans to the English settlement at Jamestown, Virginia; they become the first African Americans, and slavery begins in the American colonies.

1781   Holy Roman Emperor Joseph II abolishes serfdom, a form of slavery tied to land ownership, in the Austrian Habsburg dominions.

1789   On August 26, during the French Revolution, the French National Assembly adopts the Declaration of the Rights of Man, one of the fundamental charters of human liberties. The first of seventeen articles states, "Men are born and remain free and equal in rights."

1803   Denmark becomes the first country in Europe to ban the African slave trade. A law passed in 1792 takes effect in 1803 to forbid trading in slaves by Danish subjects and to end the importation of slaves into Danish dominions.

1804   After a slave revolt expels the French from the island of Saint Domingue, the island is declared independent under its original Arawak name, "Haiti."

1807   After prolonged lobbying by abolitionists in Britain, led by William Wilberforce and Thomas Clarkson, the British Parliament makes it illegal for British ships to transport slaves and for British colonies to import them.

1808   The United States bans further importation of Africans as slaves. At this point, there are about one million slaves in the United States.

1811–   Operating off the Atlantic coast of Africa, the British
1867   Navy's Anti-Slavery Squadron liberates 160,000 slaves. Freed from captured slave ships, they are returned to areas under British protection on the African coast, particularly Sierra Leone.

1813   Sweden, a nation that has never authorized slave traffic, consents to ban the African slave trade.

1814   The government of the Netherlands officially terminates Dutch participation in the African slave trade.

During the Congress of Vienna, largely through the efforts of Britain, the assembled powers proclaim that the slave trade should be abolished as soon as possible. The congress leaves the actual effective date of abolition to negotiation among the various nations.

1820   The government of Spain, pursuant to a treaty with Britain, abolishes the slave trade south of the Equator. Slave trade in Cuba continues until 1888.

1825   Argentina, Peru, Chile, and Bolivia abolish legal slavery.

1833   The British Parliament's Factory Act of 1833 establishes a normal working day in textile manufacture. The act bans the employment of children under the age of nine and limits the workday of children between the ages of thirteen and eighteen to twelve hours. The law also provides for government inspection of working conditions.

1834   In Britain, the Abolition Act of 1833 abolishes slavery throughout the British Empire, including its colonies in

1834 North America. The bill emancipates the slaves in all
(cont'd) British colonies and appropriates a sum equivalent to
nearly $100 million to compensate slave owners for their
losses.

1837 Thomas F. Buxton begins a campaign to abolish coolie
labor in India. After the abolition of slavery, coolies (un-
skilled Far Eastern laborers) have become a preferred
source of cheap labor. Buxton argues that coolie labor
amounts to slavery, with workers often kidnapped,
transported to the Caribbean, and forced to toil in appalling conditions.

1840 The new British and Foreign Anti-Slavery Society calls
the first World Anti-Slavery Convention in London to
mobilize reformers to monitor and assist abolition and
postemancipation efforts throughout the world. A group
of abolitionists from the United States travels to London
to attend the convention, but Elizabeth Cady Stanton and
Lucretia Mott, as well as several male supporters, leave
the meeting in protest when women are excluded from
seating on the convention floor.

1845 Thirty-six British Navy ships are assigned to the Anti-
Slavery Squadron, making it one of the largest fleets in
the world.

1848 After the revolution of 1848 in France, the new government abolishes slavery in all French colonies.

1850 The government of Brazil adopts the Queirós Law, ending the country's participation in the slave trade. The law
declares slave traffic to be a form of piracy and it prohibits Brazilian citizens from taking part in the trade.

1861 By decree Alexander II, czar of Russia, emancipates all
Russian serfs, who number around 50 million. The act
begins the time of the Great Reform in Russia and earns
Alexander II the title of "Czar Liberator."

1863 During the American Civil War, President Abraham Lincoln's Emancipation Proclamation takes effect, freeing all

slaves in the Confederate States. Lincoln also announces that African Americans can be recruited into the military.

The government of the Netherlands takes official action to abolish slavery in all Dutch colonies.

1888   Slavery ends in South America when the legislature of Brazil frees the country's 725,000 slaves by enacting the Lei Aurea (Golden Law).

1909   The campaign of the Congo Reform Association (CRA) to end forced labor in the Congo Free State succeeds. Set up in Great Britain in 1904 by E. D. Morel, the CRA's main objective is the end of forced labor in the Congo Free State (later known as Zaire). King Leopold II of Belgium had undertaken personal administration of this huge territory and forced local people to produce rubber for sale in Europe, where an increasing number of cars and bicycles intensify demand for rubber tires. Workers who refused to labor for King Leopold's officials had their hands cut off and their houses burnt and pillaged.

1910   The International Convention for the Suppression of the White Slave Trade, signed in Paris on May 4, is the first of its kind. The convention obligates parties to punish anyone who recruits a woman below the age of majority into prostitution, even if she consents.

1913   Peoples' petition to the British Parliament shuts down the Peruvian Amazon Company. In 1909, W. E. Hardenburg, an American civil engineer, had arrived in London with accounts of the inhuman exploitation of indigenous Indians in Peru by the Peruvian Amazon Company, a British entity. In the ensuing four years, the Indians had been trapped by debt and forced to work for the company, which exploited and tortured the natives. When journalists take up the story, there is a public outcry in Britain. The House of Commons mandates reports from both the company and the British Consul and establishes a Select Committee to investigate the allegations.

1915   The colonial government of Malaya officially abolishes slavery.

1918   It is estimated that most households in Hong Kong that can afford one keep a young child as a household slave.

1919   The League of Nations is founded. Its existence continues until the formation of the United Nations in 1946.

The International Labor Organization (ILO) is founded to establish a code of international labor standards. Headquartered in Geneva, Switzerland, the ILO brings together government, labor, and management to solve problems and to make recommendations concerning pay, working conditions, trade union rights, safety, woman and child labor, and social security. The ILO will be brought into relationship with the UN in 1946.

1920   Buxton's campaign against coolie labor (see 1837) succeeds when the British colonial government bans the export of bonded Indian workers.

1923   The government in Hong Kong passes a law banning the selling of young girls as domestic slaves.

1926   The League of Nations approves the Slavery Convention, and more than thirty governments sign the document, defining slavery as "status or condition of a person over whom any or all of the powers attaching to the right of ownership are exercised." The convention charges member nations to work to suppress all forms of slavery.

Burma (later known as Myanmar) abolishes legal slavery.

1927   Slavery is legally abolished in Sierra Leone, a country founded as a colony by the British in the eighteenth century to serve as a homeland for freed slaves.

1929   To achieve the abolition of slavery, Burma begins to compensate slaveholders for their "losses."

1930   The Forced Labor Convention, a combined effort of the League of Nations and the International Labor Organization, meets to discuss how to protect the rights of colonial laborers.

1936   As part of an international treaty, King Ibn Sa'ud of Saudi Arabia issues a decree ending the importation of new slaves into his country, regulating the condition of existing slaves, and providing for manumission under some conditions (slavery is not abolished).

1938   The Japanese military establishes "comfort stations" (brothels) for Japanese troops. Thousands of Korean and Chinese women are forced into sexual slavery during World War II as "military comfort women."

1939–   The German Nazi government uses slave labor through-
1945   out the war in farming and industry. Up to 9 million people are forced to work until they are worn out, at which time they are sent to concentration camps.

1941   The campaign to protect children in Ceylon (Sri Lanka) from "adoption" succeeds with the passage of the Adoption of Children Ordinance Law, which ensures the registration of all children who are adopted and requires regular inspections to prevent adopted children from working as slaves.

1948   The UN produces the Universal Declaration of Human Rights. Article 4 provides, "No one shall be held in slavery or servitude; slavery and the slave trade shall be prohibited in all their forms."

1949   The Convention for the Suppression of the Traffic in Persons and Exploitation of the Prostitution of Others prohibits any person from procuring, enticing, or leading away another person for the purposes of prostitution, even with the other person's consent. The convention consolidates earlier laws and will form the legal basis for the international protection against traffic in people until the present day.

1952   It is estimated that 40,000 Japanese children are sold into slavery for prostitution in this year alone. Brothel owners pay between $25 and $100 per child.

1954   China passes the State Regulation on Reform through Labor, allowing prisoners to be used as laborers in the *laogai* prison camps.

1956   The Supplementary Convention on the Abolition of Slavery, the Slave Trade and Institutions and Practices Similar to Slavery regulates practices involving the sale of wives, serfdom, debt bondage, and child servitude.

1957   The British and Foreign Anti-Slavery Society changes its name to the Anti-Slavery Society for the Protection of Human Rights. (In the 1990s, the name will be changed to Anti-Slavery International.)

1960   Harry Wu is sentenced to serve nineteen years in the *laogai* slave labor camp system.

1962   Slavery is legally abolished in Saudi Arabia and Yemen.

1964   The sixth World Muslim Congress pledges global support for all antislavery movements. Founded in 1926, the World Muslim Congress has consultative status with the UN and observer status with the Organization of Islamic Countries.

1973   The UN General Assembly adopts the International Convention on the Suppression and Punishment of the Crime of Apartheid. The convention outlaws a number of inhuman acts committed for the purposes of establishing and maintaining domination by one racial group over another, including exploitation of the labor of members of a racial group or groups by submitting them to forced labor.

1974   Mauritania's emancipated slaves form the El Hor (freedom) movement to oppose slavery. Leaders of El Hor insist that emancipation is impossible without realistic means of enforcing the antislavery laws and providing former slaves with the means of achieving economic independence. The movement demands land reform and encourages the formation of agricultural cooperatives. (The influence of El Hor was strongest between 1978 to 1982, though the organization still exists today.)

1975   The UN Working Group on Contemporary Forms of Slavery is formed to collect information and make recommendations on slavery and slavery-like practices around the world.

1976   India passes a law banning bonded labor.

1977   The ILO adopts the Tripartite Declaration of Principles Concerning Multinational Enterprises and Social Policy, a set of recommended standards with no means of enforcement.

1980   Slavery is abolished for the fourth time in the Islamic republic of Mauritania, but the situation is not fundamentally changed. Although the law decrees that "slavery" no longer exists, the ban does not address how masters are to be compensated or how slaves are to gain property.

1983   The civil war in Sudan erupts again, pitting the Muslim north of the country against the Christian and Animist southern tribes.

1989   The National Islamic Front takes over the government of Sudan and begins to arm Baggara tribesmen to fight the Dinka and Nuer tribes in the south of the country. These new "militias" raid villages, capturing and enslaving the inhabitants.

1990   The UN Convention on the Rights of the Child seeks to promote the basic health care and education of the young, as well as their protection from abuse, exploitation, or neglect at home, work, and in armed conflicts.

The Clean Clothes Campaign is begun in the Netherlands. The organization, which puts pressure on clothing retailers to take responsibility for the conditions in which

1990   their merchandise is manufactured, has since spread to
(cont'd) nine other countries in Western Europe.

1992   The Pakistan National Assembly enacts the Bonded Labor Act, abolishing indentured servitude and the *peshgi*
(bonded money) system. However, the government fails
to provide for the implementation and enforcement of
the law's provisions.

1994   Anti-Slavery International presents extensive evidence of
slavery in Nepal to the UN.

1995   The U.S. government issues the Model Business Principles, a voluntary model business code (apparently to
pacify human rights and labor activists in the United
States who protest the renewal of China's trade status).
The principles urge all businesses to adopt and implement voluntary codes of conduct, including the avoid-
ance of child and forced labor as well as discrimination
based on race, gender, national origin, or religious beliefs.
The principles also promote respect for the right of association and the right to organize and bargain collectively.

The organization Free the Children is begun by Craig
Kielburger and classmates and begins its work to rescue
children from exploitation.

1996   The International Organization of Employers, a subsidiary of the ILO, calls on employers and employers' organizations to immediately end slavelike, bonded, and
dangerous forms of child labor and simultaneously to
develop formal policies with a view toward the eventual
elimination of child labor in all sectors. The resolution
notes, however, that "attempts to link the issue of working children with international trade and to use it to impose trade sanctions on countries where the problem of
child labor exists are counter-productive and jeopardize
the welfare of children" (International Organization of
Employers 1996).

The Rugmark campaign is established in Germany to ensure that handwoven rugs are not made with illegal

(slave) labor. The Rugmark seal guarantees that the entire production of the rug was accomplished without slave or child labor.

The World Congress Against Commercial Sexual Exploitation of Children is held.

1997   The UN establishes a commission of inquiry to investigate reports of widespread enslavement of people by the Myanmar (Burmese) government.

A bill entitled the International Child Labor Elimination Act (H.R. 2678) is introduced in the U.S. House of Representatives to prohibit U.S. assistance, except for humanitarian aid, to countries that utilize child labor. It dies in committee.

Imported goods made by child-bonded laborers are banned by the United States.

1998   The Myanmar (Burmese) government refuses to allow the UN Commission of Inquiry to enter its borders.

The Global March Against Child Labor is established. This organization plans and coordinates demonstrations against child labor worldwide. One aim is a new Convention in the UN on the Worst Forms of Child Labor.

1999   A consortium of nongovernmental agencies calls for international aid and a cease-fire in Sudan to help end slavery there.

Despite being barred from entering Myanmar (Burma), the UN collects sufficient evidence to condemn government-sponsored slavery there. The official report states that the Myanmar government "treats the civilian population as an unlimited pool of unpaid forced laborers and servants at their disposal as part of a political system built on the use of force and intimidation to deny the people of Myanmar democracy and the rule of law" (International Labor Organization 1999, 35).

1999   The ILO passes the Worst Forms of Child Labor Conven-
(*cont'd*) tion. This convention establishes widely recognized in-
        ternational standards protecting children against forced
        or indentured labor, child prostitution/pornography, use
        of children in drug trafficking, and other work harmful
        to the health, safety, and morals of children.

        The book *Disposable People* by Kevin Bales receives histor-
        ical acknowledgment for its part in bringing attention to
        contemporary slavery in all regions of the world and is
        translated into ten languages.

        It is estimated that 15 million child laborers are exploited
        in Pakistan.

        The Protocol to Prevent, Suppress, and Punish Traffick-
        ing in Persons, Especially Women and Children, Supple-
        menting the United Nations Convention Against
        Transnational Organized Crime is signed with the pur-
        pose of combating trafficking in women and children, as-
        sisting trafficking victims, and promoting cooperation
        between countries for the purpose of accomplishing anti-
        trafficking goals.

2000   The government of Nepal bans all forms of debt bondage
        after a lengthy campaign by human rights organizations
        and freed bonded laborers.

        The Trafficking Victims Protection Act (TVPA) is passed
        by the U.S. Congress for the purpose of combating the
        trafficking in persons as a modern form of human slav-
        ery and punishment of traffickers and protection of traf-
        ficking victims.

        Free the Slaves, the American sister organization of Anti-
        Slavery International, is launched in the United States.

2001   The documentary film *Slavery: A Global Investigation* is
        broadcast in the United States and Europe, breaking the
        story of slavery and forced child labor in the cocoa and
        chocolate industry leading to immediate action by large

numbers of students. It receives a Peabody Award and two Emmy Awards.

The Child Soldiers Protocol is adopted by the UN General Assembly, establishing eighteen as the minimum age for engagement in armed conflict or compulsory recruitment into armed groups. As of spring 2004, the United States and Somalia are the only nations not to have ratified the protocol.

2002   The countries of the Economic Community of Western African States (ECOWAS) agree on an action plan to confront slavery and human trafficking in the region.

The Cocoa Protocol is signed by chocolate manufacturers and NGOs to ensure the elimination of slavery and child labor from the cocoa supply chain.

The Optional Protocol on the Convention of the Rights of the Child is promulgated with specific attention paid to the sale of children and child prostitution. The protocol is ratified in the United States in 2003.

The International Cocoa Initiative commits large chocolate manufacturers to cooperate with NGOs and local governments in establishing standards for cocoa manufacturing and monitoring production in order to ensure that child and slave labor is eliminated from the process.

By this time, more than 3 million carpets bearing the Rugmark label have been exported from Nepal, India, and Pakistan to North America and Europe.

Between 2002 and 2003, a dramatic upswing occurs in the reporting on contemporary slavery in major publications.

2003   The year that the Pakistani government has assured the United Nations that "all bonded labor will stop" in its country. It does not.

In November, the U.S. Congress issues the Reauthorization Bill approving continued funding for the Trafficking

2003   Victims Protection Act of 2000. This bill also enhanced
(*cont'd*) TVPA by facilitating closer contact between foreign gov-
        ernments on the topic and providing assistance for fam-
        ily members of victims of trafficking.

        The Protect Act is passed, enhancing the tools used to
        protect children from sex offenders and sex traffickers, as
        well as strengthening laws punishing those who travel
        abroad as sex tourists exploiting children.

        In September, *National Geographic* magazine publishes a
        major article on contemporary slavery; it registers the
        second highest amount of positive feedback the maga-
        zine has received.

        The U.S. government enacts economic sanctions against
        Myanmar for their use of forced labor.

        Mauritania passes a law that makes slaveholding punish-
        able by fines and prison.

2004   February 27 is declared National Anti-Slavery Day in the
        United States.

        A significant number of universities begin offering un-
        dergraduate courses in modern slavery.

        Government actions lead to the freeing of enslaved chil-
        dren and workers in Brazil and Bangladesh.

        The UN appoints a Special Rapporteur (Reporter) on Hu-
        man Trafficking.

        No prosecutions of any slaveholder in Mauritania had
        occurred by December 2004.

References

International Organization of Employers. "Policy Statement on the Social Clause" (Press Release). Geneva: IOE, June 3, 1996.

Report of the Director-General to the members of the Governing Body on measures taken by the government of Myanmar following the recommendations of the Commission of Inquiry, which was established to examine its observance of the Forced Labour Convention, 1930 (No. 29). International Labor Organization, Geneva, May 21, 1999.

5

Biographical Sketches

Who are the new abolitionists? Around the world men, women, and children are actively fighting slavery, liberating slaves, pressing governments for action, studying bondage, rehabilitating freed slaves, and developing strategies to end slavery. Most of these people are little known outside their own organizations and the networks that join these groups together. Many of them have firsthand knowledge of slavery, and many have faced and suffered threats, physical violence, political pressure, and defamation in their fight against slavery. Today most of us only know about the great antislavery figures of the past: everyone remembers Abraham Lincoln, and most know about Frederick Douglass and Harriet Tubman. Many of the great antislavery workers of the past inspire the abolitionists of today. For that reason, included here are the stories of just four of these historical figures whose lives are especially worth knowing, but most are the abolitionists of today. Some are old, and some are very young. Some are widely known, and others are known only in their local areas. All are working to bring slaves into freedom.

Swami Agnivesh (1939–)

Coming from a well-off Hindu family in India, the young man named Shyam Vepa Rao—who would become Swami (Holy Man or Teacher) Agnivesh—studied in Calcutta and earned degrees in law and economics. He then renounced his family status and became a "priest" (taking vows of chastity and poverty) in a Hindu group dedicated to social justice. He began his career as a

71

college teacher but, in 1977, was elected as a representative to his state legislature. In 1979, he was made the state Minister for Education. In that year, police shot down workers protesting bonded labor, and he felt compelled to meet the workers and came to support their plight. When he confronted the state government about the terrible suffering of the bonded workers, he was told to "shut up and stick to education." Faced with government inaction, he resigned his post and went to work on the problem of debt bondage.

Angering powerful interests, he was soon arrested and imprisoned as a "subversive." At the time the Bonded Labor Law was being passed in the Indian Congress, Agnivesh was in jail, reading the works of Ghandi and contemplating his role in the struggle for freedom. Upon his release, he decided to devote himself to the poorest of the poor. Turning his attention to workers enslaved in stone quarries, he found extensive debt bondage and violence used against workers. Soon he was again persecuted for his work; a false charge of murder was made against him and he spent eight months in hiding before being acquitted. In 1981, he founded the Bonded Labor Liberation Front (BLLF) of India. The BLLF has liberated thousands of bonded laborers, including children, and trained hundreds of activists. It works through direct action as well as the courts. After liberation, the freed workers are given basic education, skill training, and social and legal support.

In his saffron-colored robes, Swami Agnivesh is now a well-known representative for the poorest workers in debt bondage. He personifies an active religion that seeks to affirm human dignity for everyone. "I have never been able to compartmentalize religion, politics, and social action," he says. "They all exist together in the web of social realities" (Hallegren 1996, 5). This social reality has included two assassination attempts on his life, but Agnivesh does not give up. He has been given numerous human rights awards and is now the chair of the United Nations Trust Fund on Contemporary Forms of Slavery. A tireless traveler, he has led mass campaigns against bonded labor, child labor, consumerism, ecological destruction, and racial and religious discrimination. Agnivesh is especially critical of religions that ignore human suffering. "What good," he once wrote, "is all of this great talk about simplicity, love, meekness, sharing and cooperation, if it cannot be applied in daily life because of an economic ideology that puts profit before human happiness?" (Hallegren 1996, 6).

Jean-Robert Cadet (1955–)

Jean-Robert Cadet was born in Haiti, the son of a wealthy white businessman and a black mother who died when Cadet was only four. His father sent the young Cadet to a former mistress to become a *restavec*, a child slave. *Restavec* is a French term that means "staying with," a term that disguises the reality of slavery. Under his master's control, Cadet was forced to perform a range of menial tasks; if he made any mistake, he was beaten severely. Unfortunately, this incident of slavery is not unique—there are more than 250,000 restavec child slaves in Haiti. For the most part, these are children of the very poor who are given to well-off families in the hope that they will be given an education and a chance at a better life. Once handed over, most of the children lose all contact with their families and, like the slaves of the past, are sometimes given new names. In many ways, the restavec children are treated worse than the slaves of the past since they cost nothing and their supply is inexhaustible. They receive very little food or food of poor quality. Their health is usually poor and their growth stunted. Girl restavecs are worse off because they are sometimes forced to have sex with the teenage sons of their owners. If they become pregnant, they are thrown into the street. At maturity, most restavec children are thrown out and have to make a living any way they can—shining shoes, gardening, or as prostitutes.

As a restavec, Cadet served the family but was not part of it. He slept under the kitchen table or on the back porch. Though a small child, he received no affection or care from his owner. His sole possessions were a tin cup, an aluminum plate, a spoon, and the rags he was given to wear. In the stress and abuse of his situation, Cadet became a regular bed-wetter, which only increased the punishments he was given. Once Cadet's only friend, another restavec child named Rene, stole two dollars and bought food that he then shared with Cadet. When he was caught, he was whipped severely and then forced to kneel on hot rocks so that he would confess with whom he shared the food. When he did not implicate Cadet, he was sent to the police station for a beating; he returned terribly injured and then disappeared.

Cadet's salvation was the occasional chances he had to attend a charity school. Showing a native intelligence, he learned to read and write quickly, even in the small amount of time he had managed to keep up with schoolwork. His life changed dramatically at the age of fourteen when he was taken to the United States to continue serving his owner there. Upon arrival in the United States, his owner discovered that minors had to attend school, so Cadet was sent to junior high even though he spoke no English. Before and after school, he was still a full-time servant and cleaner. By the age of sixteen, he was required to work at cleaning jobs before and after school. Finally, he was thrown out, but with the help of the school guidance counselor, Cadet attained welfare benefits and was able to finish high school. After graduation, he joined the army, and while he was there he became a U.S. citizen.

In the army and afterward, as he pursued a college degree, he had to confront the racism of the United States. When he received his bachelor's degree, he confronted the woman who had enslaved him, showing her his degree and what he had made of his life. This confrontation was the first of many steps in the recovery of his confidence and self-esteem. With more study, he became a teacher and met the woman he would marry. But the psychological burden of his childhood in slavery still had a damaging impact on his life and relationships. In 1993, he began to write a letter to his newborn son explaining his past. This letter turned into the book *Restavec: From Haitian Slave Child to Middle-Class American*; the book deeply moved many readers, generating several television reports about slavery in Haiti. In 2000, he left his job as a teacher to devote himself full-time to the cause of restavec slave children.

Thomas Clarkson (1760–1846)

If there was one person most responsible for the abolition of legal slavery in the West, it was Thomas Clarkson. Abraham Lincoln, William Wilberforce, and others followed the lead of the man the poet Samuel Coleridge called "the moral steam engine—a Giant with one idea" (Hochschild 2005, 89). Clarkson's "one idea" was to end slavery. In the 1780s, Great Britain was the world's preeminent slave trader. Its empire was held together by slavery, and vast fortunes were being made from slaves and slave products such as sugar and cotton. The British government received a large part of its taxes from slave owners and slave-made products. Even those who thought slavery to be wrong tended to believe that it was too important for the national economy to be abolished.

While at university, Clarkson entered an essay contest; the question to be answered was, "Is it lawful to make slaves of others against their will?" As the young student researched the subject, he was shocked and absorbed by what he learned. After winning first prize, he developed the work further, publishing it as a book in 1786. Though trained to be a minister, Clarkson, aged twenty-five, decided to devote his life to ending slavery. Through this work he came into contact with a committee set up by the Quakers in 1783 to seek abolition of the slave trade. Joining this committee and gaining the promise of William Wilberforce to bring the matter to Parliament, Clarkson became the campaigner who rallied people to the cause. Traveling by horseback, he covered 35,000 miles in the next seven years. He studied the slave trade firsthand in ports like Liverpool, England, and organized antislavery groups wherever he went. Within a few years, the government was being bombarded by petitions and letters urging an end to slavery.

When Parliament defeated a law in 1791 that would abolish the slave trade, Clarkson increased his efforts, crisscrossing the country again and again to speak publicly and organize local groups. A national boycott of slave-made sugar was mounted, resulting in a reduction of sugar consumption in some parts of the country by up to one-half. In 1794, Clarkson, exhausted by the work, retired temporarily from his campaign and spent the next few years living in the countryside and writing a book about the Quakers. He returned to the fight in 1804, supplying evidence to the government and organizing support for abolition. In February 1807, after many delays, Parliament passed a law abolishing the slave trade throughout the British Empire. This law stopped the trade in slaves, but not slavery itself, so Clarkson turned his attention to full emancipation. By the 1820s, a full antislavery campaign was underway. Now in his sixties, Clarkson embarked on another grueling tour of speaking and organizing, and thousands of petitions rained down on the government. In 1833, slavery itself was abolished in the British Empire. In the 1840s, the now grand old man of the antislavery movement presided over the first world antislavery convention and pressed for an end to slavery in the United States. He continued campaigning until days before his death.

Lou DeBaca (1967–)

Lou DeBaca didn't think he was going to fight slavery when he was growing up in Iowa. His father taught animal science, and

Lou was especially interested in international agricultural development: "I thought I was going to do cattle work" he says. Being in Iowa as a boy meant adjustments. "We were the only Hispanic family in the entire state, for a while" (Basu 2003). While he was studying at Iowa State University, the farm crisis struck the Midwest and Lou decided to go to law school. For a while he worked as an intern in the office of Senator Tom Harkin, a congressional champion in the fight against child labor and slavery, afterwards feeling that the right move for him was to be a lawyer serving the public.

Soon after, DeBaca joined the Justice Department, working on civil rights cases. These are tough crimes and sometimes controversial: police brutality, hate crimes, and cases involving the far-right militias. After building up experience, he began to prosecute cases of human trafficking and forced labor, and helped found the U.S. government's Worker Exploitation Task Force. Soon his cases set the pattern for antislavery legal work and helped lead to the passing of the Trafficking Victims Protection Act in 2000. His cases brought many human traffickers to justice and helped build new lives for many victims: teenage girls from Mexico who were tricked into coming to the United States only to be enslaved and forced into prostitution; hundreds of young women who were abused and harassed in American factories on the island of Samoa; deaf Mexicans who were forced to peddle trinkets on the streets of New York; men from Central America who were enslaved as agricultural workers in Florida—all of these cases, prosecuted by DeBaca, helped to define the way U.S. law attacks slavery today. Currently, DeBaca is the United States' leading expert in prosecuting human trafficking cases and has been given awards from the Attorney General and the Justice Department. In addition to his law enforcement efforts, he is assisting other countries in setting up antitrafficking efforts using the victim-centered approach that he himself pioneered.

Frederick Douglass (1817–1895)

Born a slave in Maryland, Douglass spent his childhood as a domestic servant in Baltimore. In spite of the laws against slave literacy, he began to secretly teach himself to read using old newspapers and any other printed matter he could find. At about the age of thirteen, he found a discarded book on rhetoric (public speaking) and carefully worked through all of the exercises, becoming a skilled speaker in the process. When he was fifteen, he was sent to work on a plantation. There he organized a secret slave school that was discovered by slaveholders; he was punished and sent to another plantation. Upon returning to Baltimore, he escaped from slavery at the age of twenty using the papers of a free black sailor. He settled in Massachusetts, changing his last name to Douglass from Bailey, his master's name, to conceal his background and confuse slave catchers.

Soon after coming to Massachusetts, he became involved with the emerging antislavery movement. His speech at an Abolitionist convention in 1841 impressed the Abolitionist organization so much that he was hired to be a traveling lecturer. From that point forward, he gave hundreds of speeches around the country, though he was often met with assaults, rotten vegetables, and mob violence. His public profile meant he was in constant danger of recapture. At age twenty-six, he wrote the story of his life, *Narrative of the Life of Frederick Douglass,* which sold more than 30,000 copies and was translated into several other languages. *Narrative* made him the most famous black person in the world and increased his danger of being caught. After he toured Great Britain, antislavery activists purchased his freedom from his original owners, giving him more security. He started his own antislavery journal, and then began to drift away from many of the more conservative abolitionists with his calls for public resistance and slave revolts. With the imminence of the Civil War, he greatly encouraged blacks to be armed and included in the military. After the war, he campaigned for equal treatment and citizenship for ex-slaves and worked with select politicians to carry forward civil rights. Shortly after the death of his wife, he married his white former secretary, alienating some blacks and whites but not lessening his influence. The most influential African American of the nineteenth century, Douglass spent his life confronting the public conscience with the facts of slavery and discrimination. Less than a month before his death, when a young black man asked his advice on how to move ahead, he replied "Agitate, agitate, agitate!" (Ryan 1997).

Given Kachepa (1986–)

Given Kachepa was born in Kalingalinga, Zambia, one of six children. His mother died when he was six and his father died when he was eight; with his brothers and sisters he moved in with his aunt, who also had six children. As a ten-year-old, Given began to sing in his local church choir and, strangely, it was this that led to his enslavement.

A charity group from Texas called Teaching Teachers to Teach (TTT) had begun to help build schools in Zambia. When some of the TTT staff heard the boys choir, they were impressed with the beauty of their voices and the rich sound they made singing *a cappella,* that is, without any instrumental accompaniment. One couple from TTT decided to bring a choir to the United States and produce concerts in order to raise funds for school building in Zambia. They were right about the choir; in America, people were willing to pay a lot of money for concerts and to make large donations. Sadly, the money proved too great a temptation: instead of sending money back to the boys' families and building schools, the couple began to keep the money and to demand more and more work from the boys.

Given, aged eleven, was the youngest member of a choir that came to the United States in 1998. The rosy promises made to the choirboys before they left home turned into a nightmare in America. For nineteen months, the boys were made to sing in three to five concerts a day. If they were tired or sick, they would be threatened. When not singing, they were made to dig a swimming pool hole by hand. Housed in a trailer, if they complained their "boss" would cut off the gas so they couldn't cook. Denied any medical care, several of the boys become seriously ill, and when they were subsequently freed and given checkups, three of the boys tested positive for tuberculosis.

The boys kept singing in the hope that some of the funds collected were being sent home to ease the poverty of their families. After more than a year of bad treatment, the boys realized that no money had been sent home to their families and they began to resist their "boss," who quickly moved to deport the three oldest boys. His crime unraveled when the U.S. immigration officials began to question the boys and discovered what had happened. At first, it was difficult for officials to believe that a *choir* had been caught up in human trafficking and exploitation, but as the facts mounted, the boys were cared for and given a chance to stay in the United States. Given now lives with his foster-family in Texas, attends high school, and speaks out against human trafficking whenever he can. When I asked him how he had made it through his enslavement, he explained, "I had to stay focused and know what I believed in. There will always be people that will try to make you feel you are not worth anything, so you have to know your own worth. Having to sing like that many times, and missing my family, I had to stick it out and I knew that God would be there for me in the end. I was eleven when I came over. It was hard. Before I left, my brothers were trying to take care of me, they said they didn't want me to come, but I was thinking I could help my family and help myself and other people back home too, those that didn't have the opportunity to go to school" (Interview with author, April 2004). Today Given Kachepa does just that, raising funds to help build schools in his native Zambia.

Cheikh Saad Bouh Kamara (1944–)

Born in the West African country of Mauritania in 1944 and educated there and in France, Kamara is a leading human rights and antislavery activist. For standing up for human rights, this teacher was put into prison by his own government. Slavery exists across Mauritania on a very large scale. One of the last places on earth where chattel slavery is practiced, slaves can be inherited, hired, or lent out. Slavery is often passed down through generations of a family. In Mauritania, ethnic differences are also important in slavery, most slaveholders being Arab Berbers and most slaves being the descendants of black Africans. Slavery has been legally abolished several times—the latest in 1981—but no law has been put in place for the prosecution of slaveholders, for the rehabilitation of freed slaves, or for setting up the law enforcement necessary in order to free slaves.

Kamara, a professor of sociology at the main university in Mauritania, was a founding member of the Mauritanian Human Rights Association (MHRA). This association was established in the wake of mass killings and the expulsion of thousands of black Mauritanians from the country in the early 1990s. At first, the association had to operate in secret and, when it went public, most of its initiatives were blocked by the government—especially research into secret executions and the "disappearance" of political prisoners. Though never allowed to be a legal association in Mauritania, the MHRA was recognized by outside bodies such as the Organization of African Unity. Speaking out around the world about the slavery in Mauritania, Kamara was asked to join the United Nations Trust Fund on Contemporary Forms of Slavery.

In 1998, the president of an antislavery organization in Mauritania gave an interview to a French television program. The bad publicity angered the Mauritanian government, which responded by arresting several human rights workers, including Kamara, even though he had nothing to do with the interview. Charged with running an unlawful organization (the MHRA), he was held in jail for two months and put on trial. All of the activists were convicted and sentenced to thirteen months in prison. A few days later, they were set free on the orders of the Mauritanian president, but their convictions were still in place, which meant that not only could they be rearrested at any time, but their organizations were permanently banned from operating or doing any more human rights activity. Upon his release, Kamara left Mauritania, and he continues to work for human rights. In late 1998, he was presented with Anti-Slavery International's Anti-Slavery Award.

Craig Kielburger (1982–)

Craig Kielburger was just twelve years old when he and other students founded Free the Children (FTC), an international children's organization now active in more than twenty countries, whose mission is to free children from poverty and exploitation and to empower young people to become leaders in their communities. Kielburger first became an advocate for children's rights when he read about the murder of child labor activist Iqbal Masih in April 1995 (see Masih's biography later in this chapter). Moved by Masih's story, he worked with fellow students to start the campaign that became Free the Children. At first they found that no one, especially adults, would take a group of twelve-year-olds seriously, but they learned that by assembling the facts and making clear presentations, they could gain the attention of the public. Since then, Kielburger has traveled to more than thirty countries around the world visiting street children and child laborers and speaking out in defense of children's rights. He gained international recognition from his appearances on television in North and South America and Europe. His efforts on behalf of working, poor, and marginalized youth have been featured in many newspapers, and he has received many awards for his work. Kielburger's first book, *Free the Children*, written with Kevin Major, was published in 1998.

Free the Children has initiated projects all over the world, including the opening of schools and rehabilitation centers for children, the creation of alternative sources of revenue for poor families to free children from hazardous work, leadership programs for youth, and projects linking children on an international level. Young people affiliated with the organization have helped to convince members of business communities to adopt codes of conduct with regard to child labor, and governments to change laws to better protect children from sexual exploitation. Free the Children also initiated a "Friendship Schools Campaign." To date, students taking part in this campaign have raised funds to build twenty schools in Latin America. They have put together and shipped more than 5,000 school kits to South Africa, the Philippines, Latin America, and India. Believing that education is the key to breaking the cycle of poverty and eliminating child labor, they have built more than 400 schools and shipped 200,000 school and health kits around the world.

Young people from FTC have also raised money to set up a pipe-and-reservoir system to bring clean water from the mountains into two villages in Nicaragua and to build a medical clinic. FTC raised over $100,000 to build a rehabilitation and education center for freed bonded child laborers in India. The center, which accommodates up to 100 children at any given time, provides counseling, education, medical aid, and vocational training and thereby facilitates the reintegration of these children into society. The rehabilitation center was completed in the fall of 1998. During the Kosovo crisis, students in more than 100 schools put together 10,000 health care and hygiene kits, 8,000 stuffed animals, 2,000 baby kits, 50,000 items of clothes, and thousands of other items for the Balkan refugees. The health kits and other necessities were distributed to children in camps in Kosovo, Belgrade, and North America. In 2000, FTC joined with international development agencies representing 180 countries to launch the Campaign for Education. This campaign aims to have basic education provided for all children by 2015 and to get western governments to forgive the heavy international debt that prevents poor countries from spending more on education.

Dona Pureza Lopez Loyola (1943–)

When her son disappeared in 1993, Pureza Lopez Loyola set off to find him. She left her youngest daughter at home to go in search of her youngest son, Abel, who had disappeared after going to work on an estate in Para state, Brazil. "No matter how many children there are," she said, "the mother's heart is so big and her love so strong that she goes looking for the one that is lost, no matter where he or she may be." A poor woman with relatively little education, she sold most of her possessions to fund her trip, and with a camera and a tape recorder she traveled thousands of miles, often risking her life, but sustained by her faith. "When I was in the middle of the jungle, I used to say, 'Jesus, hold that jaguar so that I can pass.' And he did it. No animals did me harm, and even the gunmen let me go" (Interview with author, November 1998).

She sought out isolated and heavily guarded estates where she found hundreds of enslaved workers but not her son. "Many were beaten or starved," she said, "and on one estate I heard how workers who were too exhausted to work further were hung up on trees and used by gunmen for target practice." Despite her efforts, she had to return home without Abel. But in May 1996, she suddenly received a telephone call from her son, and shortly afterward Abel escaped from his forced labor and returned to her. "I had encountered hundreds of slave laborers, hidden away from prying eyes. Many were beaten or starved," she said. Assisted by the Pastoral Land Commission (an agency of the Catholic Church), she began registering official complaints, leading to the release of many enslaved laborers. After her son was located and freed from slavery, she also began to confront politicians over the lack of enforcement of antislavery laws. "After two years on the road, I had already seen enough suffering. I had seen how my son would have died. I was desperate and I began to cry out in newspapers, radio, and TV stations so that the problem was widely publicized. I have no doubts that the majority of Brazilians know about it nowadays . . . There is labor and human rights legislation, but they don't use it." Now in her fifties, she has become a fearless advocate for the enslaved and, in 1997, was given Anti-Slavery International's Anti-Slavery Award.

Iqbal Masih (1982–1995)

At the age of four, Iqbal Masih was placed in debt bondage to a carpet maker in rural Pakistan. His parents, poor laborers, received the equivalent of $12 for Iqbal. For the next six years, he worked at a carpet loom for twelve or more hours per day. Sometimes chained to the loom, regularly beaten, he was fed little and worked in terrible conditions, leaving him stunted and underdeveloped for his age. In 1992, when he was ten years old, Iqbal escaped from his slaveholder and attended a meeting organized by a Pakistani human rights group that was pressing the government to enforce its laws against bonded labor. Learning of his rights, he refused to return to the loom despite pressure from the slaveholder. He enrolled in a school, learned to read and write, and became active in campaigns to free other child workers.

Over the next two years, he helped to liberate hundreds of children from bonded labor. His youth and activism inspired people around the world and gained international attention. In 1994, he was given the Human Rights Youth in Action Award by the Reebok Foundation and was named "Person of the Week" by ABC News. Around the world he visited schools and spoke to students about the problem of child labor and bondage. After his call for a boycott of Pakistani carpets, exports from that country fell.

On April 16, 1995, a few months after his return to Pakistan from the United States, Iqbal was gunned down while riding a bicycle with a friend near his grandmother's village. Some Pakistani human rights workers claim that his murder was the work of the "carpet mafia"—angry loom owners whose ability to enslave children had been hampered by Iqbal's work. The Pakistani government says there is no evidence of this, but the government has also jailed or persecuted those people who have called for an investigation of Iqbal's murder.

While in the United States, Iqbal had visited the Broadmeadows Middle School in Quincy, Massachusetts, and talked to the children there about debt bondage and child labor. Shocked by his murder, the students there organized the "School for Iqbal" campaign in order to build a school in his home village of Muridke. They raised thousands of dollars over the next two years; the school was built, equipped, and opened in 1998. Broadmeadows students have been honored for their campaign with many awards and, in 1998, they joined the Global March Against Child Labor. You can visit their campaign online at http://www.digitalrag.com/iqbal/index.html.

Keshav Nankar (1961–)

Keshav Nankar was born into a debt-bonded family in Maharashtra state, India. When Nankar was two years old, his father died, thereby transferring his debt to Nankar and his mother. When he was six, he attended school and was considered a bright student, but the moneylender demanded that he leave school in his second year and work full-time grazing animals. At age sixteen, Nankar became a bonded laborer in his own right, and his decision to marry further bound him to his landlord. Despite having worked for ten years, he had no money because his labor supposedly went to repaying his father's debt, and he had to borrow 700 rupees (about $20) from his master to pay the "bride price." There was no written agreement for the loan, and he was only given food for his work.

Seven years later, Vivek and Vidyullata Pandit visited Nankar's district, where they identified forty bonded workers in his village (see the Pandits' biography later in this chapter). In July 1983, the Pandits were able to secure Nankar's release. In revenge, local landlords organized a labor boycott in the area and refused to employ any of the former bonded laborers. The Pandits arranged to provide food for them and their families so they would not have to reenter the cycle of bonded labor. Nankar organized a campaign in his village demanding work for all of the ex-bonded laborers at minimum wage. His success led him to become a labor activist organizing the people in his area, and he set up a cooperative growing watermelons that is still in operation. Thanks to his activism, the workers in his area are receiving a fair wage and a meal in return for their labor. He is currently the chairman of the labor union and an executive member of organizations that campaign against bonded labor. He has ensured that his children, who are now in school, do not return to a life in debt bondage. When Vivek and Vidyullata Pandit received the 1999 Anti-Slavery Award from Anti-Slavery International, they immediately presented it to Keshav Nankar, who received it on behalf of bonded laborers in India.

Vivek (1957–) and Vidyullata (1957–) Pandit

Vivek and Vidyullata Pandit are a husband-and-wife team who have touched and changed the lives of thousands of bonded laborers. Vivek was born in 1957 in Maharashtra, India, Vidyullata in Bombay the same year. Vivek's uncle had bonded laborers who served Vivek food as a child, but he did not realize until later that they were enslaved. Vivek and Vidyullata met in a political youth movement in Bombay, where he was studying sociology and she was studying science at a university. In 1975,

Vidyulatta went to jail for two-and-a-half months in protest of government actions. Soon disillusioned with India's political parties and standard answers, the couple decided to start out on their own. They left their jobs and moved to a small village in the countryside.

Working with like-minded friends, they established medical camps and preschool classes and organized a leprosy detection campaign. Getting to know the young people of the village, they realized that there was a widespread problem with debt bondage. Together they decided to devote their energies to bonded laborers and, ever since, they have put their lives at stake to help people out of bondage and into freedom. More than 1,500 people have been liberated through their efforts.

The Pandits have set up three integrated organizations based in Thane District that operate throughout Maharashtra, creating a framework that first liberates bonded laborers and then ensures that they can lead a free life: Vidhayak Sansad, set up in 1979, identifies and releases bonded laborers; Shramajeevi Sanghatana, a trade union founded in 1982 for former bonded laborers and other marginalized groups, secures equal and fair wages for men and women; and Samarthan, formed in 1993, lobbies state officials for the development and implementation of legislation against this system of enslavement.

The Pandits believe that in order for bonded laborers to be truly free, they must be released from the psychological bonds as well as the physical. They must be made to believe that it is possible to stand up to their former landlords and to adjust to a life of freedom. As Vidyullata Pandit says, "the three most important things people need to fight bonded labor are knowledge of the law, self-confidence to bring about change, and . . . conviction to ensure they don't go back to bonded labor once they are released" (Interview with author, September 2000). The Pandits have devised a program of education that prepares the former bonded laborers for a life of freedom. They are taught basic science to increase their curiosity and attention for detail, role-playing to stimulate problem solving, and games to develop strategic thinking and teamwork. Those who want to become active in the trade union receive further training, and there are former bonded laborers working in all three organizations. The Pandits' philosophy is based on self-worth. They teach bonded laborers that they have the same value as any other member of society and that no human being deserves to be exploited and oppressed. By providing these structures, the Pandits have enabled former bonded laborers to break free from the cycle of bonded labor.

Father Edwin Paraison (1962–)

Father Paraison, a Haitian Episcopal priest, braved armed guards to rescue and repatriate over a hundred children separated from their families and forced to work on sugar plantations in the Dominican Republic. Haitian workers, including children, are lured with offers of work and then enslaved in the sugar harvest. Haiti and the Dominican Republic are located on the same island and share a border. Traditionally rivals, poor Haitians are treated badly in the Dominican Republic.

Edwin Paraison was born in Haiti in 1962 and later studied theology at seminary. His first church was in Romana, Haiti, where he developed a strong relationship with the sugar workers at the local sugar processing plant. A change of bishops and some political friction meant that Paraison was transferred to Barahona, in the Dominican Republic, to establish a local church. Here he became more involved in the plight of Haitians enslaved to work on the sugar harvest in the Dominican Republic. Since the Haitian government was receiving a payment for every worker provided and the Dominican government was keen to avoid any exposure of the use of slave labor that would threaten their market for sugar in the United States, Paraison faced deadly opposition. To counter the abuse, Paraison set up programs to help Haitian workers with their basic needs and to educate them about their rights. With other priests, he monitored the movement of people, especially children, into the Dominican Republic, and set up a twenty-four-hour helpline. The work immediately generated many cases of enslaved workers and children, who Paraison freed. After more than sixty-five cases had been resolved, an armed attack killed one of Paraison's coworkers, and a wounded coworker who was taken into police custody after the attack "committed suicide" while in jail. Threatening phone calls explained that Paraison was next.

Paraison conducted research at this time to discover how many Haitians were being held in Dominican prisons, often without having been charged. He then sought to free these prisoners. When the Haitian government was overthrown in 1991, very large numbers of Haitians fled into the Dominican Republic, and Paraison found himself the key spokesperson for this refugee community. His work there revealed the serious violations of human rights suffered by the refugees even after the Dominican Republic passed laws to protect them. After U.S. network news broadcast a report on his work, he was called to testify before the U.S. Congress, but in Haiti a foreign coworker was expelled for helping him carry out research. In 1992, he received a special award from the City of Boston and was asked to advise the European Community. In 1994, he received the Anti-Slavery Award from Anti-Slavery International. He still lives in the border region between Haiti and the Dominican Republic, helping migrants and refugees.

Shakil Patan (1956–1998)

Born in Hyderabad, Pakistan, Shakil Patan was the child of refugees from India at the time of the division of India and Pakistan. He was born with the last name Khan but changed it as a protection for his family when he became involved in human rights work. He received a master's degree in political science and was active in student campaigns for democracy and rights, becoming a leader in the fight to restore democracy in Pakistan during the military dictatorship of the 1970s. While still a teenager, he was jailed by the government for a month, then later for two months; then in his twenties, he spent twenty-one consecutive months in jail. His crime was calling for democracy and civil rights.

In 1986, he was one of the cofounders of the Human Rights Commission of Pakistan (HRCP); in 1991 he organized the HRCP Task Force on the Sindh. The Sindh is a rural state within Pakistan that has large amounts of slavery through debt bondage. Patan collected documentary evidence in Sindh of debt bondage, imprisonment of workers, buying and selling of people, rape of women in bonded families, and terror and torture committed by landlords. This evidence was submitted to the government according to Pakistan's law against bonded labor, but the corruption of local officials is such that no action has been taken. More often than not, exposed landlords have simply made threats and sold their bonded families to get rid of the evidence. Patan worked closely with one village inhabited by oppressed minority families, leading raids that freed more than 2,000 people in all. Television coverage of these raids resulted in Patan becoming well known, and death threats began to follow him. In 1998, he was killed in a car accident. His widow, Nasreen Patan, has taken over the leadership of the HRCP Sindh Task Force.

Father Ricardo Rizende (1952–)

Rizende is a Roman Catholic priest who fought for human rights in the Para state of Brazil. Despite repeated threats to his life from well-known killers in Para's lawless frontier, Father Rizende persistently denounced the enslavement of workers in mining and ranching since his arrival in the Amazon. The Brazilian-born Rizende took a course in religious studies and philosophy and later earned a master's degree in agricultural and social development. He moved to the town of Rio de Maria in Para to assume his first job as a priest in 1977. Working with trade unions and lawyers, he has freed and helped to rehabilitate hundreds of slaves. The cost has been high—since the mid-1980s, seven of the activists in the local rural workers' union have been killed, other priests and lawyers have been gunned down, and several attempts have been made on Rizende's life. Rio de Maria became known as the "town of death foretold" because the published threats were so often followed by murder.

In 1996, Rizende left Para when his colleagues convinced him that the danger had become severe and that his death was next. He moved to Rio de Janeiro and gained a doctorate degree with research into human rights. From Rio, he has continued to campaign and speak out against the enslavement of workers in Brazil. The author of several books, he has grown from a local parish priest into an international expert on human rights and slavery. He was given the Anti-Slavery Award in 1992.

Salma Mint Saloum (1956–)

Like her mother and grandmother before her, Salma Mint Saloum, was a slave in Mauritania. In 1997, desperate to find a way to freedom for her family, she escaped. A heroine in the likeness of Harriet Tubman, Salma bravely crossed the river border into Senegal, and then smuggled herself across the Atlantic Ocean on a cargo ship to freedom, arriving in America in 1999. A pillar of courage, determination, and strength, she has worked to free her children from slavery in Mauritania and now wants to bring them to live with her in the United States. Hers is the clear voice of the freed slave, her first hand testimony an indictment of the slavery in Mauritania and in our world. This is part of her story (the full version appears in Chapter 6):

> Finally I met a man in the market who told me that Senegal was just across the river. I decided I had to try again. I ran to the river, where a man with a small wooden boat agreed to take me to Senegal. There I made my way to a safe house run by a former slave from Mauritania. I stayed in Senegal for a few years, earning my keep by doing housework. But I never felt safe. Always I was afraid that the master of the family would pay people to find me and bring me back to his house.
>
> When I got to the U.S., I worked braiding hair. The first time I was paid for work I had done, I cried. I had never seen a person paid for her work before in my life. It was a very good surprise.
>
> In Mauritania, I didn't dare go to the government, because they wouldn't listen. It doesn't matter what the laws say, because they don't apply the laws. Maybe it's written that there is no slavery, but it's not true. Even in front of the president of Mauritania I can say in full voice that there is slavery in Mauritania, because now I am as free as he is. (Provided to the author by Salma Mint Saloum)

In 2000, Salma sought legal asylum in the United States, through the New York Association for New Americans (NYAYA). Though Mauritania had suffered U.S. trade sanctions for its appalling human rights abuses, her hearings came as the United States resumed trade, choosing to ignore slavery for political reasons. An immigration judge ruled Salma was a slave entitled to U.S. protection and freedom. She is now building a new life, learning English, and devoting herself to working and speaking out against slavery.

Amar Saran (1954–)

Amar Saran comes from the city of Allahabad in India. He studied sociology at a university in New Delhi, then later earned a law degree, following in the footsteps of his father and grandfather. For many years he practiced law, mostly criminal law, and had nothing to do with questions of slavery. But in 1995, he was asked to join the state Vigilance Committee on Debt Bondage.

These committees are supposed to watch for and prosecute cases of bondage, but the committee in the state of Uttar Pradesh had become quiet and the state government had announced that Uttar Pradesh was free of bondage. Not long after he joined the Vigilance Committee, a local human rights activist told Saran he could show him some bonded labor. Not far into the countryside they discovered entire villages bonded and working at making gravel and quarrying.

Shocked by what he found, Saran began to press a case for their release and soon discovered that the moneylenders and landlords had powerful friends. He found that the raja (or prince) of Shankargarh, which included the local area, had secured perpetual leases for the minerals in the land under more than forty villages. Because the land is poor for farming, mining is the only way that local people can make a living. The local people were threatened with expulsion by the raja's middlemen and then led into bondage to work the gravel pits and quarries. The little money gained by the adults was not enough to support their families, and all the children of the villages were also pressed into the work. When Saran brought legal cases to abolish the debts and bondage, the courts delayed taking action. Gaining no help from the courts, Saran began working with a local group to organize the villagers into small-scale credit unions. Although it seems hard to imagine that bonded laborers could benefit from a credit union, they managed to put tiny amounts into the "bank" each week and slowly built up a sum that could be borrowed without terrible interest or false accounting. Even greater than the amount of pooled savings was the sense of empowerment gained by the credit union members. After a portion of the savings had been used to buy some members out of their bondage, most of the other members simply freed themselves, refusing to work any longer unless it was for a decent wage, thus canceling their own debts.

Faced with united workers, the middlemen backed down, and soon villages were building schools and taking their children out of the quarries. But being freed of debt did not always mean that the villagers could earn a good living. Soon it became clear that in order to gain any security, the workers would need to lease their own quarries and work for themselves. But here they collided again with the raja, who controlled all of the mineral rights and would only give leases for huge sums. Since it is Indian government policy to support poor people with grants of mineral leases, to make rehabilitation payments to freed bonded workers, and to support credit unions, and given that little of this had happened, Saran filed a major lawsuit. The lawsuit asked that the existing laws be enforced and that the question of leases be resolved. The families in the one village that has been able to get a lease to some government land have seen their lives transformed and their incomes greatly increased. The lawsuit is still not resolved, for delaying tactics are being used by the landlords. Saran continues to press the case and to work with local groups to help them free themselves from bondage.

Suman (1961–)

This remarkable young woman has guided almost 2,000 children freed from slavery into their new lives. The daughter of a government employee, Suman was born in New Delhi, India. While attending university, she volunteered to help when a flood destroyed many homes nearby. Many of the victims were poor migrants, whose temporary shelters and few possessions had been swept away. She was struck both by their resilience and by the lack of interest shown by the government in their condition. The experience made her reconsider her plan to enter government service.

One day in 1982, Suman was waiting for a bus and began to talk with two little boys. The boys were wearing ragged clothes and carrying bundles. When she asked where they lived, they replied, "In the garbage dump." Forgetting about the bus, she went with them to see their "home" and found more children working in the dump sorting the rubbish and picking out any sort of material that could be sold. She discovered that, because they were illiterate, they were regularly cheated when they sold their goods. Raising some funds through grants and loans, Suman bought gloves and shoes for the children and began to teach them to read and write.

After a few years, Suman learned about the release of children from slavery in the carpet industry. While attending a conference, she met others concerned about children in slavery as well as released bonded laborers. In 1989, she co-founded the South Asian Coalition on Child Servitude (SACCS) and led the development of Mukti Ashram, a rehabilitation center for freed child slaves. Since then, she has managed the center, developing the techniques for helping child slaves reclaim their place in the world. As they grow, the children take much of the responsibility for maintaining the center.

Suman uses only one name because the caste system in India is sometimes used to justify the enslavement of people from so-called lower castes. Since a person's last name usually indicates his or her caste position, she has given up her last name in order to demonstrate the equality of all people. When asked about her plans for the future, she responds, "I will work until child labor is abolished and all the kids are in school. My dream is that the children here at the center will become natural leaders, participating in all levels of decision making." Her advice to any young person who wants to make a difference is this: "Have confidence and clarity in your desire to do the right thing; get experience by helping others. You don't have to be special—anyone can do it!" (Interview with author, September 2000).

Moctar Teyeb (1959–)

Moctar Teyeb was born an *abd*, or slave, in Mauritania. As a child, one of his duties was to take his master's children to school each morning; if he tried to listen to the lessons through the window of the school, he was driven away. When he tried to attend the local Koranic (religious) school, he was beaten. During most of his youth, Teyeb lived a nomadic life, traveling with his master's livestock, walking long distances and doing the hardest work. As he grew older, his interest in education increased and he began to clash with his master. Then in the early 1970s, Teyeb's father escaped to Senegal. Like Frederick Douglass, Teyeb continued to educate himself in any way he could, secretly teaching himself to read. When he told his master in 1977 that he wanted to become a teacher, he was ridiculed and sent away to the capital city to work there. Slave life in the city was less controlled than in the countryside and, in 1978, Teyeb took the opportunity to follow his father and escape to Senegal.

After reuniting with his father, they set off together for the Ivory Coast, where they believed there would be a chance for Teyeb to attend school. After a harrowing trip across country, they reached their destination. At the age of twenty-two, Teyeb attended school for the first time in his life. He learned French and then persuaded the French Embassy to give him papers that stated he was Mauritanian (Mauritania was once a French colony). His academic skills were so good that he was soon awarded a scholarship to study in Libya and then Morocco. Though overjoyed at the chance to learn, his time in Libya and Morocco was made difficult by the fact that Arab classmates resented having an ex-slave in class and condemned him for his antislavery activism. Ultimately earning a law degree, he returned to Mauritania and found himself in a strange situation: Though he was regularly picked up and questioned by the police, he was not imprisoned. While his old master did not attempt to reclaim him, he found he did not fit into any community. He was able to continue contact with the underground antislavery movement.

Finally receiving a Mauritanian passport, he gained a visa to the United States and came to live with a relative in New York. Taking any sort of job, he devoted himself to studying toward an American law degree and improving his English. He also began speaking out and educating others about slavery in Mauritania. Before high school and university audiences as well as in various public gatherings, Teyeb discusses the deep-rooted slavery system from the unique perspective of an ex-slave. He often makes presentations about slavery in Mauritania. Speaking out in this way takes courage—the Mauritanian government is already trying to silence him. But every opportunity to tell his story brings more support for the antislavery movement. He continues to live in New York where he works and studies.

Harriet Tubman (1820–1913)

Harriet Tubman was the most courageous and daring of the "conductors" on the Underground Railway, which brought American slaves to freedom in the early nineteenth century. She was born Araminta Ross, a slave, in Maryland. Physically abused and starved as a child, she was partially disabled. Her life almost ended at fifteen when she blocked an overseer pursuing an escaping slave and received a terrible blow to the head. For years, she was dull-witted and unproductive, but family support and a strong will guided her to a slow but miraculous recovery. In the 1840s, she was angered to learn that her mother had been freed by a previous owner's will, but her mother had never been told, and that her family was about to be sold again. In 1849, she escaped to Philadelphia and took her mother's name, Harriet.

Within two years, she had joined with William Still, the black abolitionist and organizer of the Underground Railway in Pennsylvania. In 1851, she sneaked back into the slave states and came back with a group of escaped slaves; it was the first of many such trips. Though illiterate, she was a superb strategist and planned her trips carefully, carrying them through with rigid determination. Making at least nineteen trips, she freed hundreds of slaves, including her own parents and other relatives. More than $40,000 was offered for her capture—the equivalent of $4 million in today's money. While taking slaves to the North, she met and worked with Frederick Douglass as well as Susan B. Anthony and Elizabeth Cady Stanton. During the Civil War, she organized a group of black spies and scouts who carried out espionage and gained valuable information for the Union forces. She personally guided a group of black soldiers into a Confederate-held town and disabled the rebel supply line. After the war, Tubman worked to get women the right to vote. She was buried in 1913 with military honors.

John Woolman (1720–1772)

John Woolman was a Quaker and pioneer abolitionist born in colonial New Jersey. He has been described as having been an odd young man. During his youth, he tried to find simplicity and an ethical way of life that often led him to curious decisions, such as choosing to wear only clothes that had not been dyed with colors. After some time as a shopkeeper, he gave it up in order to travel more among the Quakers in colonial America. He took up "conveyancing"—the writing up of bills of sale, deeds, and leases—as a way to support himself. When his first employer asked him to draw up a bill of sale for a slave, Woolman did so but was very troubled at the time and afterward. From that point forward, he refused to write up any legal document regarding slavery, and he would take every opportunity to convince his clients of the immorality of slavery and urge them to free their slaves.

In 1746, he traveled in the southern colonies, where slavery was more prominent, and stayed with slaveholding Quaker families. He was so disturbed by what he saw that he wrote a pamphlet against slavery that was published, and then followed it with a call to all Quakers to renounce slavery. By 1758, his quiet but urgent campaigning among Quakers paid off with a general rule against keeping slaves or participating in the slave trade. By this action, the Quakers became the first organized body to oppose slavery in North America. Woolman also campaigned for equal treatment for Native Americans, and for living simply so that a person's resources could be better put to helping others. "The business of our lives," he wrote, is "to turn all the treasures we possess into the channel of universal love" (Religious Society of Friends 1999, 14, 23). Though a quiet and simple person, Woolman's example led the Quakers to become the mainstay of the coming abolitionist movement. Quakers are still active today in antislavery work.

References

Basu, Rekha. "Hometown Kid Fighting the New Face of Slavery." *Des Moines Register,* August 1, 2003, also available at: http://www.dmregister.com/opinion/stories/c5917686/21878226.html.

Hallegren, Bo. "Child Labor and the Situation of the Textile Industry in India." *Human Rights Solidarity,* Vol. 6, No. 3. Asian Human Rights Commission, New Delhi, September 1996, also available at: http://www.ahrchk.net/hrsolid/mainfile.php/1996vol06no03/164.

Hochschild, Adam. *Bury the Chains: Prophets and Rebels in the Fight to Free and Empire's Slaves.* New York: Houghton Mifflin, 2005, p. 89.

Religious Society of Friends, *Quaker Faith and Practice.* London: The Yearly Meeting of the Religious Society of Friends (Quakers) in Britain, 1999.

Ryan, Barbara. "Douglas, Frederick." In *The Historical Encyclopedia of World Slavery*, Vol. 1, Junius Rodriguez (ed.) Santa Barbara, CA: ABC-CLIO, 1997, p. 221.

6

Facts, Data, Evidence, and Testimony about Contemporary Slavery

The material included here aims to give the reader a sense of the scale and diversity of slavery in the modern world—and some insight into its inhumanity—at the beginning of the twenty-first century. This chapter offers an overview of the main forms of slavery, both old and new, that exist around the globe. It draws on a wide range of documents including book extracts, reports to United Nations committees, interviews with modern-day slaves, speeches from antislavery campaigners and their supporters, press stories, and briefings.

It begins with some key facts and figures, followed by a summary of the most important documents in international law and conventions that define and condemn slavery. This helps provide the context for the individual and collective stories of slaves and antislavery activists that follow.

These stories and evidence are divided into different kinds of slavery, although in practice there is a good deal of crossover between them. Traditional-style slave ownership in Mauritania, bonded labor in rural Asian societies, forced labor in Bosnia or Burma, the trafficking and sexual slavery of young girls from Thailand to the United States, domestic slavery in countries as diverse as the Philippines, Haiti and the United Kingdom—all of these variations on contemporary slavery have much in common. But they in their different ways show the many forms that slavery as a social and economic relationship can take.

The section concludes with a brief examination of the complex issue of child labor and two recent campaigns aimed at ending the use of young children in the production of goods sold to consumers. Not all child labor is slavery. But children enslaved in bonded labor or forced prostitution are two particularly pernicious kinds of slavery which have received a significant amount of attention worldwide.

Facts and Figures

The Slavery Index

Estimated number of slaves taken from Africa during the 400-year Atlantic slave trade: 13 million

Estimated number of slaves in the world in 1999: 27 million

Maximum estimated number of slaves transported from Africa by British slave traders at the height of the Atlantic trade (1730s–1740s), per year: 23,000

Estimated number of people trafficked across borders worldwide in 2004: 600,000 to 800,000

Estimated number of slaves transported into the United States each year: 20,000

Number of human traffickers arrested and charged by the U.S. government in 2003: 111

Number of human traffickers convicted of their crimes in 2003: 77

Number of international treaties enacted between 1815 and 1957 "for the suppression of the slave trade": 300

Cost of a 19-year-old agricultural slave in Mississippi in 1850 in 2004 dollars: $43,000

Cost of a 19-year-old agricultural slave in West Africa today in 2004 dollars: $40

Average profit of the British slave trade, 1761–1807: 9.5 percent

Average profit of Thai brothel using enslaved prostitutes, today: 856 percent

Cost of bringing an Indian slave family into freedom and economic stability: $32 (does not mean buying them out or paying off their illegal debt)

Cost of freeing all the slaves in the world at $32 each: $864 million

Total box-office earnings of the film *Finding Nemo* in 2003: $864 million

Amount the U.S. Congress approved for spending on nanotechnology research in 2006: $864 million

Wage bill in 2003 of the Texas "hunting industry": $864 million

The Spread of Slavery

Figure 6.1 shows the percentage of countries in the world having different amounts of slavery. Fewer than one country in five has no reported slavery, and a little under a third of all countries have very little or rare slavery. Slavery is a regular and persistent feature of life in just over half of all countries. A little less than one country in ten has slavery regularly contributing to many sectors of their economy. About two fifths of all countries have smaller amounts of slavery, which are, nonetheless, constant features in their national economy.

But why do some countries have more slavery than others? Why do some countries have persistent regular slavery and some countries have none at all? If we look at all the countries around the world and ask what things most strongly predict whether or not slavery exists in a country, a statistical test finds the strongest predictors of slavery in a country (in this order):

- Government and police corruption
- High level of infant mortality
- Population has high proportion of young people and children
- Country has low gross domestic product (GDP) per capita

What this indicates are the very factors discussed in Chapter 1 that have led to the emergence of new forms of slavery and an in-

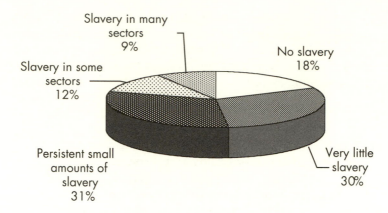

Figure 6.1   Percentage of countries with different levels of slavery (192 countries in total)

crease in slavery worldwide. Countries with a high proportion of children under the age of fourteen are countries experiencing the bulk of the population explosion. For those countries that also suffer from extremes in poverty and a lack of welfare services (measured by GDP and infant mortality), economic and social vulnerability becomes a regular part of life. When this large, poor, vulnerable population lacks protection from government and suffers police corruption, one result can be slavery.

Another pressure that seems to push countries toward a higher level of slavery is international debt. Many countries in the developing world must carry large debts to the World Bank or other lenders, and so must put most of their national income to paying the interest on these debts. If we look at those countries that are named by the World Bank as having a heavy debt load and compare them with countries that do not have large international debts, there is a marked difference with regard to slavery. Half of the countries with a heavy debt load have slavery as a regular feature in their economies, compared to only 12 percent of those countries with a small amount of international debt. Almost three quarters of countries with a large international debt find that their citizens are regularly trafficked into slavery in other countries, compared with less than a third of those with low international debt. The chart depicted in Figure 6.2 shows how international debt and slavery are related.

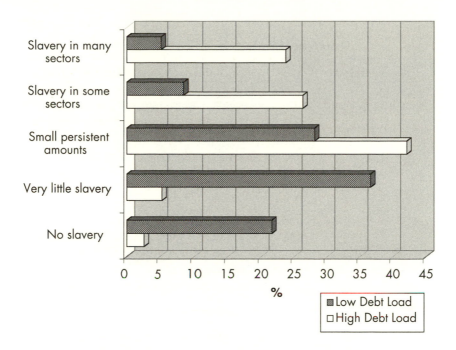

Figure 6.2   Amount of slavery in countries with high and low international debt

With slavery so widespread, it is fair to ask what laws and international agreements have been passed against it, and to wonder whether they are, in fact, effective. The next section reviews the many, and often confused, laws and conventions that exist concerning slavery.

Key International Laws and Conventions on Slavery

Slavery has not always been defined in the same way in international conventions. Table 6.1 shows how the definition of slavery has changed over time.

These different definitions and the naming of other activities as "slavery" means that many things have been called slavery that we may or may not think actually constitute slavery. Table 6.2

TABLE 6.1
Summary of the Evolution of Slavery Conventions

Slavery Convention	Definition/Declaration Regarding Slavery
Slavery Convention (1926)	Slavery defined: The "status or condition of a person over whom all of the powers attaching to the right of ownership are exercised" Forced Labor added: States should "prevent compulsory or forced labor from developing into conditions analogous to slavery"
Universal Declaration (1948)	Servitude added: "No one shall be held in slavery or servitude; slavery and the slave trade should be abolished in all their forms"
Supplementary Convention (1956)	Servile Status added: Practices referred to as servile status should be abolished: a. debt bondage b. serfdom c. unfree marriages d. the exploitation of young people for their labor
Economic, Social and Cultural Covenant (1966)	Freedom to choose work added: Recognizes "the right of everyone to the opportunity to gain his living by work which he freely chooses or accepts."
Trafficking Protocol of the UN Convention on Transnational Organized Crime (came into effect 2003)	Trafficking added: "the action of recruitment, transportation, transfer, harboring, or receipt of persons by means of the threat or use of force, coercion, abduction, fraud, deception, abuse of power or vulnerability, or giving payments or benefits to a person in control of the victim for the purposes of exploitation, which includes exploiting the prostitution of others, sexual exploitation, forced labor, slavery or similar practices, and the removal of organs"

shows most of the activities that have been called "slavery" by international agencies and compares them to our definition:

> Slavery: A social and economic relationship in which a person is controlled through violence or its threat, paid nothing, and economically exploited.

There are literally hundreds of international laws and conventions that variously define, condemn, and outlaw slavery in its various past and present forms. The following selected ex-

TABLE 6.2
Practices Defined as Forms of Slavery in International Conventions

Practice/Criteria Y = Yes N = No	Totally controlled (Y/N)	Paid nothing, economically used (Y/N)	Violence or threat of violence (Y/N)
Chattel Slavery	Y	Y	Y
"White Slavery"	Y	Y	Y
Forced Labor	Y	Y	Y
Debt Bondage	Y	Y	Y
Child Prostitution	Y	Y	Y
Forced Prostitution	Y	Y	Y
Sexual Slavery	Y	Y	Y
Migrant Workers	Y/N	Y/N	Y/N
Prostitution	Y/N	Y/N	Y/N
Forced Marriage	Y/N	Y/N	Y
Apartheid	Y/N	N	Y
Incest	Y/N	N	Y
Organ Harvesting	Y/N	N	Y/N
Caste	N	N	Y
Prison Labor	N	Y/N	Y

Source: "No One Shall Be Held in Slavery or Servitude: A Critical Analysis of International Slavery Agreements." *Human Rights Review*, Vol. 2, No. 2, January 2001, with Peter Robbins.

tracts mark key moments in the evolution of international law on slavery.

Slavery Convention of the League of Nations (1926)

Article 1 For the purpose of the present Convention, the following definitions are agreed upon:

(1) Slavery is the status or condition of a person over whom any or all of the powers attaching to the right of ownership are exercised.

(2) The slave trade includes all acts involved in the capture, acquisition or disposal of a person with intent to reduce him to slavery; all acts involved in the acquisition of a slave with a view to selling or exchanging him; all acts of disposal by sale or exchange of a slave acquired with a view to being sold or exchanged, and, in general, every act of trade or transport in slaves.

Article 2 The High Contracting Parties undertake, each in respect of the territories placed under its sovereignty, jurisdiction, protection, suzerainty or tutelage, so far as they have not already taken the necessary steps:

(a) To prevent and suppress the slave trade;

(b) To bring about, progressively and as soon as possible, the complete abolition of slavery in all its forms.

Article 3 The High Contracting Parties undertake to adopt all appropriate measures with a view to preventing and suppressing the embarkation, disembarkation and transport of slaves in their territorial waters and upon all vessels flying their respective flags.

(The 1926 Convention was adopted with slight amendments by the UN in 1953.)

The Universal Declaration of Human Rights (1948)

Article 1 All human beings are born free and equal in dignity and rights.

Article 4 No one shall be held in slavery or servitude; slavery and the slave trade shall be prohibited in all their forms.

Article 13(I) Everyone has the right to freedom of movement and residence within the borders of each state.

Article 23(I) Everyone has the right to the free choice of employment, to just and favourable conditions of work and to protection against unemployment.

Supplementary Convention on the Abolition of Slavery, the Slave Trade, and Institutions and Practices Similar to Slavery (1956)

Section 1—Institutions and Practices Similar to Slavery

Article 1 Each of the States Parties to this Convention shall take all practicable and necessary legislative and other measures to bring about progressively and as soon as possible the complete abolition or abandonment of the following institutions and practices, where they still exist and whether or not they are covered by the definition of slavery contained in article 1 of the Slavery Convention signed at Geneva on 25 September, 1926:

(a) Debt bondage, that is to say, the status or condition arising from a pledge by a debtor of his personal services or of those of a person under his control as security for a debt, if the value of those services as reasonably assessed is not applied towards the liquidation of the debt or the length and nature of those services are not respectively limited and defined;

(b) Serfdom, that is to say, the condition or status of a tenant who is by law, custom or agreement bound to live and labor on land belonging to another person and to render some determinate service to such other person, whether for reward or not, and is not free to change his status;

(c) Any institution or practice whereby:

(i) A woman, without the right to refuse, is promised or given in marriage on payment of a consideration in money or in kind to her parents, guardian, family or any other person or group; or

(ii) The husband of a woman, his family, or his clan, has the right to transfer her to another person for value received or otherwise; or

(iii) A woman on the death of her husband is liable to be inherited by another person;

(d) Any institution or practice whereby a child or young person under the age of 18 years, is delivered by either or both of his natural parents or by his guardian to another person, whether for reward or not, with a view to the exploitation of the child or young person or of his labor.

Article 2 With a view to bringing to an end the institutions and practices mentioned in article 1 (c) of this Convention, the States Parties undertake to prescribe, where appropriate, suitable minimum ages of marriage, to encourage the use of facilities whereby the consent of both parties to a marriage may be freely expressed in the presence of a competent civil or religious authority, and to encourage the registration of marriages.

Section II—The Slave Trade

Article 3 The act of conveying or attempting to convey slaves from one country to another by whatever means of transport, or of being accessory thereto, shall be a criminal offence under the laws of the States Parties to this Convention and persons convicted thereof shall be liable to very severe penalties.

2. (a) The States Parties shall take all effective measures to prevent ships and aircraft authorised to fly their flags from conveying slaves and to punish persons guilty of such acts or of using national flags for that purpose.

(b) The States Parties shall take all effective measures to ensure that their ports, airfields and coasts are not used for the conveyance of slaves.

3. The States Parties to this Convention shall exchange information in order to ensure the practical co-ordination of the measures taken by them in combating the slave trade and shall inform each other of every case of the slave trade, and of every attempt to commit this criminal offence, which comes to their notice.

Article 4 Any slave who takes refuge on board any vessel of a State Party to this Convention shall ipso facto be free.

Section III Slavery and Institutions and Practices similar to Slavery

Article 5 In a country where the abolition or abandonment of slavery, or of the institutions or practices mentioned in article 1 of this Convention, is not yet complete, the act of mutilating, branding or otherwise marking a slave or a person of servile status in order to indicate his status, or as a punishment, or for any other reason, or of being accessory thereto, shall be a criminal offence under the laws of the States Parties to this Convention and persons convicted thereof shall be liable to punishment.

Article 6 1. The act of enslaving another person or of inducing another person to give himself or a person dependent upon him into slavery, or of attempting these acts, or being accessory thereto, or being a party to a conspiracy to accomplish any such acts, shall be a criminal offence under the laws of the States Parties to this Convention and persons convicted thereof shall be liable to punishment.

2. Subject to the provisions of the introductory paragraph of article 1 of this Convention, the provisions of paragraph 1 of the

present article shall also apply to the act of inducing another person to place himself or a person dependent upon him into the servile status resulting from any of the institutions or practices mentioned in article 1, to any attempt to perform such acts, to being accessory thereto, and to being a party to a conspiracy to accomplish such acts.

Section IV Definitions

Article 7 For the purposes of the present Convention:

(a) "Slavery" means, as defined in the Slavery Convention of 1926, the status or condition of a person over whom any or all of the powers attaching to the right of ownership are exercised, and "slave" means a person in such condition or status:

(b) "A person of servile status" means a person in the condition or status resulting from any of the institutions or practices mentioned in article 1 of this Convention;

(c) "Slave trade" means and includes all acts involved in the capture, acquisition or disposal of a person with intent to reduce him to slavery; all acts involved in the acquisition of a slave with a view to selling or exchanging him; all acts of disposal by sale or exchange of a person acquired with a view to being sold or exchanged; and, in general, every act of trade or transport in slaves by whatever means of conveyance.

Convention on the Rights of the Child (1989)

Article 27 1. States Parties recognize the right of every child to a standard of living adequate for the child's physical, mental, spiritual, moral and social development.

Article 28 1. States Parties recognize the right of the child to education, and with a view to achieving this right progressively and on a basis of equal opportunity, they shall, in particular: (a) Make primary education compulsory and available free to all . . .

Article 32 1. States Parties recognize the right of the child to be protected from economic exploitation and from performing any work that is likely to be hazardous or to interfere with the child's education, or to be harmful to the child's health or physical, mental, spiritual, moral or social development.

ILO Convention Concerning the Prohibition and Immediate Action for the Elimination of the Worst Forms of Child Labor (1999)

Article 1 Each Member which ratifies this Convention shall take immediate and effective measures to secure the prohibition and elimination of the worst forms of child labor as a matter of urgency.

Article 2 For the purposes of this Convention, the term *child* shall apply to all persons under the age of 18.

Article 3 For the purposes of this Convention, the term *the worst forms of child labor* comprises:

(a) all forms of slavery or practices similar to slavery, such as the sale and trafficking of children, debt bondage and serfdom and forced or compulsory labor, including forced or compulsory recruitment of children for use in armed conflict;

(b) the use, procuring or offering of a child for prostitution, for the production of pornography or for pornographic performances;

(c) the use, procuring or offering of a child for illicit activities, in particular for the production and trafficking of drugs as defined in the relevant international treaties;

(d) work which, by its nature or the circumstances in which it is carried out, is likely to harm the health, safety or morals of children.

United States Trafficking Victims Protection Act (2000)

At the end of 2000, the U.S. Congress passed the law known as the Trafficking Victims Protection Act. This law was a breakthrough for the United States, bringing a much more clear definition of what constituted human trafficking. It called for the establishment an interagency taskforce at the top level of government and an Office to Monitor and Combat Trafficking in Persons within the State Department, and required that office to make an annual report on all countries, demonstrating how well they were doing in the global fight against human trafficking. If countries were not taking serious actions against trafficking, it allowed the President to impose economic and other sanctions against them. Such sanctions have now been imposed on Burma, Cuba, Liberia, North Korea, and Sudan. The full text of the law can be seen at http://www.state.gov/g/tip.

Excerpts from the Act
SEC. 102. PURPOSES AND FINDINGS.

(a) PURPOSES—The purposes of this division are to combat trafficking in persons, a contemporary manifestation of slavery whose victims are predominantly women and children, to ensure just and effective punishment of traffickers, and to protect their victims.

(b) FINDINGS—Congress finds that:

(1) As the 21st century begins, the degrading institution of slavery continues throughout the world. Trafficking in persons is a modern form of slavery, and it is the largest manifestation of slavery today. At least 700,000 persons annually, primarily women and children, are trafficked within or across international borders. Approximately 50,000 women and children are trafficked into the United States each year.

(2) Many of these persons are trafficked into the international sex trade, often by force, fraud, or coercion. The sex industry has rapidly expanded over the past several decades. It involves sexual exploitation of persons, predominantly women and girls, involving activities related to prostitution, pornography, sex tourism, and other commercial sexual services. The low status of women in many parts of the world has contributed to a burgeoning of the trafficking industry.

(3) Trafficking in persons is not limited to the sex industry. This growing transnational crime also includes forced labor and involves significant violations of labor, public health, and human rights standards worldwide.

(4) Traffickers primarily target women and girls, who are disproportionately affected by poverty, the lack of access to education, chronic unemployment, discrimination, and the lack of economic opportunities in countries of origin. Traffickers lure women and girls into their networks through false promises of decent working conditions at relatively good pay as nannies, maids, dancers, factory workers, restaurant workers, sales clerks, or models. Traffickers also buy children from poor families and

sell them into prostitution or into various types of forced or bonded labor.

(5) Traffickers often transport victims from their home communities to unfamiliar destinations, including foreign countries away from family and friends, religious institutions, and other sources of protection and support, leaving the victims defenseless and vulnerable.

(6) Victims are often forced through physical violence to engage in sex acts or perform slavery-like labor. Such force includes rape and other forms of sexual abuse, torture, starvation, imprisonment, threats, psychological abuse, and coercion.

(7) Traffickers often make representations to their victims that physical harm may occur to them or others should the victim escape or attempt to escape. Such representations can have the same coercive effects on victims as direct threats to inflict such harm.

(8) Trafficking in persons is increasingly perpetrated by organized, sophisticated criminal enterprises. Such trafficking is the fastest growing source of profits for organized criminal enterprises worldwide. Profits from the trafficking industry contribute to the expansion of organized crime in the United States and worldwide. Trafficking in persons is often aided by official corruption in countries of origin, transit, and destination, thereby threatening the rule of law.

(9) Trafficking includes all the elements of the crime of forcible rape when it involves the involuntary participation of another person in sex acts by means of fraud, force, or coercion.

(10) Trafficking also involves violations of other laws, including labor and immigration codes and laws against kidnapping, slavery, false imprisonment, assault, battery, pandering, fraud, and extortion.

(11) Trafficking exposes victims to serious health risks. Women and children trafficked in the sex industry are exposed to deadly diseases, including HIV and AIDS. Trafficking victims are sometimes worked or physically brutalized to death.

(12) Trafficking in persons substantially affects interstate and foreign commerce. Trafficking for such purposes as involuntary servitude, peonage, and other forms of forced labor has an impact on the nationwide employment network and labor market. Within the context of slavery, servitude, and labor or services which are obtained or maintained through coercive conduct that amounts to a condition of servitude, victims are subjected to a range of violations.

(13) Involuntary servitude statutes are intended to reach cases in which persons are held in a condition of servitude through nonviolent coercion. In United States v. Kozminski, 487 U.S. 931 (1988), the Supreme Court found that section 1584 of title 18, United States Code, should be narrowly interpreted, absent a definition of involuntary servitude by Congress. As a result, that section was interpreted to criminalize only servitude that is brought about through use or threatened use of physical or legal coercion, and to exclude other conduct that can have the same purpose and effect.

(14) Existing legislation and law enforcement in the United States and other countries are inadequate to deter trafficking and bring traffickers to justice, failing to reflect the gravity of the offenses involved. No comprehensive law exists in the United States that penalizes the range of offenses involved in the trafficking scheme. Instead, even the most brutal instances of trafficking in the sex industry are often punished under laws that also apply to lesser offenses, so that traffickers typically escape deserved punishment.

(15) In the United States, the seriousness of this crime and its components is not reflected in current sentencing guidelines, resulting in weak penalties for convicted traffickers.

(16) In some countries, enforcement against traffickers is also hindered by official indifference, by corruption, and sometimes even by official participation in trafficking.

(17) Existing laws often fail to protect victims of trafficking, and because victims are often illegal immigrants in the destination country, they are repeatedly punished more harshly than the traffickers themselves.

(18) Additionally, adequate services and facilities do not exist to meet victims' needs regarding health care, housing, education, and legal assistance, which safely reintegrate trafficking victims into their home countries.

(19) Victims of severe forms of trafficking should not be inappropriately incarcerated, fined, or otherwise penalized solely for unlawful acts committed as a direct result of being trafficked, such as using false documents, entering the country without documentation, or working without documentation.

(20) Because victims of trafficking are frequently unfamiliar with the laws, cultures, and languages of the countries into which they have been trafficked, because they are often subjected to coercion and intimidation including physical detention and debt bondage, and because they often fear retribution and

forcible removal to countries in which they will face retribution or other hardship, these victims often find it difficult or impossible to report the crimes committed against them or to assist in the investigation and prosecution of such crimes.

(21) Trafficking of persons is an evil requiring concerted and vigorous action by countries of origin, transit or destination, and by international organizations.

(22) One of the founding documents of the United States, the Declaration of Independence, recognizes the inherent dignity and worth of all people. It states that all men are created equal and that they are endowed by their creator with certain unalienable rights. The right to be free from slavery and involuntary servitude is among those unalienable rights. Acknowledging this fact, the United States outlawed slavery and involuntary servitude in 1865, recognizing them as evil institutions that must be abolished. Current practices of sexual slavery and trafficking of women and children are similarly abhorrent to the principles upon which the United States was founded.

(23) The United States and the international community agree that trafficking in persons involves grave violations of human rights and is a matter of pressing international concern. The international community has repeatedly condemned slavery and involuntary servitude, violence against women, and other elements of trafficking, through declarations, treaties, and United Nations resolutions and reports, including the Universal Declaration of Human Rights; the 1956 Supplementary Convention on the Abolition of Slavery, the Slave Trade, and Institutions and Practices Similar to Slavery; the 1948 American Declaration on the Rights and Duties of Man; the 1957 Abolition of Forced Labor Convention; the International Covenant on Civil and Political Rights; the Convention Against Torture and Other Cruel, Inhuman or Degrading Treatment or Punishment; United Nations General Assembly Resolutions 50/167, 51/66, and 52/98; the Final Report of the World Congress against Sexual Exploitation of Children (Stockholm, 1996); the Fourth World Conference on Women (Beijing, 1995); and the 1991 Moscow Document of the Organization for Security and Cooperation in Europe.

(24) Trafficking in persons is a transnational crime with national implications. To deter international trafficking and bring its perpetrators to justice, nations including the United States must recognize that trafficking is a serious offense. This is done by prescribing appropriate punishment, giving priority to the prosecu-

tion of trafficking offenses, and protecting rather than punishing the victims of such offenses. The United States must work bilaterally and multilaterally to abolish the trafficking industry by taking steps to promote cooperation among countries linked together by international trafficking routes. The United States must also urge the international community to take strong action in multilateral fora to engage recalcitrant countries in serious and sustained efforts to eliminate trafficking and protect trafficking victims.

SEC. 103. DEFINITIONS.

In this division:

(1) APPROPRIATE CONGRESSIONAL COMMITTEES—The term 'appropriate congressional committees' means the Committee on Foreign Relations and the Committee on the Judiciary of the Senate and the Committee on International Relations and the Committee on the Judiciary of the House of Representatives.

(2) COERCION—The term 'coercion' means—

(A) threats of serious harm to or physical restraint against any person;

(B) any scheme, plan, or pattern intended to cause a person to believe that failure to perform an act would result in serious harm to or physical restraint against any person; or

(C) the abuse or threatened abuse of the legal process.

(3) COMMERCIAL SEX ACT—The term 'commercial sex act' means any sex act on account of which anything of value is given to or received by any person.

(4) DEBT BONDAGE—The term 'debt bondage' means the status or condition of a debtor arising from a pledge by the debtor of his or her personal services or of those of a person under his or her control as a security for debt, if the value of those services as reasonably assessed is not applied toward the liquidation of the debt or the length and nature of those services are not respectively limited and defined.

(5) INVOLUNTARY SERVITUDE—The term 'involuntary servitude' includes a condition of servitude induced by means of—

(A) any scheme, plan, or pattern intended to cause a person to believe that, if the person did not enter into or continue in such condition, that person or another person would suffer serious harm or physical restraint; or

(B) the abuse or threatened abuse of the legal process.

. . .

(8) SEVERE FORMS OF TRAFFICKING IN PERSONS—The term 'severe forms of trafficking in persons' means—

(A) sex trafficking in which a commercial sex act is induced by force, fraud, or coercion, or in which the person induced to perform such act has not attained 18 years of age; or

(B) the recruitment, harboring, transportation, provision, or obtaining of a person for labor or services, through the use of force, fraud, or coercion for the purpose of subjection to involuntary servitude, peonage, debt bondage, or slavery.

(9) SEX TRAFFICKING—The term 'sex trafficking' means the recruitment, harboring, transportation, provision, or obtaining of a person for the purpose of a commercial sex act.

United Nations Convention on Transnational Organized Crime (2000)

Also in 2000, the United Nations brought forward the Convention on Transnational Organized Crime. This Convention dealt with organized crime in three areas: the illegal sale and traffic of weapons; drug trafficking; and human trafficking. To come into force (be recognized as international law), a Convention has to be approved (signed and ratified) by a minimum number of national governments. Sometimes this process of ratification will take many years, but unlike many conventions, the Convention on Transnational Organized Crime came into force quickly—on September 29, 2003—but it has *not* been ratified by the United States.

One part of the Convention is the Protocol to Prevent, Suppress and Punish Trafficking in Persons, Especially Women and Children. A protocol is a distinct part of a Convention that has to be signed and ratified separately. This Protocol was a major step in bringing forward a clear definition and plan for the international effort to end human trafficking. Known as the Trafficking Protocol, it aims to prevent and combat trafficking in persons, to protect and assist the victims with full respect for their human rights, and to facilitate international cooperation against trafficking.

The Protocol to Prevent, Suppress and Punish Trafficking in Persons, Especially Women and Children defines trafficking in persons in this way:

Trafficking in persons is (Art. 3.a):

- The action of recruitment, transportation, transfer, harbouring, or receipt of persons
- By means of the threat or use of force, coercion, abduction, fraud, deception, abuse of power or vulnerability, or giving payments or benefits to a person in control of the victim
- For the purposes of exploitation, which includes exploiting the prostitution of others, sexual exploitation, forced labour, slavery or similar practices, and the removal of organs
- Consent of the victim is irrelevant where illicit means are established, but criminal law defences are preserved (Protocol Art. 3.b, Convention Art. 11.6)

The definition is broken down into three lists of elements: criminal acts, the means used to commit those acts, and goals (forms of exploitation). This definition of trafficking is a key element of the Protocol. It represents the first clear definition at the international level. It will greatly assist in the fight against trafficking by standardizing approaches to the problem. As it is adopted it will help ensure that legislative and administrative measures are consistent from country to country, and it will help provide a common basis for statistical and research purposes.

When a country ratifies the Trafficking Protocol, it is agreeing to take specific actions:

- To make trafficking in persons a criminal offense
- To protect and assist the victims of human trafficking
- To help repatriate victims when this is appropriate
- To prevent trafficking through information and mass media campaigns to alert and educate officials and potential victims, addressing factors such as "poverty, underdevelopment and lack of equal opportunity," which make people vulnerable to trafficking, and using "legislative . . . educational, social or cultural" or other measures to reduce the demand that leads to trafficking in the first place
- To have their enforcement agencies cooperate with other countries through information exchange and helping with training

- To strengthen their own border controls, imposing requirements on commercial carriers to check passports and visas, and to considering the denial or revocation of visas of persons involved in trafficking

The Trafficking Protocol entered into force on December 25, 2003, and it has *not* been ratified by the United States.

Reports, Evidence, and Testimony about the Different Types of Slavery

Bonded Labor

Bonded labor is the most common form of slavery in the modern world. A person pledges him or herself against a loan of money but the length and nature of the service is not defined and the labor does not reduce the original debt. The debt can be passed down through the generations, and "defaulting" can be punished by seizing or selling children into further debt bonds. It is most common in India and Pakistan.

Testimony about Bonded Labor in India

Keshav Nankar is an ex-bonded laborer who now works to liberate others from such slavery. Vivek Pandit works with bonded laborers in the Thane district of India (see also their biographical sketches in Chapter 5). They made the following speeches to an audience in London on jointly receiving the annual Anti-Slavery Award for 1999.

> **Keshav Nankar.** Today, I am here in front of you, speaking to you, after travelling thousands of miles. This is unbelievable considering who I was in 1983. Today, I have the capacity and the confidence to address thousands of brothers and sisters. I am proud that today I can deal with government officials at various levels. And, if they do not pay attention to my community's genuine demands, we will protest and demand our rights. Furthermore, I have become actively involved in the political process. I contested the elections for the State Assembly. I teach my fellow farmers the latest, modern techniques of

farming practices. Looking back at my past I cannot believe my present today. It seems unreal but it's not a dream, it is a reality born out of a lot of pain, a lot of struggle and a lot of dreams put together.

I remember as a child, when I was six or seven years old, my father enrolled me in the village school. I used to like my school very much. I especially loved the singing, dancing, and playing. But my father needed some money. He asked his landlord—for whom he had worked his entire life—for some money. The landlord gave him the money but took me in return. He asked my father, "What would your child do in school?" and "How will he feed himself?" He said, "Remove him from school, send him here to look after my cattle and I will give him one meal a day." That is how I was taken out of school when I was seven years old and I was not allowed to study beyond my first standard.

I continued working with the landlord. I got married and my wife and I worked in the fields and at home. Through marrying me, my wife also became a bonded laborer to my landlord. From dawn to midnight, we used to fetch water, clean the utensils, wash clothes, collect firewood and remove cow dung. We also had to prepare the ground for sowing the seeds, transplanting the saplings, nurturing the plants, harvesting the field, and finally husking the grains. The other agricultural laborers, who were lucky not to be bonded, worked much less and earned much more than me.

Once, to earn a bit more, I went to work with another landlord. This angered my landlord. He sent his henchmen to fetch me. They brutally assaulted me and verbally abused me during the journey back to my landlord.

My wages were not sufficient to feed my family even once. My debt kept increasing. I was getting sucked into a whirlpool. As a result, I became suppressed, with no voice of my own. I wanted to break the shackles and get out of this misery but I could not see any way out. In 1983, I met a few workers of Shramjeevi Sanghatana, a trade union that had started mobilizing bonded laborers, agricultural laborers and small farmers in the neighboring areas. They built our confidence and our powers. They taught us to say NO and not to bow to any injustice. They gave us the strength to fight against all sorts of atrocities that have been committed against us for generations. The landlords troubled us in many ways but the Sanghatana members remained with us through all our sufferings and hardships. When we were beaten severely, they were there getting beaten with us. When we had no food, they starved with us. This is how our struggle continued.

Today, in our area nobody dares to keep a bonded laborer. We proudly run the village Gram Panchayat (Council). I contested the assembly elections based on the credibility of Sanghatana, not on the power of money. I lost the elections but it is not the result, but the process that is important. I proved that a poor person once without any rights, suppressed beyond imagination, could also emerge stronger and exercise his democratic rights to the fullest.

Today, I also do collective farming, along with the other freed bonded and agricultural laborers. The landlords who were keepers of bonded labor now come to me for advice on farming. This is not my story alone but a story of thousands of changed lives. (Acceptance speech given at the 1999 Anti-Slavery Awards Ceremony, London, England, October 27, 1999. Reprinted by permission of Anti-Slavery International.)

Vivek Pandit. When I went to get my visa before coming here I was interviewed by a lady at the Consulate who asked me in wonder, "Are there still slaves in India?" Perhaps some of you would ask the same question. The answer my friends is yes. Even after fifty years of freedom from colonial rule there are still millions of men, women, and children who live lives of bondage. When we went to work in the rural areas in the late seventies we knew nothing of bonded labor or slavery, what we saw in the villages was that they were not a homogenous community. We saw that the landlord belonging to the upper caste, with more money and political connections owned the tribals who were landless, abjectly poor and belonged to the lowest stratum of the caste system. The power was literally concentrated at the core even geographically. All resources came to villages where the landlords lived, while the tribals (indigenous people) were pushed to the far-flung hamlets, in the interior and inaccessible forests.

We learned from the people how they took small sums of money from the landlord during illness or marriage and then were bonded to him for generations. The bonded laborer was less than an animal. The landowner's bullocks were better taken care of than the human beings. After the season transplantation of paddy the bullocks were rested for a month or more and all this time the bonded laborer was expected to gather the green fodder for the cattle. I remember that the tribals would work without respite till their feet rotted by being continuously in the water. Ironically, the owners would beat the tribals who could not work.

These were the slave citizens of a free country. This was the irony in the largest democracy in the world. When we began working for the release of bonded laborers we realized we were challenging the vested interests in the area. The release of bonded labor is a process from slavery to freedom, and freedom is never gifted away. Freedom can only be won through struggle, by building the strength of the people. We realized that those in bondage have to be prepared to overthrow their chains at any cost, even at the cost of their lives. My advice to those who say they want to free bonded laborers but are unable to do so because of police cases or threats by landlords, I ask them, "What else did you expect?" It is only natural that the powerful will react to keep their interests intact. Dr. Martin Luther King had said, "Freedom has always been an expensive thing." Indeed we have to prepare to pay the highest price for it.

The essential condition of bondage is in the minds of the people. While recording the statements of the hundreds of bonded laborers, whenever we asked, "What is your problem?" invariably they replied, "Nothing." A bonded laborer has no dreams and torture is a way of life. They have been conditioned to accept that their place is at the periphery of society. The process of release and rehabilitation of bonded labor is to restore the personhood of the person, to restore self-esteem, confidence, and the feeling that they too can win. Until yesterday we had nothing but we can build for a better to-morrow for our children. Release from bondage can only come through collective action saying 'no' to an in-human system. Thus, there were uniting slogans that brought together the bonded laborers:

Tribals are human beings not cattle

We are demanding our rights as human beings.

Slogans and songs like these are helpful in reinforcing the feeling of dignity in the bonded labor. When the landlords attacked them a tribal woman said, "We will eat bitter roots and crabs, but we will not bow down be-fore the landlords." That became another powerful slo-gan in the struggle against bonded labor. The system of bonded labor could not be fought in isolation. The struggle against bonded labor was linked to the larger struggle for rights of agricultural laborers, for minimum and equal wages, for the restoration of tribal land grabbed by the landlords and so on. The movement grew, not strength in members, but strength in feeling, belief and solidarity. More and more marginalized people joined it and strengthened it. We learned that bonded laborers do not become free because they are not convinced that they can remain in freedom. The message that goes across to the bonded laborer is that the entire system is against them.

The landlords are obviously exploiting them, but the law enforcement agencies do not help them either. They know that they are being tortured but there is no one to listen to their plight. They are not even convinced that social workers or NGOs will listen to them. I remember when we first came across the issue of bonded labor, we spent nearly two whole years trying to convince the tribals to become free. The landlords were angry that we were campaigning against them, and the tribals ran away whenever they saw us because my uncle was a bonded labor keeper. They thought we were the agents of the landlords. A bonded laborer does not become free overnight. In this period of transition we have to help them in every possible way. Once they are free, the bonded laborers become part of the larger community of the workforce and are free to sell their labor to any person. The issues of the larger community become theirs. The poverty, illiteracy, disease and exploitation that are the lot of the free labor also become their lot.

Another lesson we learned was that social legislation by itself cannot destroy slavery. While powerful laws are important and useful, without an insistent and equally powerful voice to demand their implementation, laws have remained on paper. Similarly, any other tool like using the media, public interest litigation or using legislative devices have to be linked to collective action if they are to bring long lasting change in the lives of the people. Releasing bonded laborers is not a project. It is entering into the politics of tilting the balance of power in favor of the marginalized. This requires knowing the various democratic institutions, the laws, and the pulse of the people, the mind of the opponent. But once bonded laborers are free the sky is the limit. They do not wait for alternative employment or rehabilitation packages. Freed bonded laborers in Thane (our district in Maharashtra) have helped other bonded laborers all over the country in their struggle for freedom. They have even collected one Rupee each as a token contribution in the freedom struggle of Nelson Mandela and the African National Congress. They have truly understood in their hearts that no one is free till every one is free. (Acceptance speech given at the 1999 Anti-Slavery Awards Ceremony, London, England, October 27, 1999. Reprinted by permission of Anti-Slavery International.)

Contract Slavery

Contract Slavery in Brazil

Contract slavery shows how modern labor relations are used to hide slavery. Contracts are offered that guarantee employment, but when the workers are taken to the place of work they find themselves enslaved. This is the second largest but also the most rapidly growing form of slavery today.

The main form of slavery found in modern-day Brazil is contract slavery based on debt bondage. In a country where an estimated one in five of the population lives in absolute poverty, workers from areas hit by recession or natural disasters such as drought are enticed into accepting verbal contracts on the basis of false promises of well-paid work. They are then transported thousands of miles in trucks to work on estates in isolated parts of the Amazon states. Recruitment is carried out by a *Gato* (cat). The workers are then told they are in debt for their transportation, tools, food, and other inflated living costs while working and forced into a cycle of bonded labor. In 2003, newly elected President Luiz Ignacio Lula da Silva (known as "Lula") announced dramatic increases in funding and efforts aimed at fighting slavery. Despite the increased activity, at least 25,000 people are thought to be enslaved clearing land in the Amazon and making charcoal for the nation's steel industry. The work to end slavery in Brazil is hampered by the fact that many of the large landowners are also powerful politicians who block national and local efforts.

Evidence and Testimony from Brazil about Contract Slavery

From the early 1980s, as the wave of development swept into Mato Grosso do Sul, recruiters began to appear in the slums of Minas Gerais seeking workers with some experience of charcoal making. These recruiters are called *Gatos* and are key players in the process of enslavement. When they drive into the slums with their cattle trucks and announce that they are hiring men or even whole families, the desperate residents immediately respond. The *Gatos* will go from door to door or use loudspeakers to call people into the street. Sometimes the local politicians, even local churches, will let them use public buildings and help them to recruit workers. The *Gatos* explain that they need workers in the ranches and forests of Mato Grosso. Like good salesmen they lay out the many advantages of regular work and good conditions. They offer to provide transport to Mato Grosso, good food on site, a regular salary, provision of tools, and a free trip home every month to see the family. For a hungry family it seems a miraculous offer of a new beginning. In a charcoal camp in Mato Grosso do Sul I spoke with a man named Renaldo who told me about being recruited by the *Gato*:

> My parents lived in a very dry rural area and when I got older there was no work, no work at all there. So I decided to go to the city. I went to São Paulo but that was even worse, no work and everything was very expensive, and the place was dangerous—so much crime! So then I went up to Minas Gerais because I heard that there was work there. If there was I didn't find it, but one day a Gato came and began to recruit people to

work out here in Mato Grosso. The Gato said that we would be given good food everyday, and we would have good wages besides. He promised that every month his truck would bring people back to Minas Gerais so that they could visit their families and bring them their pay. He even gave money to some men to give to their families before they left and to buy food to bring with them on the trip. He was able to fill up his truck with workers very easily and we started on the trip west. Along the way, when we would stop for fuel, the Gato would say 'Go on into the cafe and eat as much as you like, I'll pay for it.' We had been hungry for a long time, so you can imagine how we ate! When we got to Mato Grosso we kept driving further and further into the country. This camp is almost fifty miles from anything, it is just raw cerrado for fifty miles before you get to even a ranch, and there is just the one road. When we reached the camp we could see it was terrible: the conditions were not good enough for animals. Standing around the camp were men with guns. And then the Gato said, 'You each owe me a lot of money, there is the cost of the trip, and all that food you ate, and the money I gave you for your families—so don't even think about leaving.'

Renaldo was trapped. With the other workers he found he could not leave the camp or have any say in the work he was given to do. After two months, when the workers asked about going home for a visit they were told they were still too deeply in debt to be allowed to go. (Bales 1999; © The Regents of the University of California. Reprinted by permission.)

Chattel Slavery

This is the form of slavery closest to the old slavery. A person is completely owned by their master or mistress. They are sold, captured, or born into a lifetime of slavery. The slave children are usually also treated as property and can be traded like cattle between owners. Chattel slavery is most commonly found in parts of northern and western Africa and some Arab countries. It represents a small proportion of today's slaves.

Evidence of Chattel Slavery in Mauritania

Mauritanian society is made of three groups, the Arab Moors from the north, slaves and ex-slaves called Haratines, and the Afro-Mauritanians in the south. Slavery has been abolished many times in Mauritania, most recently in 1980 when perhaps as many as one third of the country's population of 2 million became ex-slaves on paper. But many remain enslaved, either unaware of their rights or unable to translate legal freedom into practical action. Salma Mint Saloum and Moctar Teyeb are former Mauritanian slaves, and their biographical sketches appear in Chapter 5.

Bill of Sale for Two Slaves. In the name of Allah, most gracious and most merciful, salutation and peace upon him:

Mohamed Vall Ould Nema, son of Sidiba, bought from Mohamed Lemine Ould Sidi Mohamed, son of Taleb Ibrahim, a slave with her daughter named Kneiba in the price of 50,000 [$30] Ouguiya received entirely by the seller from the buyer. Therefore, it becomes effective: his ownership of the two slaves listed. The two parties did receive my witness and the buyer before accepted the hidden defects of the slaves. The contract was made at the end of the month of Hija of the year 1412 [1992] by Abedrabou Montali Ould Mohamed Abderrahmane, son of Berrou. God forgive me and my father and all the believers.

Here is the finger[print] of the buyer's left hand.

(Unpublished translation of bill of sale from Arabic dated 1992. Reprinted by permission of Anti-Slavery International.)

Testimony about Chattel Slavery in Mauritania. My name is Salma. I want you to read this attentively. If you want to meet me, I am here. I am a witness, before the whole world, to the fact of slavery in Mauritania.

I was born a slave. I was born in Mauritania in 1956. My mother and father were slaves for one family, and their parents were slaves of the same family. Ever since I was old enough to walk, I was forced to work for this family all day, every day. We never had days off. We hardly knew that it was Saturday or Sunday, because we had to work every day. Even if we were sick, we had to work.

When I was still a child, I started taking over my mother's job, taking care of the first wife of the head of the family, and her 15 children. Every day at 5 AM I had to make their breakfast. First, I had to get water, and wood to make a fire. We were in the desert, and the well was far away, so often I had to walk a long way. I had to cook all their meals, and clean their clothes, and watch all the children. Even if one of my children was hurt or in danger, I didn't dare help my child, because I had to watch the master's wife's children first. If I didn't, they would beat me. I was beaten very often, with a wooden stick or leather belt. One day they were beating my mother and I couldn't stand it, I tried to stop them. The head of the family got very angry with me, and he tied my hands, and branded me with a burning iron, and he hit me across the face. The ring on his finger left a scar on my face.

When I was a slave, I was never allowed to go to school or learn anything more than some Koran verses and prayers. But I was lucky, because the eldest son of the master had gone to school away from our village and had different ideas than his father. This eldest son decided to help me. He saw that I was smart, and he secretly taught me to speak French, and to read and write a little. I think that everyone thought he was raping me, but he was teaching me.

I always thought about liberty. Other slaves were afraid of liberty. They were afraid that they wouldn't know where to go or what to do or who to talk to. But I was never afraid. I told my mother that one day I would be free. I always believed that I had to be free, and I think that helped me to escape.

The first time I tried to escape was about ten years ago. When I left the family's village, I didn't know where to go, and I went in the wrong direction. I didn't know how close I was to Senegal, just on the other side of the river. So instead of going to Senegal, I walked for two days in the wrong direction. I found another family with slaves, and I hid with the slaves, but that family found me and sent me back. The head of the family punished me terribly. They bound my wrists and ankles and tied me to a date tree in the middle of the family compound, and left me there for a week. He cut my wrists with a razor, so that I bled terribly. I still have scars on my arms.

Finally I managed to escape. I met a man in the market who told me that Senegal was not far away, that it was just across the river, and that I could escape. So I decided that I had to try. I ran away from the family compound and went to the river. At the river, a man with a small wooden boat agreed to take me into Senegal. There I made my way to a safe house run by a former slave from Mauritania.

I stayed in Senegal for a few years. I lived in this house, and I earned my keep by doing work around the house. But I never felt safe there. I knew that Mauritania wasn't far away. Always, I had in my head that the master of the family could come and pay people to look for me and bring me back to his house. I was afraid all the time in Senegal.

When I got to the U.S., I found liberty. I worked when I got here, braiding hair. That was the first time I had been paid for work I had done. To be paid for my work, that was really liberty. To work for someone and be paid, and I can't even explain it. I had never believed in that. Even here, in New York, I believed that I would be treated like I was in Mauritania. The first time I was paid here, I cried that day. I had never seen a person paid for her work before in my life. It was a very, very good surprise. Now I am used to that. It has really made me happy.

To work, and to learn things, to go to school, to learn, to talk with people I choose to talk to: these things are liberty to me. To have the liberty to discuss with people, to be free to go where I want, to eat what I want, to sleep where I want. Before, I didn't have that. Really, seriously, before, I didn't have that. Also, to have my children with me. One of the hardest things for me was leaving my children behind in Mauritania, but I knew that I had to escape first and then figure out how to get them out of there.

In the three years I have been here, I have been working to secure the liberty of my children, so that they would be as free as me. I had to pay people in Senegal so that they would find them and bring them to Senegal. Now most of my children are in Senegal. Every morning I get up early, and buy a phone card, and I speak with my children. All my children tell me that they would rather die in the street than to return to Mauritania. Also I have been paying for them to go to school in Senegal. They never went to school in Mauritania, there they got nothing. For them, they love to go to school, to learn.

One of my children is now in the United States with me. I want very, very much that the others will join us. That is also liberty for me. In Mauritania, I never had the right to make decisions concerning my own children. Here, it is incomparably different.

I myself went to school in the U.S. I have been learning English. I want to continue learning English. I want to learn many things. I want to learn to speak English well, like everyone. I want to become an interpreter somewhere. I also want to learn how to use computers. These are things that would never ever have been possible for me in Mauritania.

In Mauritania, I didn't dare go to the government, because they wouldn't listen. Because for them, slavery is normal. It doesn't matter what the laws say there, because there they don't apply the laws. Maybe it's written that there is no slavery, but it's not true. Even in front of the President of Mauritania I can say in full voice that there is slavery in Mauritania, because now I'm as free as he is.

In the beginning in the U.S. I was afraid of going to Immigration. I was so afraid that I would be sent back to Mauritania. After I met my lawyer, I learned that that wasn't true. Here, if you are honest and correct and you tell the truth, you will really have your liberty. Here, it's freedom. The judge was honest, and he did his job. The judge demanded proof, but then he paid attention and listened. I met a doctor who helped me, and Kevin Bales, and the Bellevue Program for Torture Survivors.

It was a big difference from Mauritania, and a big surprise to me. A big difference.

I would like to be a citizen of the United States one
day. I want to learn English. I want my children to learn
English better than me. I want my children to be citizens. I came here and got total liberty. I see that here
there is democracy, which to me means freedom of ex-
pression. In Mauritania, there was no liberty of expres-
sion. In Dakar, I was afraid to speak out, because we
were so close to Mauritania. I had to be cautious. I had
to be far, far, far from Mauritania. Here in America, I can
speak out. (Provided to the author by Salma Mint Saloum, 2003)

War Slavery

Slavery has been a feature of war for thousands of years. A special form of slavery exists in southern Sudan—a chattel slavery
revived from the past and reborn to serve a war economy. The
civil war in Sudan between the Muslim North and the Christian
and Animist South (particularly the Nuer and Dinka peoples) began in 1955, a year before the country gained its independence. A
peace accord in the early 1970s led to a ten-year cessation in fighting, but collapsed in 1983. In the current round of the civil war,
slavery emerged as a weapon used by Northern militias against
Southern villages. It was a new factor in the war but also the re-
vival of one of the most ancient processes of enslavement. In assaults on "enemy" villages, government-supported militias have
attacked and killed people, destroyed crops, taken livestock, and
captured and enslaved some of the inhabitants as a tactic of war.
In 2002, the U.S. Congress passed the Sudan Peace Act that provided for a major new diplomatic effort to bring the war in Sudan
to an end. Pressure was brought to bear on all parties and, in late
May 2004, a deal was signed between the government and the
rebel Sudan People's Liberation Army (SPLA) that involved pro-
tocols on power-sharing and the administration of three disputed
areas in central Sudan. However, as the Peace Accords were being signed, conflict was breaking out in the western Darfur Region of Sudan. This area is not covered in the peace treaty, and
progovernment militias began a campaign of murder, mass rape,
and "ethnic cleansing" aimed at driving hundreds of thousands
of people out of the region.

A fifteen-year-old in Darfur described what happened when she was captured by progovernment militia in February 2004:

> When Kaileck was attacked, I fled towards the mountains, but five horsemen caught me and took me far away in a field." All five of them raped me twice. They kept me for 10 days. They whipped me. I could not say anything because they were armed. All I could do was to cry. They tied up my arms and my legs and would only release me when they raped me. They called me *Abeid* [slave in Arabic]. Eventually they abandoned me. Someone told my mother where I was and she came to take me back. I could not walk by myself. (BBC News 2004)

International action has now been taken to reduce the conflict in the region and food aid has been rushed to the refugee camps filled by the displaced people, but it is unclear how the situation will be resolved as Sudan lurches toward the end of its civil war.

Testimony about Slavery in Sudan

Testimony of Ahok Akok, a woman interviewed at Khartoum.
Our family was captured about six years ago [that is, about 1994] when we were already fleeing north and had crossed into the North into Kordofan. I was captured with my son, Akai, and my two daughters, this one called Abuk [present at the interview], who was about eight at the time, and a younger one, about two. We were taken by a tribe called Humr [that is, Misseriya Humr], who split the three of us up. The man who took me subsequently sold me on to some other nomads to look after cattle, for about 130 Sudanese pounds. I had to look after their cows and spent about six years with them before I managed to escape to Makaringa village.

Meanwhile, my three children had been taken away by others. For six years, until I reached Makaringa village, I had no news of them. When I reached the village, my son Akai heard where I was and joined me there. He is with us at this CEAWC center. We then contacted the Dinka Committee and they were able to find my daughter Abuk, who had been renamed Khadija. She had initially been put to work looking after livestock, but had got into trouble when some animals had escaped—she was too little to look after them. After that, she was employed as a domestic servant. She hardly speaks any Dinka language now, only Arabic. I still have no news of my youngest daughter and am still hoping to find her.

Testimony of Gabriel Muong Deng, a young man interviewed in Ad-Dha'ein. I am from Warawar [possibly Wedweil], near Marial Bai [in North Bahr El Ghazal]. I was abducted about five years ago and spent about four years working for a man called Adam Mohamed. I am about 15 now, and was about nine or ten when taken.

At the time I was seized, I was attending Grade 1 school in Kwel. My father was already dead and my mother was living with her brother. I was studying at home on the day attackers came. Four others were taken as well as me: two boys and two women. We thought the noise was some distance away but the attack surprised us. I had my hands tied and was put on a horse. I was eventually taken all the way to Jebel Mara [in the centre of Darfur, in West Darfur State]. We started by going to Mellam [Merem], I was told. It took about a month to get there, accompanied by five men. Once in the Jebel Mara, I was taken to a place called Rijit by Adam Mohamed. He had a family of five boys and two girls living in a tent. They belonged to the Salamat tribe and spoke Arabic, which I gradually learned to speak. One of the girls was called Howa.

Each year we moved to and from the south in about June and October. I was given about 30 cows to graze. Adam Mohamed had a rifle, which he taught me to use, so that I could scare off wild animals [translated as "wolves"]. To start with he would only let me have one bullet at once, but eventually let me have more. The family renamed me Mohamed and taught me to pray. I was never sent to school. I did not meet other Dinka boys looking after cattle.

One day [probably during 1998], I lost a cow and was told to go and search for it. I asked if I might take the gun, and was told I couldn't. When I refused to go out,

Adam Mohamed took a stick and hit me extremely hard here [he indicated his right collar bone, where he has a protuberance, apparently as a result of a badly set bone]. This took almost a year to heal, and when I was better I was determined to escape.

One night, when Adam Mohamed was away at the beginning of the rainy season [probably about June 1999], I hid in the trees and left. I traveled by finding other Dinka who would guide me. I went through Greda and found Dinka from my own clan who helped me. I arrived in Ad-Dha'ein in about September 1999. (Anti-Slavery International, 2001. Reprinted by permission.)

Evidence about Slavery in Sudan

PRESS RELEASE—UNICEF hails new research on missing children in Sudan

NEW YORK, 28 May 2003—UNICEF praised new research released today by the Rift Valley Institute that shows that over 10,000 children and adults abducted by militia groups in Sudan over the past 20 years are still missing.

UNICEF said the new information would make the ongoing search for those still missing "far more effective, far more meaningful, and far more hopeful."

"This has been an absolutely vital initiative," said JoAnna van Gerpen, the UNICEF Representative in Sudan, speaking of the Rift Valley Institute's efforts. "For the first time since 1983 the true extent of the abductions has been documented. It's a huge step in helping us search for the missing children and women. It drives home the fact that they are real people with real names and stories—not just statistics."

The children's agency called on the Government of Sudan, as well as major international donors and friends of Sudan's peace process, to seize the new data as an opportunity to make headway in finding those still missing.

The findings are the result of over 18 months of work by the Rift Valley Institute to identify the names and details of individuals who were abducted in southern Sudan over the last 20 years.

The number of children and adults whose families do not know where they are—some 10,380 according to the data released today by the Institute—demonstrates how serious the problem of abduction remains, even though the incidence of abduction has fallen over the past two years, UNICEF said.

Since the formation of the Government of Sudan's Committee for the Eradication of the Abduction of Women and Children in May 1999, UNICEF has supported work by the authorities and tribal communities in western Sudan to find abducted children and women and to reunify them with their families.

Over the past four years, over 700 people have been reunified with their families in southern and western Sudan. The most recent family reunifications took place in mid-May, when UNICEF and Save the Children UK flew 62 children across the cease-fire lines to their families in parts of northern Bahr al-Ghazal held by the Sudan People's Liberation Army (SPLA).

However, UNICEF has become increasingly concerned about lack of progress and wants to see significantly more effective work on abduction by the Sudanese authorities. "In our view, empowering local governments and genuine community leaders—people who know their area and feel a responsibility toward it—is essential to progress," van Gerpen said. "Knowledge of the names, clans and villages of nearly every missing child is an extraordinary tool. It should now be possible to search for every individual by name—although it will be a massive task."

UNICEF believes donors and friends of Sudan's peace process have a responsibility to keep the issue of abduction alive in their relations with both the Sudanese government and the SPLA. This means taking a rigorous look at how effective action against abduction can best be encouraged and implemented, setting benchmarks for progress and providing financial support. "We are grateful to our fellow humanitarian organizations for the tremendous work they have done in carrying out this research and giving these abducted women and children their names back," van Gerpen said. "We hope it will be a major step toward giving them their lives back." (UNICEF)

Slavery Linked to Religious Practice

Evidence and Testimony about the Trokosi System in Ghana

Slavery can also be linked to religion, as in the case of the young girls given by their families as slaves to local fetish priests in southeastern Ghana, Togo, Benin, and southwestern Nigeria. Trokosi is a religious system and a traditional form of "justice" whereby young girls in Ghana are dedicated to a shrine—and its priest—to atone for offenses usually committed by men in their family, often rape. The girl, who must be a virgin, may herself be the product of the rape and the slavery is seen as a way of atoning the gods and society. In other cases, the crime can be trivial but the girl often remains a fetish slave for the rest of her life, cooking, cleaning, farming, and serving the priest sexually until he frees her, usually after she has borne children. At that point, the girl's family must provide another slave to take her place. Ghana's constitution forbids slavery but the practice continues to be justified at the village level on religious grounds. Since 2000, a new law against Trokosi has been passed in Ghana, and the government has taken steps to end the practice.

Testimony about Trokosi

The following two testimonies involve women from the Volta region in eastern Ghana who have all been released by International Needs, a local NGO based in Accra that has joined forces with other organizations to oppose the abuse of women and children through harmful culture practices or religious beliefs.

Julie Daobadri, 24, was sent to the Tsaduma Trokosi shrine. Mercy Senahe, 23 years old, spent 12 years at the Avakpe shrine. She is now training to be a dressmaker. All three accounts were published in the *Anti-Slavery Reporter*, July 1998.

Julie Daobadri. I was only seven when I was sent to the shrine because my grandfather, who I had never met, had allegedly stolen four cedis (about 1 pence) from a Trokosi slave. I was taken to the shrine to prevent my family being killed. Between the age of 10 and 12, I labored in the fields for the priest. Then the priest started to sexually abuse me. If I refused his almost daily sexual demands, was beaten mercilessly.

There was no food for me in the shrine. I was left in tattered clothes and my parents, who promised to visit me regularly with essential items, abandoned me. It dawned on me that if I didn't try and change the situation, I would die in slavery. So I escaped to a nearby village where a young man made me pregnant. He accepted me into his house and fed and clothed me.

The priest sent young men after me and I was taken back to the shrine where I was beaten until I collapsed. I still have the scars that remind me of those evil days. I wish I could erase those terrible years from my mind. The young man was summoned to the shrine, fined and warned to stay away from me or die. At the age of 21, after more than 14 years in the shrine I escaped and sought refuge at the International Needs Vocational Training Center.

Mercy Senahe. I was sent to the shrine when I was nine years old because my grandmother stole a pair of earrings. I was made to work from dawn until dusk in the fields and when I came home there was no food for me to eat. When I was 11, the priest made his first attempt to sleep with me. I refused and was beaten. The other girls in the shrine told me it was going to keep happening, and if I refused I would be beaten to death and so the next time he tried I gave in. The suffering was too much so I tried to escape to my parents but they wouldn't accept me and sent me back to the shrine. I couldn't understand how my parents could be so wicked. (*Anti-Slavery Reporter*, Anti-Slavery International, London. Reprinted by permission.)

Evidence about Trokosi Slavery

"Liberating Ghanaian girls from 'trokosi'"

Hundreds of families and guests came to Adidome, Ghana, to celebrate with 128 women freed from years of forced labor in the service of local priests. The women were graduating from a vocational centre run by a local non-governmental organization, International Needs Ghana (ING), which helps women reclaim normal lives in their communities.

"Changing centuries old customs and practices is not easy," said Fiaga Togbe Kwao, the chief of the Mepe Traditional Area in his address at the graduation ceremony.

He urged the crowd, gathered on 10 November 2001, to support efforts to raise the status of women throughout Ghanaian society.

The women at the vocational centre had all been taken to serve as *trokosi*, literally "wife of the gods" in the local Ewe language. According to the customary practice in Ghana's Volta region, which has lasted some 300 years, if someone commits a serious crime or social infraction, traditional leaders order that a young girl from that family be sent to the shrine as a form of atonement. She is expected to serve the priest for three to five years, after which the family might redeem her.

The practice, however, has commonly resulted in exploitation and sexual abuse of the young girls. Ms. Dora Galley, now 22 years old and one of the women who learned hairdressing skills at the vocational centre, spent seven years in a shrine. She says she was compelled by the priest to work on the shrine's farm from morning until evening without any payment or food.

"I had to cut down trees and uproot tree stumps to burn into charcoal to sell and make some money to take care of myself," she says. "I did not have the right to take crops from the farm unless the priest allowed me to. Occasionally my parents sent me some food, but that was kept in the priest's room and I had to request it any time I needed some. I was forced to have sex with the priest as one of the rituals in the shrine, but luckily I did not get pregnant."

Ms. Patience Akope, now 31, tells a similar story. She spent 21 years at a shrine and has one 15-year-old child. "The priest did not allow me to visit the clinic for prenatal care or go to the hospital," she explains. "Throughout the pregnancy, I had to fend for myself."

Trokosi is also practiced in Benin, Nigeria and Togo, but most information on it comes from Ghana. Since its inception, the ING has liberated and rehabilitated 2,800 trokosi women and children, although thousands more are thought to exist.

All the graduates in Adidome spent between 6 months and 3 years in the ING's vocational centre. They were taught skills such as batik, tie dyeing, soap and pomade making, hairdressing and baking, which will be valuable as they try to build a new, independent life.

In June 2001, the ING received US$50,000 from the UN Development Fund for Women (UNIFEM) to improve its anti-trokosi programs, including vocational centers, psychological counseling, schools for trokosi children, and campaigns to educate people on laws and activities aimed at changing trokosi practices.

Ms. Florence Butegwa, UNIFEM's regional program coordinator in Lagos, Nigeria, notes that trokosi is just one kind of abuse against women, among many around the world. In other places, she told Africa Recovery, it might be widow burning, female genital mutilation or physical assault by family members. "Women's rights abuses are not unique to Africa," she says. Nevertheless, when viewed as "violations of the rights of women," practices such as trokosi are simply unacceptable.

Ms. Akope is adamant: "The practice of trokosi is a crime and it should be stopped completely. Human beings are not animals to be sacrificed. The government should move quickly to arrest and jail those who are still perpetuating this evil and dehumanizing practice of keeping and abusing young innocent girls in the shrine."

Laws are not enough

Members of the ING and other activists in Ghana have influenced the government to outlaw the trokosi practice. In 1998, the Ghanaian parliament passed a law banning all forms of ritualized forced labor.

In early 2001, President John Agyekum Kufuor, commenting on the practice of trokosi, declared, "Girls should go to school, not to a shrine." He pledged to enforce the law. So far, however, no priest or family member has been jailed for continuing the practice.

Ending behaviour that is embedded in tradition is not simple. Cultural practices "die hard," Mr. Wisdom Mensah, the ING project coordinator, told Africa Recovery. In October 2001, he noted, the ING held a seminar for police officers in the Volta region. A majority of participants said they were not familiar with trokosi and were not aware of the law against it. The ING's focus, he explained, is to sensitize people about trokosi, aiming at its gradual elimination. Legislation alone cannot do that.

Ms. Butegwa is similarly critical of only "criminalizing the practice without understanding why the practice continues to exist." As a result, she says, trokosi may be perpetuated "in another form or underground."

Some local groups have accused the ING of trying to destroy traditional culture. "We are not against our culture," Mr. Mensah explains. "We are against servitude, slavery and child labor."

In response to accusations that his group is attacking the constitutional right of freedom of religion, he answers: "Your freedom ends where someone else's freedom begins. If you have a religion, a belief system or a traditional practice that enslaves people, puts them in servitude and reduces their dignity, then you violate our national constitution."

Because of his work, Mr. Mensah has received death threats. But he is undeterred. "It's worth devoting one's life to the cause of women." (Nirit Ben-Ari, Africa Recovery, United Nations, January 31, 2004)

Forced Labor

Much of what we call slavery also goes by the name *forced labor.* In part, this is because one part of the United Nations, the International Labor Organization, is charged with investigating and combating *forced labor.* The term originally referred to the practice of governments enslaving their own citizens or others, but has now broadened to include other types of slavery. The evidence presented here looks first at the ongoing situation of forced labor in Burma, and then at a recent report on forced labor in the United States.

In Burma, tens of thousands of men, women, and children are used as laborers or bearers in military campaigns against indigenous people or on government construction projects. They are forced to clear landmines from the roads, build military camps, and act as porters for the army. Here violence is used to enslave people whom the regime wishes to punish or eliminate for the economic benefit of the state. When a state is democratic and just and an individual commits a crime with knowledge of possible imprisonment, then they have taken on the risk of incarceration of their own free will. If, however, a state is neither democratic nor just, then incarceration may well be enforced enslavement, often for political ends.

Testimony and Evidence about Forced Labor in Burma

EarthRights International published a report, "Entrenched: An Investigative Report on the Systematic Use of Forced Labor by the Burmese Army in a Rural Area," in 2003. The report detailed the use of torture and rape by the military in their exploitation of forced labor. From the report:

Torture. Interviews describe physical violence and torture, including kicking, punching, and beating. Men were restrained while beaten either by having their hands tied or by being buried in a hole. One village head sent a letter of complaint to a higher-ranking officer about the treatment that the villagers receive from the soldiers. The letter angered the officer, who while drinking inflicted brutal punishment:

> They [soldiers] stayed in one of the village farms. They took anything they wanted from the hut. The headman was so angry at this column that he wrote a letter to the [Major]. Another village headman took the letter to send to the Major. When the Major read the letter he beat this headman. The major tied him up and beat him saying, "All of you headmen are the same." He tied him under a coconut tree and slapped his face until he was unconscious. The villagers wanted to help him but they were afraid of [the Major] because he was drinking a lot of alcohol. At four in the morning a [local] man cut him free and told him to run away because everyone thought that the Major would kill him in the morning. He went to the hospital in [nearby town], and stayed there for one week. He had to pay 6,000 kyat for an injection and tablets. The village had to give one goat to the soldiers as a punishment for letting him run away.

One head woman explained that men beg not to be headmen so that they can avoid insults and beatings:

> Last year [2001], Commander [name withheld] killed four villagers that he didn't trust in a certain village. In

August 2001, Captain [name withheld] arrested one old man in my village, age 60, and beat him up. When they let him go he started walking away but some soldiers called him back. He was old and deaf, so he didn't hear and kept walking. One soldier ran to him and shot a carbine gun very close to his ear. He fell down unconscious.

Sexual Harassment and Violence. Interviewees outline a general pattern of sexual harassment that occurs while women perform road watch duty. Women and girls are often subjected to fondling and rude remarks. Hence, villagers try their best to send men for this job.

[A] soldier came while two women were watching the road, and he grabbed one woman's hand and was touching her and saying rude things. I saw this and other people learned about this so families are afraid to send girls to watch the road. (EarthRights International 2003)

Three interviews detail specific incidents of sexual harassment by soldiers. Two cases of gang rape by the military are documented through eyewitness accounts. According to one army deserter, the same soldiers presumably raped three more women:

Then I heard a lot of noise from one house. There were some women screaming and crying. Two women came out of the house. Two soldiers started raping them. I knew the soldiers; they were [names redacted]. I saw this with my own eyes from about twenty yards away. There were three other women in the house with five more soldiers, and there was a lot of shouting and crying inside the house. After the two soldiers outside let the two women go, five soldiers and three women came out of the house and all the women ran past me into the jungle. The men were laughing and saying, "oh how nice" after the women. They also stole some necklaces from the house. We stayed in that village for two weeks. We killed all the pigs in the village and dried the meat. As we left, we burned down the whole village. (EarthRights International 2003)

Evidence of Forced Labor in the United States

In 2004, Free the Slaves and the Human Rights Center at the University of California–Berkeley released the report "Hidden Slaves: Forced Labor in the United States." This was the first report to examine the extent of slavery and forced labor in modern America.

Hidden Slaves: Forced Labor in the United States (Excerpts)

INTRODUCTION
Migrant-Camp Operators Face Forced Labor Charges
  The New York Times, June 21, 2002
Takoma Park Couple Enslaved Woman
  The Washington Post, June 10, 2003
Slavery in Florida's Citrus Groves
  The Miami Herald, Nov. 21, 2002
"Coyotes" Offer Evil Deal: Hondurans Forced into
    Prostitution
  The Washington Times, July 23, 2002

For most Americans the occasional newspaper headline is the only indication that forced labor exists in the United States. Each year forced labor generates millions of dollars for criminals who prey on the most vulnerable—the poor, the uneducated, and the impoverished immigrant seeking a better life. Held as captives, victims of forced labor toil in slavelike conditions for months and even years with little or no contact with the outside world. Those who survive enslavement face enormous challenges as they struggle to regain control over their shattered lives. Forced labor is a serious and pervasive problem in the United States for four reasons: it is *hidden*, it is *inhumane*, it is *widespread*, and it is *criminal*.

- *Forced labor is hidden.* Each year thousands of men, women, and children are trafficked into the United States and forced to work without pay in deplorable conditions. Most of them are rarely seen in public places. Hidden from view, they toil in sweatshops, brothels, farms, and private homes. To prevent them from escaping, their captors confiscate their identification documents, forbid them from leaving their workplaces or contacting their families, threaten them with arrest and deportation, and restrict their access to the surrounding community.

- *Forced labor is inhumane.* Victims of forced labor have been tortured, raped, assaulted, and murdered. They have been held in absolute control by their captors and stripped of their dignity. Some have been subjected to forced abortion, dangerous working conditions, poor nutrition, and humiliation. Some have died during their enslavement. Others have been physically or psychologically scarred for life. Once freed, many will suffer from a host of health-related problems, including repetitive stress injury, chronic back pain, visual and respiratory illnesses, sexually transmitted diseases, and depression.

- *Forced labor is widespread.* Forced labor exists in ninety cities across the United States. It is practiced in a wide range of industrial sectors, including domestic service, the sex industry, food service, factory production, and agriculture. In the last five years alone the press has reported 131 cases of forced labor in the United States involving 19,254 men, women, and children from a wide range of ethnic and racial groups. Of these 131 cases of forced labor cited in the article, 105 listed the number or the estimated number of persons who had been found in a situation of forced labor. Although many victims are immigrants, some are U.S. residents or citizens.

- *Forced labor is criminal.* Forced labor is universally condemned and outlawed. Its practice in the United States violates a host of laws including indentured servitude, money laundering, and tax evasion. Yet criminals find it a highly profitable and lucrative enterprise. Their workers are forced to be docile, and when problems arise, "employers" know they can rein workers in with threats and physical violence. Criminals also have learned that the odds are good that they will never be held accountable in a court of law.

Geographical Distribution of Victims

Our data suggest that forced labor operations have existed in at least ninety U.S. cities over the past five years. This figure was derived from a press survey of 131 cases of forced labor and a telephone survey of forty-nine service providers across the United States. The press survey located cases of forced labor in sixty-four cities within the United States and its territories of Saipan and Guam, while service providers reported forced labor in thirty-eight cities in seventeen states, with twelve cities appearing in both surveys. The survey of service providers also revealed that the length of time victims were held in forced labor ranged from a few weeks to more than twenty years, with the majority of cases lasting between two and five years.

Our data also suggest that forced labor operations are concentrated in the states of California, Florida, New York, and Texas—all of which are transit routes for international travelers. Cities where reported forced labor occurred also tended to be in states with large populations and sizable immigrant communities. Our data is consistent with findings of the U.S. government. The U.S. Department of Justice (DOJ) reports that in 2003, the largest concentrations of survivors of trafficking who received federal assistance resided in California, Oklahoma, Texas, and New York. In 2002, the DOJ reports that survivors of trafficking who received federal assistance resided in Texas (31 percent), Florida (19 percent), and California (14 percent) (U.S. Department of Justice 2003). Note that these concentrations reflect where survivors resided at the time they received federal assistance and does not necessarily reflect where the forced labor operations occurred.

Enslavement for Commercial Sexual Exploitation

Women, young girls, and young boys are held in slavery and forced into prostitution for the financial gain of others in brothels in the United States, Europe, and many developing countries such as Thailand and the Philippines. The following report touches on the enslavement of young American women into prostitution.

A Teenage Prostitution Ring in Detroit, Michigan

Not all cases of forced labor involve undocumented immigrants. In January 2003, a multistate ring of forced prostitution involving young Midwestern women and girls, some as young as thirteen years old, was uncovered when a seventeen-year-old girl pursued by a group of men and women burst into a store in a Detroit, Michigan, suburban strip mall and pleaded with a security guard to help her. Seeing that the girl was terrified and battered, the guard evicted the group of pursuers from the store and took her to the police (Schmitt and Hackney 2003).

The teenager told authorities that a man and a woman had abducted her while she was waiting at a bus stop in downtown Cleveland, Ohio. Her captors drove her to Detroit, where she was held in a house with other female captives and forced to have sex with male visitors (Schmitt and Hackney 2003). The captives were always escorted around the house, even to the bathroom, and the older women kept the younger ones in line by threatening and sometimes beating them. Each day the girls were given a new assignment. Some would go to malls in the metro Detroit area to sell jewelry and trinkets, others would be forced to dance and strip for private parties and to have sex with men who visited the Detroit house (Schmitt and Hackney 2003).

The girls' captors "did that punishment-reward thing," a police investigator said. "They would get their nails and hair done. If they stepped out of line, they got beat down. Some of the senior women acted as enforcers" (Schmitt and Hackney 2003). In fact, the young woman escaped when she and several other young women were taken to the mall to get their hair done and to buy clothes. When the group stopped at the mall to sell some jewelry, she seized the opportunity and ran (Hackney 2003a). The young woman's mother remarked, "The whole thing is unreal—it's like slavery. They lure and coerce these girls into doing whatever they want. It's a sick game they are playing with our children" (Hackney 2003a). Once in police custody, the young woman led the police to the house where they arrested Henry Davis, 32, otherwise known as "Chicago," "Tony," or "Daddy," the alleged leader of the ring, and Jamal Rivers, 17. They were charged with multiple felonies, including first-degree criminal sexual conduct, kidnapping, and transporting women for prostitution (Hackney 2003c). On further investigation, the police discovered that Davis had been operating a forced prostitution ring as early as 1995 by kidnapping teenage girls and transporting them to cities throughout the Midwestern United States (Schmitt 2003; Hackney 2003b). The case never went to trial. In August 2003, Davis entered into a plea agreement and was sentenced to serve forty years in prison (Hackney 2003d). Despite his detention and his plea agreement, most of the teenagers reported being so afraid of Davis that they did not attend his formal sentencing hearing. Some of Davis's victims say they now sleep with nightlights on or crawl into bed with their mothers. Others say they are experiencing emotional problems. One young woman, who was raped repeatedly at the Detroit house, is pregnant and believes she is carrying Davis's child. "The devastation [Davis] has brought on these young women is just immeasurable," the local prosecutor said (Hackney 2003d).

Evidence of Enslavement for Sexual Exploitation in Thailand

Thailand is well-known as a destination for *sex tourism*, which exploits large numbers of women and children. What is less known is the widespread use of prostitutes by working-class Thai men, and the way that young women are enslaved to work in the working-class brothels. The following is an excerpt that details the economics of a brothel using enslaved prostitutes in a provincial city in Thailand:

> Forced prostitution is a great business. The overheads are low, the turnover high, and the profits immense. In this research I have tried to detail for the first time the business side of this form of slavery and to expose the scale of exploitation and its rewards. It is far, far different from the capital intensive slavery of the past which required long-term investments and made solid but small profits. The disposability of the women, the special profits to be made from children, all ensure a low risk, high return enterprise. For all its dilapidation and filth the brothel is a highly efficient machine that in destroying young girls turns them into gold.
>
> To set up a brothel requires a relatively small outlay. About 80,000 baht ($3,200) will buy all the furniture, equipment, and fixtures that are needed. The building itself will be rented for anywhere from 4,000 to 15,000 baht per month ($160 to $600). In addition to the prostitutes the brothels need a pimp (who often has a helper), a cashier/book-keeper, and sometimes employs a cook as well. Pimps will get from 5000 to 10,000 baht per month in salary ($200 to $400), cashiers about 7000 baht ($280) and the cook about 5000 baht ($200) or less. For electricity and other utilities about 2000 baht ($80) is needed each month. Beer and whisky must be bought which is re-sold to clients. This leaves only two other outgoings—food and bribes.
>
> Feeding a prostitute costs 50 to 80 baht per day ($1.50 to $3.20). Slaveholders do not skimp on food since men want healthy looking girls with full figures. Healthy

looks are important in a country suffering an HIV epidemic, and young healthy girls are thought to be the safest. Bribes are not exorbitant or unpredictable, in most brothels a policeman stops by once a day to pick up 200 to 400 baht ($8–$16), a monthly expenditure of about 6,000 baht ($240) which is topped up by giving the policeman a girl for an hour if he seems interested. The police are interested in the stability of the brothels: a short side-street generates $32,000 to $64,000 each year in relatively effortless income. The higher priced massage parlors and night-clubs pay much larger bribes and will usually require a significant start-up payment as well. Bribe income is the key reason that senior police officials are happy to buy their positions and compete for the most lucrative.

Income far exceeds expenses. Each of the twenty girls makes about 125 baht ($5) for the brothel with each client she has, and each day she has between ten and eighteen clients, making 1250 to 2250 baht ($48 to $104). A single day's return is 25,000 to 45,000 baht ($1000 to $1800) just on sex. And as can be seen from the table below, there are a number of other ways for the brothel to turn a penny.

Monthly Income and Expenditure (in Baht) for the Always Prospering Brothel

Outgoings (per month)	Income (per month)
Rent 5,000	Commercial sex* 1,050,000
Utilities and bills 2,000	Rent paid by prostitutes 600,000
Food and drink 45,000	Sale of condoms 70,000
Pimp's salary 7,000	Sale of drinks 672,000
Cashier 7,000	Virgin premium 50,000
Cook 5,000	"Interest" on debt-bond 15,000
Bribes 6,000	
Payments to taxis and the like 12,000	
Beer and whisky 168,000	
Total Outgoings 257,000	Total Income 2,457,000
(in US dollars $10,280)	

Monthly Profit 2,200,000 (in U.S. dollars $88,000)

* Average 14 clients per day at 125 baht per client for 20 prostitutes for 30 days

The amount which is made on drinks, mostly the sale of beer and whisky, is difficult to measure. In the table above the half a million baht is a conservative estimate based on each client buying a single beer, which has been bought by the brothel for 20 baht and sold for 80 baht. The prostitute's rent averages 30,000 baht per month for their rooms, and if half the girls are repaying a debt-bond the amount made by the brothel each month on the 'interest' would be at least 15,000 baht. The sale of condoms is pure profit. Condoms are provided free of charge to brothels by the Ministry of Health in an attempt to slow the spread of HIV. Clients are charged 10 baht for a condom and most clients are required to use one. Siri explained that she got through three to four boxes of condoms each month, there are 100 condoms in each box.

The income shown as the virgin premium requires some explanation. Some customers, especially Chinese and Sino-Thais, are willing to pay very large amounts to have sex with a virgin. There are two reasons for this. The first is the ancient Chinese belief that sex with a virgin will reawaken sexual virility and prolong life. According to this belief, a girl's virginity is a strong source of yang (or coolness) and it quenches and slows the yin (or heat) of the ageing process. Wealthy Chinese and Sino-Thais (as well as Chinese sex tourists from Taiwan, Singapore, Malaysia, and Hong Kong) will try to have sex with virgins as regularly as possible and will pay well for the opportunity. When a new girl is brought to the brothel she will not be placed out in the selection room with the other prostitutes, but kept back in another room, the *hong bud boree sut,* the 'room to unveil virgins.' Here she will be displayed, possibly with other children, and her price will be negotiated with the pimp. To deflower a virgin these men pay between 5,000 and 50,000 baht ($200 to $2,000). Deflowering often takes place away from the brothel in a hotel room rented for the occasion. The pimp or his assistant will often attend as well since it is usually necessary to beat the girl into submission.

The second reason the brothel can make a virgin premium is the general fear of HIV/AIDS. While Thai men or other non-Chinese customers do not hold the same beliefs about yin and yang, they do fear HIV infection. It is assumed that virgins cannot carry the virus, and even after a girl has lost her virginity, she can be sold at a higher price as pure or fresh. One Burmese girl reported being sold as a virgin to four different clients. The younger the girl, or the younger looking she is, the higher her price can be, as in Siri's case. The premium might also be paid to a brothel by another, higher class, commercial sex business. Special 'Members Clubs' or massage parlors might take an order from a customer for a virgin, a pure girl, or a child. If the brothel doesn't have a suitable young girl on hand, it might arrange with a broker for one to be recruited, or if time is pressing, kidnapped. The more expensive establishments don't normally want to get involved in procurement and are willing to pay the brothels to find the young girls. Once used in this way, the girl is put to work with the other prostitutes in the brothel to feed the normal profit stream.

This profit stream makes sex slavery very lucrative. The Always Prospering Brothel nets something like 26,400,000 baht a year ($1,056,000)—a return of 856% on outgoings. Key to this level of profit is the low cost of each girl. A new girl, at a cost of 100,000 baht, requires a capital outlay of less than 5% of one month's profit. Just counting the sale of her body and the rent she must pay, a brothel recovers the cost of buying a girl within two or three months. Within the sex industry it is the slave-holder that makes the highest profits. Voluntary prostitutes in night-clubs and massage parlors charge higher prices, but have only three to five clients a day. Escort girls may have only one client a night. Voluntary sex workers also keep a much larger proportion of the money they make, and exercise some discretion over which clients they will take. By contrast, for the slave-holder, total control of the prostitute, over the volume of clients she must take, over the money she makes, means vast profits. There is no good estimate of the part the sex industry plays in the Thai economy, and the total number of sex workers is hotly debated. But if we look just at the estimated 35,000 young women held in debt bondage, the annual profits they generate are enormous. If their brothels follow the same scheme as the Always Prospering, the annual profit made on these girls is over 46 billion baht ($1.84 billion). There is one other cost to be laid against this profit, the price the girls pay with their bodies, minds, and health. (Bales 1999; © The Trustees of the University of California. Reprinted by permission.)

Testimony about Sexual Slavery in Cambodia

A member of the Sex Workers Union of Cambodia gave the following speech, published in the local press, to the First National Conference on Gender and Development in Cambodia, held in Phnom Penh in September 1999.

I came here today as a woman, a Khmer woman. I came here today to tell you my story, in the hope that after you listen to me you can understand my situation and the situation of thousands of Khmer women and other women around the world.

It is very difficult for me to come here and speak to you; but I am doing this because I want you to listen, to me the real person; and I want you to remember me and what I say to you today when you are in your offices talking about policies and strategies that affect me and my sisters.

I want you to remember we are not "problems," we are not animals, we are not viruses, we are not garbage.

We are flesh, skin and bones, we have a heart, and we have feelings, we are a sister to someone, a daughter, a granddaughter. We are people, we are women and we want to be treated with respect, dignity and we want rights like the rest of you enjoy.

I was trafficked, I was raped, beaten, and forced to accept men. I was humiliated and forced to be an object so men, yes men, could take their pleasure, I brought profit to many and brought pleasure to others. And for myself I brought shame, pain and humiliation.

But worst of all I receive demeaning comments from you: you discriminate against me, you give yourselves a job because of me and you are busy thinking about the best way to protect the community from me.

The police come to Toul Kork [an area where prostitution is common] almost every day. They always have a reason to come, but they come more frequently before festivals like Pchum Ben, because we are an easy target to extract money from.

In a public forum the chief of these police stands up and states "We do not arrest the girls": lies and more lies. They arrest us and take our money, our jewelry, sometimes even our few possessions we have in our room like our bed covers.

If we cannot pay then they detain us for a day or two, they give us no water. When they are convinced we simply have no money to pay they take us to another brothel and sell us to a new *maebon* (pimp), usually for US$100 for one girl. Then we become indebted once again and have to pay off that debt to the new *maebon*.

This is trafficking. The police, yes, the police sell us for another cycle of slavery. Do you think it is in their interests to see my occupation decriminalized? Of course not: then they lose their share of the money.

In one day we pay almost 15,000 riel in bribes to the district police, to the municipal authorities and the local authorities. Then another group of police come and arrest us. If we do not run and hide we are re-sold to slavery.

Your solution is to ask these people to protect us. Think again. They live off our blood. Money is too important to everyone, money and more money. It is not enough to eat: people demand more because they want nice things.

I come from a poor family; they sent me to study at a cultural school in Phnom Penh. I was living with a family but I could not contribute to my living, so they helped me find a job in a nearby hotel washing dishes. This hotel had many sex workers. But I just washed dishes and went to school.

One night a man followed me when I was on my way home and raped me. I was only 17 years of age. You cannot imagine how I felt and what impact this had on me. But after that, I was lured to becoming a sex worker under false promises.

I was sent to Stung Treng; I was beaten when I refused to accept men. Shortly after I was taken to Stung Treng a man came to pay for me to go with him. He paid my *maebon*.

He took me to the pig slaughter house where he worked and locked me in a dirty smelly cell. Then he came back with six other men. They all, one by one, raped me; one man raped me twice. After a whole night of gang rape I was faint with pain.

When the morning came I heard the workers preparing to start their work. I heard the pigs being pushed into the pens, they were screaming. I knew what that feeling was like: I was no better than the pigs to these men; they could have killed me. Something inside me did die, and I will never be the same.

I am 24 years old and my life has been like this since 1993. I did not know the Khmer Rouge years but I have heard the stories of suffering. People say they were slaves.

Compared to my life for the last five years I think I and my sisters have suffered and are suffering more than you have. I know starvation, I know slavery, I know being forced to work all day. But I also know physical violation and torture every day, I know discrimination and hatred from my country-people, I know not being wanted and accepted from my society, the society that put me in this condition. I know fear, I feel it every day, even now that I dare speak my life is in danger.

This is a crime, but no one is punished. I fought the Khmer Rouge [the communist dictatorship that controlled Cambodia in the past], I was a soldier fighting to protect you from the Khmer Rouge and risking my life. I fought for the freedom of the Cambodian people, this is what the commander told us we were to do and I was proud I was fighting for freedom. I fought for your freedom—only to become enslaved and abused by you.

After all these years I now work as a sex worker. I also run a union to unite sex workers to fight for basic rights and for freedom. We bring our voices to forums like this to educate people like you, with the hope you can learn from us. Many of my sisters are scared to join our struggle because they live in constant fear of abuse and threats.

Some of you think that I am bad because I choose to remain a sex worker. My answer to those people is: I think your society, my society, my motherland Cambodia, is bad because it does not give girls like me choices; choices that I see are better for me.

I think it is bad that my country allows men to rape young women like me and my sisters and go unpunished. I think it is bad that my society lets men seek and demand the services of women like me. I think it is criminal that we are enslaved to make money for the powerful.

I think it is bad that my family are so poor and getting poorer because they can not survive as farmers with little resources which are getting smaller because more powerful people move them off their land.

I think it is bad the police treat me and my sisters like we are criminals but those who exploit us and take our dignity, our money and sometimes our lives live in freedom, enjoying their lives with their families. Because why? Because they have a powerful relative, because they have money.

Is this right? Is this justice? My sisters and I we do not create the demand, we are the objects; the demand comes from the men, the men come to us. We are cheated, deceived, trafficked, humiliated and tortured. Why? Because men want us and we bring money to the powerful. But we are the powerless.

You give us AIDS; when we are no longer profitable you leave us to die, but we do not die in peace: you point your finger and you blame us. You, the development organizations, give us condoms and teach us all the time about AIDS. We do not want your words, we do not want your judgment, we do not want you to tell us what is better for us. We know about AIDS; we watch our sisters die from the disease.

Ask us if we have the power to demand condom use from our clients. Look at me: you see a woman, but my boss sees dollars. An extra payment to my boss and the client does not wear a condom. If I protest I receive a beating. If I die tomorrow no one cares: there are many other girls who will be tricked and trafficked like me, because we feed many people.

I do not want to go to your shelter and learn to sew so you can get me work in a factory. This is not what I want. If I tell you that you will call me a prostitute. But those words are easy for you because you have easy solutions to difficult problems you do not understand, and you do not understand because you do not listen.

My life has become this way now; for me there is no turning back, so let me continue to practice my occupation, but recognize my occupation and give me my rights, so I am protected and I can have power to demand justice. (*The Phnom Penh Post,* September 17–30, 1999)

Domestic Slavery

Enslaved domestic workers have escaped or been freed from rich households in the United States, United Kingdom, and France, among other countries. This is one of the most common types of slavery around the world. Children are especially vulnerable to being made domestic slaves. In some parts of the Caribbean and West Africa, children are given or sold into domestic service, and organizations have grown up to free them and provide them with an education. In Haiti and the Dominican Republic, these children are called *restavecs*. Ownership is not asserted as such, but strict control, usually enforced by violence, is used. The domestic services performed by the child provide a good return on the upkeep costs. When slavery is discovered in the United States, it is often domestic slavery.

Evidence of Domestic Slavery in the United States

It is just like a fisherman going to fish. You know, he has his bait, he has his rod and also the hook itself. Now before he gets a fish, you know, he must put the bait. And that's exactly what happened, if he don't put the bait, he can't get a fish. So they tell the parents a lovely story, you know, what they will encounter when they come to the United States. But behold, when they get into the United States the picture is completely different, so anyway they're just using very lovely stories to entice the parents to get the children into the United States.

—Louis

Louis works for the phone company. He also frees slaves. When his family got together for the Thanksgiving holiday in 1999, Louis did what everyone does—he started lining up all the relatives and taking pictures. As he snapped away he noticed something strange. In the large group of family and friends one teenage girl always tried to hide when he took a picture.

And I asked myself, you know, what's wrong with the young lady? At first I asked her, where do you come from? She told me she was visiting from Indiana. That is, she was staying with my cousin there. But something stuck in my mind.

Louis had visited his cousin in Indiana several times and didn't remember ever meeting this young woman. Driving home from the party he asked his wife what she knew about the girl. His wife had heard that the girl had run away from her family, eloped actually, and now was hiding with their cousin. Yet this was a little odd as well, because the girl was obviously not from the same ethnic group as his family.

Louis came to the United States from Cameroon in West Africa in 1985, and in time became a U.S. citizen. With a degree in management from an American university he holds down a good job, and serves as an elder in his Presbyterian church. Living in the suburbs in Virginia, Louis and his family were pursuing nothing more and nothing less than the middle class dream of stability and security. Now in his late forties he found himself puzzled by the sight of this strange and troubled girl in the middle of his family's Thanksgiving holiday. Things just weren't adding up, so a few days later he drove over to visit his cousins where the young woman was staying.

And then she began to tell me the story. And I felt so bad about it . . . I mean everyone has a human feeling, if you hear a story which is so terrible, you are moved, being human. So I felt like this is wrong and she began to tell me the stories. I began to put down in writing the stories she told me and probably, if you read the whole report that I wrote, you would come to the conclusion that something was really, really wrong.

The more Louis heard, the more sickened he became. There was no elopement in this girl's past. Confused, isolated, still in shock, she painfully recounted years of slavery in the suburbs of Washington, DC.

Her name was Deborah [name changed]. Back in Cameroon, at the age of fourteen, she had just finished school for the summer vacation when a friend of her aunt stopped by her parent's house. This woman explained that there was a Cameroonian family in the United States that needed someone to help around the house. In exchange, the family would help Deborah go to school in America. It sounded like a great opportunity to Deborah and to her parents. They talked it over carefully, and then agreed she could go right away since the summer vacation had just begun. That would give Deborah time to settle in before starting school in the United States. Away from her parents, Deborah was introduced to the family she would be working for; they helped sort out her passport, bought her air ticket, and escorted her through customs and immigration when they reached the United States. Everything was nice until they reached Deborah's new home in America. Then the trap slowly closed.

The husband and wife showed Deborah the jobs they wanted her to do. Soon the jobs filled her day completely and they rapidly took complete control of her life. Up at six in the morning, Deborah would be working long past midnight. When she began to question her treatment, the beatings began. "They used to hit me," Deborah told me, "I couldn't go for three days without them beating me up." The smallest accident would lead to violence. "Sometimes I might spill a drink on the floor by mistake, they would hit me for that," she said. In a strange country, locked up in a strange house far from home, Deborah was cut off from help. If she tried to use the phone she was beaten, if she tried to write anything it was taken away from her. "It was just like she was lost in the middle of a forest," said Louis, "she was completely isolated."

Under complete violent control, paid nothing, working all hours, this fourteen-year-old schoolgirl had become a slave. The promises to help her go to school in America were just the bait used to hook her. In Cameroon her parents received no word from her, but had occasional reassuring messages from the family that had enslaved her. The beatings and constant verbal abuse broke the will of this young girl for a time, and her life dissolved into a blur of pain, exhaustion, work, denigration, and fear. Deborah lived for another four years in this state of permanent exploitation.

Someday we may know what happened in these years, but perhaps not. Deborah today is nervous and withdrawn, still suffering from the trauma of her enslavement. Her mind has deeply buried her memories. What we do know is that one day after she had turned eighteen, the woman who controlled Deborah found her trying to talk to a neighbor. Dragging her away, "she started yelling at me, started cursing me," Deborah told me, "and I couldn't take it any more, I just had to run away." Later that day she ran to the home of a friend of her "employer." She pleaded for help, but this woman called the family that had enslaved her. When Deborah realized this she ran again, this time to a nearby shopping mall. Her only hope was a Cameroonian man she had met in her "employers'" home, he had seemed nice and she had learned his phone number. Begging change from passersby to make a phone call, she managed to leave a message for him, asking him to pick her up. Without a coat, in the cold October night, she waited outside the mall, for she had nowhere else to go, no other place to turn. Four hours later, at nearly 11 PM, the man picked her up and took her home to his family. This man was Louis's cousin.

In safety, Deborah was still in limbo. The family she was staying with simply did not know what to do with her, and she feared that in time her "employers" would try to take her back. Then came Thanksgiving and the meeting with Louis. As Louis gently drew out Deborah's story it shocked and saddened him:

> I felt terrible, I mean, I felt really terrible, because I couldn't imagine, not even in my slightest imagination, that in this day-and-age someone would treat somebody's child the way she was treated. It made me sick in my stomach.

Soon Louis had taken Deborah to stay with his own family, and as she opened up to him even more shocking facts came out. It occurred to Louis to ask Deborah if she knew of any more girls in the same situation. "Oh, yes," she replied. Following up on Deborah's lead he found two more young women in slavery, and through subterfuge and daring he liberated them. Linda had been brought to the United States at seventeen and spent four years as a domestic slave, Sally had been brought at age fifteen and spent three years in bondage. Now Louis had three young women staying with his family, their care and support coming from his own pocket. His first job, he decided, was to reassure their families, so he took videos of all three, and made a trip to Cameroon. When they saw the video, the girl's families were overjoyed:

> They were very happy to see me, and especially the fact that I took the video of their children, they were extremely happy, because even if they now saw what their daughters had gone through, at least they had first hand information from their children. I felt good about it because it was like a conclusion to me that I had done the right thing. I could see their faces and I could see that they realized at least, that someone was concerned about the lives of their children.

Sally's family had been told that their daughter had died in America. Their shock and joy are hard to imagine. Meanwhile Louis was digging up the connections that had smuggled the girls into the United States. He found a network that recruited girls from poor families promising education and jobs. One woman provided a "stepping stone," a house where the girls were taken after leaving their families and prepared for the trip to America. Some of the respected members of the Cameroonian community in the United States were involved and Louis began to understand he was up against something big. (Bales, Kevin. *How We End Slavery*. Forthcoming.)

Evidence of Domestic Slavery in Haiti

In Haiti, children as young as six are given into slavery as restavecs. The term comes from the French "rester avec" meaning "to stay with." The Foyers Maurice Sixto (children's refuge project) grew out of a shelter for child domestic servants opened on the outskirts of the capital Port-au-Prince in 1989. Such shelters provide educational activities for children every afternoon. Those involved in this issue will agree that child domestic servitude in Haiti is a dominant institution whose roots go back to the time of slavery. It exposes minors of both sexes to a form of bondage that profits the adults to whom they have been entrusted.

The total number of child domestic servants fluctuates constantly. They come from rural families facing great hardship. They do not have the opportunity to go to school or acquire a practical trade. They number between 200,000 and 300,000, which is 14 percent of Haiti's young population, 85 percent of whom are young girls between six and eighteen years of age.

The *restavec*, as they are commonly called, are typically treated like young slaves. They are used as beasts of burden to perform various household tasks: cleaning, frequent trips to shop at the market and to fetch water from the well, taking care of the children at home, carrying rubbish and excrement produced by people and animals in the house, etc. They are the first members of the house to get up in the morning and the last to go to bed at night. For food, they are usually given the leftovers of the family's meals. According to a survey conducted by the *Institut-Psycho-Social de la Famille* (IPSOFA) for UNICEF, 30 percent of these children say they only receive one meal a day. All this for little or no pay. One meal a day and the promise of being sent to school are their only reward for the hard work, beatings, and humiliating insults they suffer. (Contribution by Father Miguel of the Foyers Maurice Sixto, Haiti, to the UN Economic and Social Council Commission on Human Rights, Subcommission on Prevention, Discrimination and Protection of Minorities, Working Group on Contemporary Forms of Slavery, 23 Session, Geneva, May 1998)

Child Labor and Slavery

Child labor becomes slavery in the officially recognized sense when it involves debt bondage or the child is sold into prostitution or given into domestic service. The most vulnerable children, as with adults, are those who come from indigenous and migrant communities. The UN Convention on the Worst Forms of Child Labor calls on countries to take swift and effective measures to prevent the most damaging exploitation of children, including child slavery, prostitution, and pornography. But how should governments go about stopping child labor and child slavery? When the United States began to act against child labor, the situation of some children was actually made worse.

Experience shows that blanket policies of banning all child labor led by rich countries does not work. At the beginning of the 1990s, Senator Tom Harkin of Iowa introduced a bill calling for a ban on the import of any goods which were manufactured wholly or in part by children under the age of fifteen. The U.S. Child Labor Deterrence Bill has not yet become law. However, while it was under discussion, 50,000 children in Bangladesh lost their jobs as employers fired them rather than risk having their products, mostly clothing, banned from the United States. Desperate for money, many of these children took other even more exploitative and abusive jobs in other industries or were forced into prostitution. The Harkin Bill has since been over-taken by the Sanders Amendment passed in Congress in 1997, which bans import of bonded child labor products. It also pro-vided funds for the UN Commission on Human Rights and for the ILO for activities relating to child bonded labor. The Sanders Amendment played a part in the following example:

Evidence of Child Slavery in India

Citing Child Labor, U.S. Stubs Out Bindi Beedis

At a time when the United States is set to revise its list of Indian firms facing sanctions, one company has been added to the taboo list—Ganesh Beedis—which stops the company from marketing its hand-rolled, unfiltered cigarettes (beedi) in the US for reason that it employs child labor.

The "detention" order came into effect last week fol-lowing a feature on *Tobacco Slaves in India* on the CBS television network exposing the use of child labor in In-dia's beedi industry.

The feature apparently included indentured children working for slave wages and being exploited in the Mangalore Ganesh beedi industry in Tamil Nadu (In-dia). The film showed plenty of raw footage of children toiling for up to 12 hours in abject conditions.

US Customs Commissioner Raymond Kelly said that it is morally, ethically and legally wrong to import goods made with forced or bonded labor, especially the forced labor of children, into the US.

The order against the company will continue pending the final results of an investigation. The agency however has been investigating allegations of forced child labor in the beedi industry in India even before the feature surfaced. The estimated value of all imported beedis, including those made by Mangalore Ganesh in fiscal year 1999 was $1.28 million, up from $915,000 the year before, said Customs spokeswoman Layne Lathram.

Mangalore Ganesh Beedis spokesman Priya Das, denying the charges of employing child labor for manufacturing beedis has threatened legal action against CBS. Mr Das argues that "beedi rolling is a skilled or semi-skilled job. A child cannot roll a beedi. It has to be rolled by an adult."

Mr Das also points out that beedi rolling work was given on contract and the company checks the quality when they are returned to roll. "Morally we ensure that no such irregularity like employment of child labor takes place," he said. "Ever since the company began in 1940, there was no complaint about child labor," he added. (Child Labor News Service, December 1, 1999)

References

Bales, Kevin. *Disposable People: New Salvery in the Gobal Economy*. Berkeley: University of California Press, 1999.

BBC News, June 10, 2004, quoted at: http://news.bbc.co.uk/1/hi/world/africa/3791713.stm.

Earth Rights International. "Entrenched: An Investigative Report on the Systematic Use of Forced Labor by the Burmese Army in a Rural Area," 2003.

Hackney, Suzette. (2003a). "Abducted Teen's Mother Describes House of Horrors," *Detroit Free Press*, January 15, 2003.

Hackney, Suzette. (2003b). "Fourteen-year-old Tells of Terrors in Sex Ring," *Detroit Free Press*, January 16, 2003.

Hackney, Suzette. (2003c). "More Sex Ring Arrests Likely Today," *Detroit Free Press*, February 4, 2003c.

Hackney, Suzette. (2003d). "Man Sentenced in Sex-Ring Case," *Detroit Free Press*, September 16, 2003.

Schmitt, Ben, and Suzette Hackney. "Sex Ring Busted by Kidnapped Girl's Tip," *Detroit Free Press*, January 15, 2003.

Schmitt, Ben. "More Charges in Sex Ring," *Detroit Free Press*, February 15, 2003.

U.S. Department of Justice, *Report to Congress from Attorney General John Ashcroft on U.S. Government Efforts to Combat Trafficking in Persons in Fiscal Year 2003*, 9.

7

Directory of Organizations, Associations, and Agencies

S ome of the organizations listed here are based outside the United States. If you wish to contact any of the following organizations by telephone from the United States, first dial the international access code 011, then the country code, then the city code, then the local phone number. To make the listings more clear, I have put the country code in square brackets and the city or area code in parentheses.

The first two organizations listed are the two main antislavery groups with a global approach; after that, intergovernmental organizations are listed first, then governmental organizations, and finally nongovernmental organizations are listed according to the region of the world where they are based.

Global Antislavery Groups

Free the Slaves
1012 14th St. NW, Suite 600
Washington, DC 20005
Phone: (866) 324-FREE; (202) 638-1865
Fax: (202) 638-0599
E-mail: info@freetheslaves.net
Web site: www.freetheslaves.net

Free the Slaves is the main American organization working to end slavery across the globe. Founded in 2000, Free the Slaves collaborates with other antislavery organizations through funding and networking, raises public awareness of contemporary slavery, promotes slave-free trade, aids policy makers in enforcing and drafting new legislation to prevent slavery, and continues research to understand forms of slavery and devise ways to eliminate it. The strategy this organization uses to target slavery is based upon the idea that adequate access to basic needs reduces vulnerability of poor people to enslavement. Also employing more direct methods, Free the Slaves operates according to the principles that:

- All people have the right to be free from any form of slavery, and to assert that right
- All people who are or have been enslaved should have the opportunity to realize their full potential

and seeking to:

- Create an inclusive and diverse movement, respecting the dignity and views of all people involved in eradicating slavery
- Base all our strategies on accurate research
- Support sustainable solutions, preventing adverse repercussions for those we aim to assist
- Attain guidance and ideas from agencies around the world that are carrying out local and regional antislavery programs

Working in the firm belief that slavery can be eradicated in this lifetime, Free the Slaves supports other organizations that investigate slavery and carry out rescue missions to free enslaved children and workers as well as helps freed slaves to begin their lives outside of slavery.

Publications: Free the Slaves publishes a monthly electronic newsletter providing updates in the campaign/fight against slavery that is available at the Web site.

Web site: The Web site provides a wealth of information on slavery, its history and evolution, and its relevance today in the products we consume. The site also offers educational resources, links to partner organizations, important antislavery and human rights documents, and details on how to take action against slavery. Updates regarding projects of partner human rights organizations as well as positive events in the fight to end slavery are regularly published on the site. A link is also provided to the Free the Slaves activism page, which is dedicated to bringing awareness to the greater population in an effort to combat slavery. Regular reports on activities and scheduling for future events as well as practical ways to introduce antislavery activism to groups and communities may be found there. Antislavery videos may be purchased at the online store, and the online gift catalog shows ways to contribute to the effort to free children, provide housing for freed children, and purchase practical instruments of change for communities of former slaves.

Anti-Slavery International
Thomas Clarkson House
The Stableyard
Broomgrove Road
London SW9 9TL UK
Phone: [44] 020 7501 8920
Fax: [44] 020 7738 4110
E-mail: info@antislavery.org
Web site: www.antislavery.org

Anti-Slavery International is the European sister-organization of Free the Slaves and is a key organization concerned with contemporary slavery. Anti-Slavery is the oldest human rights organization in the world. It was responsible for the abolition of slavery within the British Empire in 1833 and was established in its present form in 1839 to carry the fight to other parts of the world. It gave inspiration to the Abolitionist movement in the United States and Brazil, and has contributed to the formulation of all the relevant international standards on slavery.

Throughout its history, it has campaigned relentlessly and intervened effectively on behalf of enslaved people. Generally, the most marginalized and dispossessed groups fall victim to slavery, and the antislavery movement has always been closely allied with the struggle of indigenous people.

Anti-Slavery promotes the eradication of slavery and slavery-like practices and supports freedom for everyone who is subjected to such practices. The abuses that Anti-Slavery opposes include slavery and the buying and selling of people as objects, trafficking of women and the predicament of migrant workers who are trapped into servitude, debt bondage and other traditions that force people into low-status work, forced labor, forced prostitution, abusive forms of child labor, and early or forced marriage and other forms of servile marriage. Anti-Slavery focuses on the rights of people who are particularly vulnerable to exploitation of their labor—notably women, children, migrant workers, and indigenous peoples.

Anti-Slavery pursues its objectives by

- Collecting information about these abuses, bringing them to the attention of the public, and promoting public action to end them
- Identifying ways in which these abuses can be brought to an end and influencing policymakers in governments or other institutions at national and international levels to take action accordingly
- Supporting victims of the abuses that Anti-Slavery opposes in their struggle for freedom, in particular by working with organizations they establish and other organizations campaigning on their behalf

Publications: Anti-Slavery publishes more works on contemporary slavery than any other organization. Many of its publications are listed in Chapter 8. The organization also has the most complete archive of materials concerned with the historical anti-slavery movement.

Web site: The Anti-Slavery International Web site provides access to its publications (an extensive catalog of books, research reports, exhibitions, videos, and other materials), news of ongoing campaigns and recent successes, an explanation of policies, links to other groups, and a sound introduction to antislavery work around the world.

Intergovernmental Organizations

International Labor Organization (ILO)
1828 L. St. NW
Washington, DC 20036
Phone: (202) 653-7652
Fax: (202) 653-7687
E-mail: burrylee@ilo.org
Web site: www.ilo.org/public/english/index.htm

The ILO's main purpose is to promote and develop policies inspired by ideals of social justice aimed chiefly at improving the position of workers within member states. The International Labor Conference, which is the permanent secretariat of the ILO, meets once a year. Every three years it elects the Governing Body, which includes ten member states designated as "states of chief industrial importance."

Publications: The Publications Bureau of the ILO presents an extensive array of materials including books, CD-ROMS, journals, radiographs, and videos dealing with such areas as employment policy, developments in industrial relations, occupational health and safety, and labor statistics and methods, as well as information on child labor practices. The Web site has a fully searchable online shopping catalog for easy purchase.

Web site: The ILO Web site has links to news and contact information, as well as a large, scrolling menu of links to worldwide branches of the organization.

UNESCO

2 United Nations Plaza, Room 900
New York, NY 10017
Phone: (212) 963-5995
Fax: (212) 963-8014
E-mail: e.minchenberg@unesco.org
Web site: www.unesco.org

The United Nations Educational, Scientific, and Cultural Organization (UNESCO) came into being in 1946 when twenty states ratified its constitution. As of October 19, 1999, the organization has 188 member states. UNESCO's stated goal is "to contribute to peace and security in the world by promoting collaboration among nations through education, science, culture and communication in order to further universal respect for justice, for the rule of law and for the human rights and fundamental freedoms that are affirmed for the peoples of the world, without distinction of race, sex, language or religion, by the Charter of the United Nations" (UNESCO Strategy 2005).

Publications: UNESCO uses its publications to foster international public awareness of its major programs in literacy, bioethics, education, human rights, women, the environment, sustainable development, and peace. UNESCO's publications catalog includes more than a thousand titles in English, French,

Spanish, Russian, Chinese, and Arabic, published under its own imprint or copublished. UNESCO produces books, CD-ROMs, periodicals, and scientific maps derived from UNESCO programs and generally aimed at specialized users. For the general public, UNESCO has recently developed a news series on key world issues, such as Cultures of Peace. Full listings of UNESCO's publications are available on the Web site.

Web site: UNESCO has an extensive Web site listing the organization's goals, history, and constitution; current events, activities, and programs; and links to related organizations. It is available in English, Spanish, French, Russian, Arabic, and Chinese.

UNICEF: United Nations Children's Fund
UNICEF House
3 United Nations Plaza
New York, NY 10017
Phone: (212) 326-7000
Fax: (212) 887-7465
E-mail: information@unicefusa.org
Web site: www.unicef.org

Founded in 1946, UNICEF is an advocate of children's rights; it works to protect those rights and helps the young meet their basic needs for sustenance and education and to expand their opportunities to reach their full potential. The organization uses the Convention on the Rights of the Child as its guide in establishing international standards of behavior toward children. UNICEF provides primary health care, basic education, and sanitation in many developing countries.

Publications: UNICEF compiles and makes readily available information on the situation of children, the performance of countries in fulfilling the promise to children, the protection of children's rights, and its own contributions in programs for children. In addition to various news articles, UNICEF's publication program includes annual reports such as *World Summit for Children, Promise and Progress: Achieving Goals for Children, The State of the World's Children, The Progress of Nations 1999,* and the *UNICEF Annual Report.*

Web site: The UNICEF Web site is full of reference materials including news articles, publications, statistics, and general and research information.

UNIFEM: Women's Human Rights Program
304 East 45th Street, Fifteenth Floor
New York, NY 10017
Phone: (212) 906-6400
Fax: (212) 906-6705
Web site: www.unifem.org

UNIFEM has worked since 1976 to empower women and to support gender equality. The organization's main goals are strengthening women's economic powers, increasing women's roles in governance and leadership, and promoting women's human rights.

Publications: UNIFEM publications include books and reports on economic capacity issues, governance and leadership issues, gender mainstreaming challenges, and human rights concerns. UNIFEM and the Center for Women's Global Leadership recently copublished a training manual on women's human rights entitled *Local Action/Global Change, Learning about the Human Rights of Women and Girls.* The manual combines development of rights awareness with issue-oriented actions and includes substantive information about the human rights of women in such areas as violence, health, reproduction and sexuality, education, the global economy, the workplace, and family life. Other publications include videos, annual reports, and speeches and statements on UNIFEM issues.

Web site: The UNIFEM Web site has a list of resources and links to the organization's mission statement, press releases, current news regarding women's rights, and other women's rights organizations.

World Trade Organization (WTO)
154 Rue de Lausanne
1211 Geneva 21
Switzerland
Phone: [41] (22) 739-5111
Web site: www.wto.org

Organized in 1995, the WTO grew from the General Agreement on Tariffs and Trade (GATT). The WTO is an international trade organization that deals with the global rules of trade between nations. It works to ensure that international trade flows as smoothly and predictably as possible. The general goal of the

WTO is to improve the welfare of the peoples of the member countries.

Publications: The extensive list of WTO publications is conveniently divided into the following categories: free publications, recent publications, legal publications, annual reports, trade policy reviews, special studies, and videos. The official WTO newsletter *FOCUS* is available in back issues online, and an online bookshop is available for immediate purchase of materials.

Web site: The WTO Web site has a hierarchical list of links under the broad heading "General Information, Trade Topics, and Resources." The categories contain news texts, trade documents and agreements, and links to other organizations.

Governmental Organizations

Office to Monitor and Combat Trafficking in Persons
U.S. State Department
Antitrafficking hotline: 888 373 7888
Web site: www.state.gov/g/tip

The Office to Monitor and Combat Trafficking in Persons was established by the Trafficking Victims Protection Act of 2000. It coordinates American government efforts against human trafficking and publishes an annual Trafficking in Persons Report documenting the current state of trafficking globally and reporting on the efforts of individual countries to fight human trafficking. It supports projects and research overseas.

Web site: The Web site includes up-to-date information on U.S. government efforts against trafficking, factsheets, and links to major reports and laws.

Nongovernmental Organizations by Region

Africa

African Network for the Prevention and the Protection Against Child Abuse and Neglect (ANPPCAN)
P.O. Box 1768
Nairobi, Kenya
Phone: [254] (2) 573-990

Fax: [254] (2) 576-502
E-mail: anppcan@africaonline.co.ke
Web site: www.anppcan.org

ANPPCAN is a Pan-African organization that advocates the protective rights of children and facilitates research and the exchange of scientific information about them. The organization conducts situation analyses on the state of child abuse in Africa, publishes the results, and advises African governments on how to improve the conditions for children in Africa.

Publications: Annual reports on the state of child abuse and neglect in Africa.

Web site: The Web site provides a mission statement, contact information for chapters throughout Africa, descriptions of organization projects, access to annual reports, and links to international organizations.

International Needs (IN)
P.O. Box 690
Dansoman Est.
Accra, Ghana
Phone: [233] (21) 226-620
E-mail: intneeds@ncs.com.gh
Web site: www.africaexpress.com/internationalneedsghana

Founded in 1974, International Needs is a Christian organization that works to eradicate poverty, disease, and oppression worldwide. It also aims to uplift the standing of women and children. IN-Ghana's work includes a Trokosi liberation project that aims to free ritual slave girls and support them to build new lives (see a description of Trokosi slavery in Chapter 6).

Publications: The organization publishes press releases regarding current projects and events. These press releases are available on the Web site.

Web site: This Web site provides the mission statement of the organization, contact information, an extensive news page, a description of IN services, and a search page for the IN Web site.

WAO-Afrique
399, 168 Rue Tokoin Solidarité
B.P. 80242
Lomé, Togo
Phone: [228] 214-113

Fax: [228] 217-345
E-mail: wao-afrique@bibway.com
Web site: www.membres.lycos.fr/waoafrique

Founded by a former child domestic, WAO Afrique works for the protection and prevention of all forms of abuse, exploitation, and trafficking of children. Preventative initiatives include campaigning, education, and awareness at the community and government levels. The organization runs education and training projects for the police and other human rights organizations in order to help them respond better to the increasing incidents of child labor, exploitation, and trafficking of children into and within Togo and other West African countries.

Web site: This is a French-language Web site.

Asia

Anti-Slavery Society of Australia
G.P.O. Box 483 C
Melbourne, Victoria 3001 Australia
Phone: [61] (03) 9642 1015
E-mail: info@childlabor.net
Web site: www.anti-slaverysociety.org

The Anti-Slavery Society is dedicated to ending slavery and the slave trade as well as bonded labor, child labor, child prostitution, and the international trafficking of women and children for prostitution. The society not only investigates and campaigns against all forms of slavery but also organizes missions to rescue slaves, reintegrate them into their communities, and raise consumer awareness about goods produced by slave labor. The society receives no government funding; it relies on private contributions to pay for its activities.

Web site: The Web site contains an extensive hierarchical table of contents describing current slavery practices and counter-methods.

Asia Monitor Resource Center (AMRC)
444 Nathan Road, Flat 8B
Kowloon, Hong Kong
Phone: [852] 2332-1346
Fax: 852] 2385-5319

E-mail: admin@amrc.org.hk
Web site: www.amrc.org.hk

The Asia Monitor Resource Center (AMRC) is an independent NGO that focuses on Asian labor concerns. The center provides information, research, publishing, training, labor networking, and related services to trade unions, labor groups, and other development NGOs in the region. Its main goal is the support of democratic and independent labor movements in the Asian arena.

Publications: Publications include a quarterly report entitled *Asian Labor Update* and various articles pertaining to labor concerns.

Web site: The AMRC Web site provides a description of the organization and a list of AMRC publications, but very little other information.

Asian Migrant Center (AMC)
4 Jordan Road
Kowloon, Hong Kong
Phone: [852] 2312-0031
Fax: [852] 2992-0111
E-mail: amc@hk.super.net
Web site: www.pacific.net.hk/~amc

The Asian Migrant Center was established in 1989 to help develop alternatives to migrant work and to empower migrants in Asia. It researches the conditions of migrant workers throughout the continent and investigates the political and social movements within their groups. The AMC supports a number of migrant worker organizations to foster reintegration of migrants and raise political awareness of their situation.

Publications: The organization's major publication is the annual *Asian Migrant Yearbook* ($55), a reference book on Asian migrant workers and migration issues. The most recent edition of the resource contains full-color maps of Asian labor migration; photographs, charts, and country statistics; analytical reports from sixteen Asian countries; and special articles on the impact of the 1997 Asian financial crisis on migrant workers, violence against women migrants, and globalization and migration.

Web site: The AMC Web site provides a resource list, information for ordering the *Asian Migrant Yearbook,* descriptions of organization activities, and links to like-minded organizations.

Europe

Burma Peace Foundation
Online Burma/Myanmar Library
85 Rue de Montbrillant
1202 Geneva, Switzerland
Phone: [41] (22) 733-2040
E-mail: darnott@iprolink.ch
Web site: www.burmalibrary.org

The Burma Peace Foundation confronts many of the same problems that the Burma Project addresses, such as human rights and economic abuses.

Web site: Acting as a searchable online index, the Online Burma Library holds over 100,000 Burma-related documents, consolidating information from over 500 Web sites of NGOs, activist organizations, and media sites.

Catholic Agency for Overseas Development (CAFOD)
Romero Close
Stockwell Road
London SW9 9TY UK
Phone: [44] (207) 733 7900
Fax: [44] (207) 274 9630
E-mail: cafod@cafod.org.uk
Web site: www.cafod.org.uk

CAFOD is the official relief and development agency of the Catholic Church in England and Wales. It is committed to justice for the world's poor, regardless of religion; CAFOD funds more than a thousand projects worldwide. It has been active in publicizing and working against slavery and bonded labor in the developing world.

Publications: CAFOD issues policy briefings covering relief and development issues; online fact sheets describing issues facing the developing world, such as racism, the environment, land mines, food, aid, poverty, and the role of women; and press articles regarding CAFOD activities.

Web site: The CAFOD Web site has links to news articles, campaigns for human rights, job opportunities, and a wealth of information for people interested in becoming part of the organization.

Child Rights Information Network (CRIN)
17 Grove Lane
London SE5 8RD UK
Phone: [44] (207) 716 2240
Fax: [44] (207) 793 7628
E-mail: info@crin.org
Web site: www.crin.org

CRIN is a global network of children's rights organizations striving to improve the lives of children by exchanging information about child rights, promoting the UN Convention on the Rights of the Child, and developing capacity building and networking tools.

Publications: CRIN maintains a publications database of the publications (journals, newsletters, articles, and reports) of member organizations. Many of these publications are available on CRIN's Web site.

Web site: Besides the publication database of member organizations, the CRIN Web site offers extensive links to human rights organizations and articles on the rights of children.

Christian Aid
35 Lower Marsh
Waterloo
London SE1 7RL UK
Phone: [44] (207) 620 4444
Fax: [44] (207) 620 0719
E-mail: info@christian-aid.org
Web site: www.christian-aid.org.uk

Christian Aid is an organization dedicated to helping people worldwide overcome poverty and human rights abuses. It has volunteers in more than sixty countries. A leader in overseas aid and development, it also provides in-depth research and has campaigned actively against bonded labor.

Publications: Christian Aid's publication program issues regular reports to support its advocacy, campaigning, and lobbying work. Recent reports have focused on the impact of debt on poor countries, proposals for rapid debt cancellation, and business ethics and ethical trading. Other areas of publication include globalization, aid, human rights and governance, gender, and participation.

Web site: The Christian Aid Web site provides newsbriefs, reports, and information concerning human rights across the globe.

Clean Clothes Campaign
P.O. Box 11584
1001 GN Amsterdam
The Netherlands
Phone: [31] (20) 412-2785
Fax: [31] (20) 412-2786
E-mail: info@cleanclothes.org
Web site: http://www.cleanclothes.org

The Clean Clothes Campaign works to improve working conditions in garment industries worldwide. The campaign works with consumer organizations, trade unions, and other groups to make sure that employers are responsible for providing safe and fair conditions for their employees.

Publications: Several reports related to the work of the Clean Clothes Campaign, including accounts of poor working conditions, discussions of labor and consumer issues, and analyses of independent monitoring models, are published on the organization's Web site.

Web site: The Web site has general news and current events sections, a list of reviewed companies, a proposed code of conduct for employers, and contact information for concerned consumers.

Comite Contre L'Esclavage Modern (CCEM)
31 Rue des Lilas
75019 Paris, France
[33] (1) 4452-8890
[33] (1) 4452-8909
Web site: www.ccem-antislavery.org

The CCEM, known in English as the Committee against Modern Slavery, fights the intolerable practice of slavery in France and abroad. Made up entirely of volunteers, the committee enlists journalists, lawyers, social workers, doctors and health professionals, students, and retired people to work toward its goal of ending slavery worldwide. Branches of this organization exist in France, Belgium, Spain, and Italy.

Publications: The CCEM publishes reports on topics related to the organization's activities and findings.

Web site: The CCEM Web site is offered in both French and English. It has sections for news, activity reports, information for people interested in joining the committee, and contact information.

Defence for Children International (DCI)
P.O. Box 88
1221 Geneva 20, Switzerland
Phone: [41] (22) 734-0558
Fax: [41] (22) 740-1145
E-mail: dci-hq@pingnet.ch
Web site: //defence-for-children.org

Defence for Children International is a nongovernmental organization working for the protection and promotion of children's rights. Established during the International Year of the Child (1979), DCI encourages concerted international action toward promoting and protecting the rights of the child. It also seeks to foster awareness and solidarity about children's rights situations by conducting research and monitoring of potentially abusive areas. DCI suggests both preventive and curative protection of all children's rights.

Publications: A regular newsletter and other information on all aspects of children's rights, through regular and ad hoc publications.

Web site: The DCI Web site is very limited in scope; it provides a mission statement and links to children's rights standards.

Foundation Against Trafficking in Women
P.O. Box 1455
3500 BL Utrecht
The Netherlands
Phone: [31] (302) 716-044
Fax: [31] (302) 716-084
E-mail: fe@stv.vx.xs4all.nl

The Foundation Against Trafficking in Women was founded in the early 1980s in response to growing prostitution tourism. The organization works with NGOs, international action groups, and other women's organizations to develop legislation and litigation addressing the issue.

Web site: None

Free Burma
(No physical address)
E-mail: FreeBurma@POBox.com
Web site: www.ibiblio.org/freeburma

Free Burma is an organization that describes itself as "a collection of hardware, software, documentation and volunteers" dedicated to information dissemination about the current tyranny of the military dictatorship in that country (Free Burma Web site). See Chapter 6 for a description of forced labor in Burma.

Web site: The Free Burma Web site provides a mission statement and description of the current situation in Burma, as well as links to documents relating to Burma, almost daily news updates, and ways to become involved in any of the organization's areas of concern. A CD-ROM is also available on the Web site containing the same information provided online.

Human Rights Information and Documentation Systems International (HURIDOCS)
48 Chemin du Grand-Montfleury
CH-1290 Versoix, Switzerland
Phone: [41] (22) 755-5252
Fax: [41] (22) 755-5260
E-mail: info@huridocs.org
Web site: www.huridocs.org

Established in 1982, HURIDOCS is a global network of human rights organizations. Its goal is to provide a "decentralized information network" to workers in the field of human rights. HURIDOCS offers the tools and techniques for information handling, training courses on documenting human rights studies, and advice and support on documentation centers and information systems.

Publications: Reference books and software on the tools for "Human Rights Information Handling," reports on HURIDOCS activities, and a regular newsletter. Publications must be ordered through the organization. Some selections from the newsletter and reports are available on the Web site.

Web site: The HURIDOCS Web site contains general information about the organization as well as guidelines and formats for human rights documentation.

International Confederation of Free Trade Unions (ICFTU)
5 Boulevard du Roi Albert II, Bte 1
1210 Brussels, Belgium
Phone: [32] (2) 224-0211
Fax: [32] (2) 201-5815
E-mail: internetpo@icftu.org
Web site: www.icftu.org

Established in 1949, the ICFTU is made up of 233 organizations in 152 countries worldwide; it has over 151 million members, over a fourth of whom are women. The ICFTU is open to all democratic trade unions. It works together with the International Labor Organization, the United Nations Economic and Social Committee, the International Monetary Fund, the World Bank, and the World Trade Organization. The confederation's main goals are to defend workers' rights, encourage equal rights for women, eradicate child labor, make education available for all, and support the environment.

Publications: The ICFTU publishes a monthly journal entitled *Trade Union World* and a number of other publications each year on particular themes. Additionally, it publishes the *Survey of Trade Union Rights* each June, which provides information on more than 115 countries violating basic trade union rights norms. An online bulletin is also available via e-mail.

Web site: The ICFTU Web site contains a history of trade unions and milestones in workers' rights. It also provides a mission statement, a calendar of workers' rights events, educational materials, labor rights resolutions, and links to associated trade union campaigns.

**International Textile Garment and
Leather Workers Federation (ITGLWF)**
8 Rue Joseph Stevens
Brussels 1000, Belgium
Phone: [32] (2) 512-2833
Fax: [32] (2) 511-0904
Web site: www.itglwf.org

Comprising 206 trade unions in 106 countries, this organization works to protect the rights of laborers in the textile and leather industries. It seeks regulations regarding child workers, overworking of laborers, and similar abuse in these industries.

Web site: The ITGLWF Web site provides news updates, a code of conduct for the industry, descriptions of the federation's priorities, and links to regional ITGLWF chapters.

La Strada Ceska Republika
P.O. Box 305
Prague, Czech Republic
Phone: [420] (2) 2272-1810
E-mail: lastrada@strada.cz
Web site: www.strada.cz

La Strada's goal is to prevent the trafficking of women in Central and Eastern Europe. It provides aid for victims and works to raise awareness of the problem by lobbying government bodies and conducting research.

Publications: The organization publishes informational brochures for women regarding the problems of trafficking.

Web site: This Web site is available in both Czech and English. It provides information on preventing women trafficking, support of victims, and international politics involved in the matter, as well as links to other offices throughout Eastern Europe.

NGO Group for the Convention on the Rights of the Child
c/o Defence for Children International
P.O. Box 88
1221 Geneva 20, Switzerland
Phone: [41] (22) 740-4730
Fax: [41] (22) 740-1145
E-mail: ngo-crc@tsicalinet.ch
Web site: www.crin.org/NGOGroupforCRC

A coalition of more than fifty international NGOs working to facilitate implementation of the Convention on the Rights of the Child, this organization is a subsidiary of DCI. Though the organization does not call for all child labor to be banned, it does support positive changes for child workers and "best interest" treatment of children. The group's major goal is to prevent exploitative and abusive child labor and improve conditions for working children.

Publications: Brochures on combating the sale of children, child prostitution, and child pornography; eliminating the exploitation of child labor; education on the Convention on the

Rights of the Child; and a guide for NGOs reporting to the Committee on the Rights of the Child are only available from the organization.

Web site: The Web site contains background information about the group, contact addresses, a list of aims and objectives, a list of NGO members, and a mailing list.

Norwegian Institute of International Affairs (NUPI)
CJ Hambros Plass 2D
P.O. Box 8159 Dep.
N-0033 Oslo 1, Norway
Phone: [47] (2) 22 99 40 00
Fax: [47] (2) 22 36 21 82
Web site: www.nupi.no/default-e.htm

The Norwegian Institute of International Affairs researches international political and economic issues. Major topics of research include the integration and sovereignty of Europe, collective security and peace operations, international economics, and development policy.

Publications: Within the field of international relations, NUPI researchers publish articles, books, and reports. Some materials are published directly by NUPI, whereas others are published by domestic or foreign publishing houses.

Web site: This Web site is offered in both Norwegian and English. It contains research information, news items, general publications and texts of working papers, transcripts of international affairs seminars, and contact information.

Rädda Barnen
Torsgatan 4
107 88 Stockholm, Sweden
Phone: [46] (8) 698-9000
Fax: [46] (8) 698-9010
E-mail: info@rbise
Web site: www.rb.se/eng

Rädda Barnen is the Swedish division of Save the Children.

Publications: Rädda Barnen publishes books, reports, videos, and a magazine. A documentation database and a newsletter on child soldiers are also available.

Web site: This Web site is similar to the Save the Children Web site but focuses on a Swedish audience. The site is available in Swedish and English.

Rugmark
Rugmark-German office
c/o TRANSFAIR e.V.
Remigiusstrasse 21
50937 Köln, Germany
Phone: [49] (221) 942040-0
Fax: [49] (221) 942040-40
E-mail: rugmark@transfair.org
Web site: www.rugmark.de

Or:

Rugmark-USA
733 15th Street NW, Suite 912
Washington, DC 20005
Phone: (202) 347-4205
Fax: (202) 347-4885
E-mail: info@rugmark.org
Web site: www.rugmark.org

The Rugmark campaign monitors the use of illegal child labor in the carpet industry. It also aims to fulfill consumer demands for socially responsible production conditions to avoid a consumer boycott of hand-knotted carpets. Rugmark has worldwide organizational support including divisions in Europe, North America, India, and Nepal.

Publications: Publications include organizational reports and information on the status of child labor in the carpet industries in India, Nepal, and Pakistan.

Web site: The Rugmark Web site is offered in both German and English. It provides general information about the campaign's goals, news, information for prospective licensees, and contact information.

Survival International
6 Charterhouse Buildings
London EC1M 7ET UK
Phone: [44] (207) 687 8700
Fax: [44] (207) 687 8701

E-mail: info@survival-international.org
Web site: www.survival-international.org

Survival International is a worldwide organization providing support of tribal and indigenous peoples. It supports self-determination of all people in regard to life, land, and human rights. The organization also offers for sale tribal goods produced under socially responsible conditions.

Publications: Publications include country-specific urgent action bulletins, press releases, and success stories. All of these are available on the Web site and are searchable by publication type and country.

Web site: This Web site describes the organization's campaigns and offers backgrounds of numerous tribes and countries. It also has sections for current news and events, application information, a catalog of goods, and links to similar organizations.

Transnational Institute (TNI)
Paulus Potterstraat 20
1071 DA Amsterdam
The Netherlands
Phone: [31] (20) 662-6608
Fax: [31] (20) 675-7176
E-mail: tni@tni.org
Web site: www.tni.org

Since 1974, the Transnational Institute has worked to find solutions to global problems dealing with militarism, poverty, social wrongs, and the environment. The U.S. branch of the institute has sponsored exchange programs and other projects between the United States and Russia. Over 850 Russian citizens participated in these exchanges, and more than 1,200 U.S. citizens have made the trip to Russia. Now, after the collapse of the Soviet Union, the Transnational Institute continues its exchange program with the Commonwealth of Independent States.

Publications: TNI's global research generates a comprehensive publication program that includes full-length books, topical reports, and a book series published in association with Pluto Press. Also available are publications by TNI fellows. Descriptions of publications and instructions for ordering are available on the Web site.

Web site: The Transnational Institute's Web site contains information and links to current news and projects, as well as an extensive online archive of articles and past publications.

North America

Amnesty International USA
322 Eighth Avenue
New York, NY 10001
Phone: (212) 807-8400
Fax: (212) 627-1451
Web sites: www.amnesty-usa.org;
www.amnesty-volunteer.org/usa/education

One of the world's largest human rights organizations, Amnesty International lists as its goals the liberation of prisoners of conscience; ensuring fair, speedy trials for political prisoners; abolition of cruel treatment of prisoners (including torture and the death penalty); and ending extrajudicial killings and disappearances.

Publications: As part of its campaign to protect fundamental human rights, Amnesty International regularly publishes country reports and other documents on human rights issues around the world. All published information is scrupulously analyzed and cross-checked by the research department and legal offices in London to ensure the integrity of the final reports. These reports are regarded by experts in various fields of study as one of the most reliable sources for information on human rights issues. The accuracy and strict impartiality with which the organization's research is conducted has made it a vital resource for many news organizations, government agencies, lawyers, professors, and students.

Web sites: The Web sites have an enormous amount of information about human rights abuses, current events, and organization activities. Links to other Amnesty International sites and other human rights organizations are also provided.

Asian-American Free Labor Institute (AAFLI)
1925 K Street NW, Suite 301
Washington, DC 20006
Phone: (202) 778-4500
Fax: (202) 778-4525

The AAFLI is the international component of the AFL-CIO. The institute works with Asian trade unions to enforce child labor standards, worker health and safety standards, and safe labor conditions.

Publications: The AAFLI publishes a quarterly newsletter, the *AAFLI News*, and other informational material.

Web site: None

Break the Chain Campaign
733 15th St. NW, Suite 1020
Washington, DC 20005-2112
Phone: (202) 234-9382 ext. 244
Fax: (202) 387-7915
E-mail: joy@ips-dc.org (Director)
Web site: www.BreakTheChainCampaign.org

Break the Chain Campaign is a coalition of legal and social service agencies, ethnically based organizations, social action groups, and individuals devoted to protecting the rights of the migrant domestic working community. Specifically, it focuses on those domestic workers carrying A-3 or G-5 visas. (See Chapter 6 for a description of domestic slavery in the United States).

Publications: The Legal Rights and Resources Available to G-5 and A-3 Domestic Workers. A handbook for work with domestic workers, available from the campaign (No ISBN).

Web site: The Web site covers the work of the campaign. It includes a contact for those who know of a case of G-5 or A-3 abuse. One section details the abuse and exploitation of G-5 and A-3 domestic workers. Information on how to contact the Campaign for Migrant Domestic Workers Rights is also given.

Burma Project
Burma Project
Open Society Institute
400 West 59th Street
New York, NY 10019
Phone: (212) 548-0632
Fax: (212) 548-4655
E-mail: burma@sorosny.org
Web site: www.burmaproject.org

The Burma Project, established by the Open Society Institute in 1994, aims to increase international awareness of conditions in

Burma (Myanmar) and to assist the country in making its transition from a closed to an open society. (See Chapter 6 for a description of forced labor in Burma.)

Publications: Publications include a bimonthly magazine, *Burma Debate,* which serves as a forum for discussion of central issues concerning Burma; *Burma: Country in Crisis,* a report that provides background information on current events in Burma; *Burma News Update,* a newsflash report that delivers timely updates regarding current developments in Burma; and *BurmaNet News,* an electronic newspaper covering Burma and providing recent articles from newspapers, magazines, newsletters, the wire services, and the Internet. Subscriptions to *Burma News Update* and *BurmaNet News* are free and available by e-mail. Most publications are available on the Web site.

Web site: The Burma Project Web site has links to a history of Burma, news reports, publications, current projects, grant/scholarship information, political and economic information, and thorough descriptions of the problems threatening the Burmese people.

Child Labor Coalition (CLC)
c/o National Consumers League
1701 K Street NW, Suite 1200
Washington, DC 20006
Phone: (202) 835-3323
Fax: (202) 835-0747
Web site: www.natlconsumersleague.org/clc.htm

Since 1989, the CLC has worked to end exploitation of child labor and to encourage education, health, safety, and general well-being for working children. The CLC researches child labor abuses and publishes its findings in order to influence policy concerning child workers.

Publications: No regular publications.

Web site: The CLC Web site offers advice of what consumers can do to combat child labor, other background information, and links to other child labor organizations.

Coalition Against Slavery in Sudan and Mauritania
P.O. Box 3293
New York, NY 10027
Phone: (212) 774-4287

E-mail: casmasalc@aol.com
Web site: http://members.aol.com/casmasalc

This human rights organization brings together abolitionists and human rights activists from all races, creeds, and nationalities to collectively fight for the eradication of the chattel enslavement of black Africans. It is a response to the centuries-old practice of buying, selling, and breeding Africans by Arab Moors and North African Arabs that never stopped in the countries of Sudan and Mauritania.

Publications: Cotton, Samuel. *Silent Terror: A Journey into Contemporary African Slavery.* New York: Writers and Readers Publishing, Harlem River Press, 1998.

Web site: The Web site contains recent news about work against slavery in Mauritania and Sudan as well as an archive of articles on the subject.

Coalition of Immokalee Workers
P.O. Box 603
Immokalee, FL 34143
Phone: (941) 657-8311
Fax: (941) 657-5055
E-mail: workers@ciw-online.org
Web site: www.ciw-online.org

The CIW is a community-based worker organization. Their members are largely Latino, Haitian, and Mayan Indian immigrants working in low-wage jobs throughout the state of Florida. CIW has been extensively involved in bringing enslaved agricultural workers to freedom. They organize actions and boycotts of companies that will not take responsibility for the human cost of the fruit and vegetables they buy.

Publications: The CIW Web site holds a large number of reports and press materials.

Web site: This Web site has a large collection of materials for student action. These include sample press releases and reports from boycotts and demonstrations at universities around the country. It is an invaluable resource for understanding the reality of slavery in modern America.

ECPAT USA
157 Montague Street
Brooklyn, NY 11201

Phone: (212) 870-2427
Fax: 212) 870-2055
E-mail: info@ecpatusa.org
Web site: www.ecpatusa.org or www.ecpat.net

ECPAT is an international institution dedicated to eliminating child pornography, child prostitution, and "the trafficking of children for sexual purposes." ECPAT is nonpolitical and nonreligious; it works with other organizations and governments to support its goals.

Publications: ECPAT has a number of books that are basic and fundamental explanations of child prostitution and trafficking, particularly *The ECPAT Story,* by Ron O'Grady (1996); *The Rape of the Innocent,* also by Ron O'Grady (1994); *Enforcing the Law against the Commercial Sexual Exploitation of Children,* ECPAT (1996); *Child Prostitution and Sex Tourism: A Series of Research Reports,* by Dr. Julia O'Connell Davidson and Jaqueline Sanchez-Taylor, 1996; *Looking Back, Thinking Forward: The Fourth Report on the Implementation of the Agenda for Action Adopted at the World Congress against Commercial Sexual Exploitation of Children* (2000); *Five Years after Stockholm: The Fifth Report on the Implementation of the Agenda for action* (2001); and *ECPAT Report on the Implementation of the Agenda for action against the Commercial Sexual Exploitation of Children 2001– 2002* (2003).

Web site: The ECPAT Web site details current efforts to end child exploitation, including the International Young People's Participation Project, which aims to increase the level of young people's participation in the campaign against the commercial sexual exploitation of children. It intends to do this by collaborating with national partners in more than thirty countries.

Free the Children
7368 Yonge Street, Suite 3000
Thornhill, Ontario L4J 8H9 Canada
Phone: (905) 760-9382
Fax: (905) 760-9157
E-mail: info@freethechildren.com
Web site: www.freethechildren.org

Set up by Canadian schoolchildren, Free the Children is dedicated to eliminating the exploitation of children around the world by encouraging youth to volunteer in, as well as to create, programs and activities that relieve the plight of underprivileged children. It is an organization run by children for children. It now employs adults to work in its central office, but only on the understanding that they are facilitators and administrators but do not take part in making policy for the organization. Free the Children funds schools, rehabilitation programs for ex-child laborers, and aid for children in situations of conflict or natural disaster around the world.

Publications: The book *Free the Children,* by organizer Craig Kielburger, is sold through the Web site, as are a video about the organization's work and a CD of songs.

Web site: The Web site has a guide to projects run by Free the Children and an explanation of its history.

Human Rights First
333 Seventh Avenue, 13th Floor
New York, NY 10001
Phone: (212) 845-5200
Fax: (212) 845-5299
E-mail: nyc@humanrightsfirst.org
Web site: www.humanrightsfirst.org

Founded in 1978, the Human Rights First works to ensure that all governments are compliant with the International Bill of Human Rights. It supports legal institutions dedicated to upholding human rights for all.

Publications: Extensive publications include books, topical reports, and papers on such varied issues as asylum, freedom of association, international justice, international financial institutions, and international refugee programs. Pertinent issues are also reported with a geographical emphasis, including papers on matters in Africa, Europe, Latin America/Caribbean, and Middle East/North Africa. Publication descriptions are available on the Web site; most must be ordered from the organization. Human Rights First's program WITNESS, a partnership with Peter Gabriel and Reebok, releases a biweekly series of human rights videos called "WITNESS Rights Alert."

Web site: The Human Rights First Web site is like a newspaper; it has links to articles about the legal aspects of worldwide human rights violations.

Human Rights Watch (HRW)
350 Fifth Avenue, 34th Floor

New York, NY 10118-3299
Phone: (212) 290-4700
Fax: (212) 736-1300
E-mail: hrnyc@hrw.org
Web site: www.hrw.org

HRW is dedicated to protecting human rights around the world. It investigates and exposes human rights violations and holds abusers accountable. The Human Rights Watch organization established the Children's Rights Project in 1994. This division of HRW examines countries and organizations suspected of children's rights violations and publishes its findings in reports distributed to governments, institutions, and NGOs capable of ending the child abuse. Human Rights Watch's Women's Rights Project examines reports of women's rights abuses worldwide. It publishes its findings along with HRW's other articles. The Women's Rights Project also keeps track of current events in the field of women's rights.

Publications: The organization regularly publishes reports on such topics as slavery, child rights, child labor, bonded child labor, abduction, and the trafficking of women and girls.

Web site: The main Web site details HRW's many divisions and has extensive links to HRW publications, campaigns, essays, country briefings, and research materials. The Children's Rights Project Web page (www.hrw.org/children) has links to some of its reports. The Women's Rights Project Web page (www.hrw. org/women) has links to news articles about women's rights abuses and transcripts of HRW's reports on the subject.

International Forum on Globalization (IFG)
1009 General Kennedy Avenue #2
San Francisco, CA 94129
Phone: (415) 561-7650
Fax: (415) 561-7651
E-mail: ifg@ifg.org
Web site: www.ifg.org

Founded in 1994, the International Forum on Globalization is dedicated to examining the impacts of economic globalization. It organizes activities to inform the general public about the effects of globalization.

Publications: Publications include a newsletter for members and papers discussing such issues as corporate governance, the World Trade Organization, and the effects of globalization on the environment, citizenship, and commerce. Descriptions of published papers are available on the Web site.

Web site: The IFG Web site has links to forum events and partner organizations.

Laogai Research Foundation (LRF)
1925 K Street NW, Suite 400
Washington, DC 20006-1132
Phone: (202) 833-8770
Fax: 202) 833-6187
E-mail: laogai@laogai.org
Web site: www.laogai.org

LRF was established by ex-*laogai* (forced labor camp) inmate Harry Wu in 1992 to carry out research, publish, and publicize the plight of the millions of Chinese held in gulags across China—home to the most extensive forced labor camp system in the world today.

Publications: The organization publishes an annual *Laogai Handbook,* a newsletter, and special reports, and assists television journalists in making documentaries exposing the abuse of human rights in the laogai.

Web site: The LRF Web site has links to foundation newsletters.

Multinational Monitor (Essential Information, Inc.)
P.O. Box 19405
Washington, DC 20036
Phone: (202) 387-8030
Fax: (202) 234-5176
E-mail: monitor@essential.org
Web site: www.multinationalmonitor.org

The *Multinational Monitor* is a monthly publication of Essential Information, Inc., an organization that aims to provide provocative information to the public on important topics neglected by the mass media and policy makers. The *Multinational Monitor* examines corporate activity, especially in the Third World, focusing on the export of hazardous substances, worker health and safety, labor union issues, and the environment.

Web site: The *Multinational Monitor*'s Web site has links to its online issues.

Save the Children Federation
54 Wilton Road
Westport, CT 06880
Phone: (800) 728-3843
Web site: www.savethechildren.org

Save the Children helps impoverished and abused children worldwide, addressing health and educational needs alongside social and economic wrongs.

Publications: The organization has extensive publications available online. This includes Champions newsbriefs, the *IMPACT* newsletter, and annual and special reports. The major report *The State of the World's Mothers* is also available on the Web site.

Web site: Save the Children's somewhat disorganized Web site has links to children's rights publications.

Sweatshop Watch
310 Eighth Street, Suite 303
Oakland, CA 94607
Phone: (510) 834-8990
E-mail: sweatinfo@sweatshopwatch.org
Web site: www.sweatshopwatch.org

Sweatshop Watch is a coalition of international human rights organizations. Its goal is to end sweatshop conditions for textile workers.

Publications: Sweatshop Watch publishes a quarterly newsletter, current and back issues of which are available online. The newsletter reports and discusses consumer and labor issues related to human rights violations.

Web site: Sweatshop Watch's Web site has links to related articles and newsletters.

WITNESS
353 Broadway
New York, NY 10013
Phone: (212) 274-1664 ext.201
Fax: (212) 274-1262
E-mail: witness@witness.org
Web site: www.witness.org

Founded in 1992 by singer Peter Gabriel, the Lawyers Committee for Human Rights, and the Reebok Human Rights Foundation, WITNESS is a nonprofit organization dedicated to strengthening human rights advocacy by providing video and communications technology for documenting human rights abuses. The videos are then used as evidence before courts, educational materials for raising awareness, and deterrents to further violations. WITNESS partner organizations, totaling 150 in all, including television stations that air the videos and help to distribute the footage internationally.

Web site: This heavily trafficked Web site (1.5 million hits per month) provides the WITNESS mission statement as well as actual video footage, news updates, partner information, details for training and getting involved, and an online store.

World Vision
34834 Weyerhaeuser Way South
P.O. Box 9716, Dept. W
Federal Way, WA 98063-9716
Phone: (888) 511-6598
Web site: www.worldvision.org/worldvision/master.nsf

World Vision is a Christian organization dedicated to ending poverty, hunger, and human rights abuses worldwide. In India, it has developed innovative programs for the liberation and rehabilitation of child bonded laborers.

Publications: Publications include an annual report, a quarterly periodical entitled *World Vision Today,* a monthly commentary and fact sheet entitled *Insider,* and policy papers on such issues as landmines and child sponsorship. Most of these publications are available in full text online.

Web site: The Web site has current and past press releases, links to current projects, articles about past activities, and links to World Vision sites worldwide.

South America

Atalaya Regional Indigenous Organization
Organization Indigena Regional de Atalaya (OIRA)
Correo Central, Atalaya, Peru
Phone: [51] (64) 573-469

Formed in 1986 as a federation of local indigenous community groups, OIRA works to organize local people into taking action against the use of slavery affecting the more than 10,000 indigenous peoples in the Atalaya region of Peru. Some of OIRA's achievements include documenting information on sixty communities where slavery was taking place, running literacy courses for indigenous bonded laborers on ranches and estates, persuading authorities to help local indigenous people to be officially registered, and winning an agreement with the authorities over indigenous land rights. OIRA has freed more than 6,000 people.

Web site: None

**National Forum on the Prevention
and Eradication of Child Labor**
SBN Quadra 01
Bloco (F)-Sala 204
Ed. Palacio da Agricultura
SENAR/CA
Brazilia/ DF CEP 70040-000, Brazil
Phone: [55] (61) 226-6815
Fax: [55] (61) 321-5775
E-mail: infantil@senar-rural.com.br

This organization is coordinated by the Brazilian Ministry of Labor and is composed of forty institutions with representatives of workers, employers, the federal government, and NGOs. A methodology of work called "integrated actions" is at the heart of this organization. It means that every institution member of the forum should make an effort to concentrate his/her actions in a specific area at the same time and with the same target group.

Web site: None

Pastoral Land Commission (CPT)
Head Office
Rue 19, No. 34, First Andar
Centro-CEP, 74030-090
Goiania
Goias, Brazil
Phone: [55] (62) 212-6466
Fax: [55] (62) 212-0421
E-mail: cptnac@cultura.com.br

One of the most powerful defenders of land reform in Brazil, the CPT reported 5,000 cases of slave labor in Brazil in 1991.
Web site: None

South Asia and Southeast Asia

Asian-American Free Labor Institute (AAFLI)
G.P.O. Box 596
Dhaka-1000, Bangladesh
Phone: [880] (2) 88-403
E-mail: aaflibd@pradeshta.net

The AAFLI is one of the AFL-CIO's four international institutes. For the past twenty-five years, the institute has been fighting for and promoting human rights in Asia. It works to eliminate child labor and rehabilitate former child workers. The AAFLI works with trade unions, human rights organizations, and both government and NGO groups to promote public policies to enforce labor rights and standards.
Web site: None

Bonded Labor Liberation Front, India (BLLF)
7 Jantar Mantar Road
New Delhi 110001, India
Phone: [91] (11) 336-6765/7943
Fax: [91] (11) 336-8355
E-mail: agnivesh@usnl.com
Web site: www.swamiagnivesh.com

Founded after police opened fire on a workers' demonstration in 1981, the BLLF-India initially aimed to free bonded laborers working in stone quarries near Delhi. It is now a nationwide organization fighting debt bondage in all parts of the economy, including agriculture, where the largest number of bonded laborers exist. It coordinates activities of local centers in identifying, releasing, and rehabilitating bonded laborers; trains activists; educates bonded laborers about their rights; runs education centers; and provides legal advice. The organization established a National Day of Children in Servitude on which rallies and demonstrations are held to highlight the injustices of the debt bondage system.

Butterflies
C-7 First Floor
Prabhataria, Mohammedpur
Green Park Extension RK Puran
New Delhi 110066, India
Phone: [91] (11) 686-3935
Phone: [91] (11) 619-6117
Fax: [91] (11) 685-8117
E-mail: bflies@sdalt.erner.in
E-mail: ritap@giasdlo1.usnl.net.in

The Butterflies NGO works specifically with street children around interstate bus terminals in India. It helps to educate the children, provide them with health care, train them in vocations, and file court petitions on their behalf.

Publications: Issues a quarterly magazine that keeps an account of child-related accidents and abuse.

Web site: None

Child Workers in Asia (CWA)
P.O. Box 29
Chantrakasem Post Office
Bangkok 10904, Thailand
Phone: [66] (2) 930-0855/6
E-mail: cwanet@loxinfo.co.th
Web site: www.cwa.tnet.co.th

CWA is a network of NGOs and individuals involved with the child labor movement in Asia. Through grassroots efforts and local advocacy, this organization works to foster development of child-focused NGOs. It also analyzes the situation of working children in order to raise awareness of the matter, advise interested organizations, and publish pertinent information.

Publications: Publications include a quarterly newsletter on child labor issues (available on the Web site).

Web site: The CWA Web site offers various declarations on children's rights, an extensive list of references regarding working children (organized by country and by topic, such as "bonded child labor"), statistical information, current research information, and links to related sites.

End Child Prostitution in Asian Tourism International (ECPAT)
328 Phyathai Road
Bangkok 10400, Thailand
Phone: [66] (2) 215-3388
Fax: [66] (2) 215-8272
E-mail: info@ecpat.net
Web site: www.ecpat.net

The End Child Prostitution in Asian Tourism (ECPAT) campaign began in 1990 in response to concern over increasing child prostitution in Thailand, the Philippines, and Sri Lanka. It aims to persuade governments to introduce effective policing to end child slavery and prostitution, make the promotion of tourism for child prostitution illegal, and encourage legal punishment of abusers, not victims. As a result of its work, these and other governments have introduced stricter laws, and Sweden, Germany, and Australia have passed laws allowing them to prosecute their citizens for sexual abuse of children in other countries. Other offices are established in forty countries, including Australia, Canada, France, Germany, Japan, Switzerland, the United States, and the United Kingdom.

Global Alliance Against Traffic in Women (GAATW)
36, Bangkok Noi Office
Bangkok 10700, Thailand
Phone: [66] (2) 864-1427/1428
Fax: [66] (2) 864-1637
E-mail: GAATW@mozart.inet.co.th
Web site: www.thai.net/gaatw

Formed at the International Workshop on Migration and Traffic in Women in 1994, the GAATW ensures that human rights of trafficked women are protected by state authorities and agencies. The organization involves grassroots women in practical support and advocacy of international organizations with similar goals.

The GAATW campaigns for a new, broader definition for "trafficked persons" and promotes and facilitates action research in the field of trafficking women.

Publications: The publication program includes practical guidebooks such as *Human Rights in Practice: A Guide to Assist*

Trafficked Women and Children and *The Migrating Women's Handbook.* The organization has also published a regional report entitled *Trafficking in Women in the Asia-Pacific Region,* presenting the background and methods of trafficking in the region, thus giving a clear picture of the conditions and circumstances that characterize the situations faced by trafficked women.

Web site: The GAATW Web site lists current activities, bulletins and newsletters, documentation and standards regarding women's rights, publications available for purchase, links to other Web sites, and a questionnaire regarding women's rights.

Human Rights Commission, Pakistan (HRCP)
107 Tipu Block
New Garden Town
Lahore, Pakistan
Phone: [92] (42) 586-4994/583-8341
Fax: [92] (42) 588-3582
E-mail: hrcp@hrcp-web.org
Web site: www.hrcp.cjb.net

The HRCP is an organization working against bonded labor, child labor, and forced marriage. A Special Task Force on the Sindh province has brought the issue of bonded labor and kidnapping of freed laborers to international attention. Over the past five years, the Human Rights Commission has succeeded in freeing over 7,000 bonded laborers.

Publications: Every year, the HRCP publishes a comprehensive report on the state of human rights in that country. In 2004, it also published a major report on child labor entitled *Rights of Pakistan Children: The Task Ahead.*

Web site: The HRCP Web site provides up-to-the-minute reports on human rights violations in Pakistan, press releases, a list of its publications, and a special secton devoted to Afghanistan.

Informal Sector Service Center (INSEC)
P.O. Box 2726
Kathmandu, Nepal
Phone: [977] 1-427-8770
Fax: [977] 1-427-0551
E-mail: insec@insec.org.np
Web site: www.insec.org.np

INSEC works to promote and protect the human rights of people in unorganized sectors of Nepal. Research into human rights abuses includes the bonded labor system. It also runs human rights and literacy training programs and works with the government to pass effective legislation banning all forms of bonded labor.

Publications: INSEC's documentation center produces and circulates an annual report on human rights issues as well as regular newsletters. It has also published a comprehensive report on bonded labor in western Nepal.

Web site: The INSEC Web site provides a history of the organization, a list of accomplishments, current INSEC programs and publications, and general human rights information.

People's Recovery, Empowerment and Development Assistance (PREDA) Foundation, Inc.
Upper Kalakalan
Olongapo City 2200, Philippines
Phone: [63] (47) 223-9629
Fax: [63] (47) 222-5573
E-mail: predair@info.com.ph
Web site: www.preda.org

PREDA is a not-for-profit human rights organization focusing on women and children's rights. It promotes just laws to empower the poor and protect their rights. PREDA also aims to protect the weak and defenseless, mainly children and women exploited in demeaning labor such as prostitution. The organization assists the sexually abused and leads investigations into allegations of abuse.

Publications: PREDA publishes a regular newsletter, available online. It also posts all articles published externally about or mentioning PREDA on its Web site.

Web site: The PREDA Web site has a history of the organization, archives of its newsletter, links to projects, campaign links, and an on-site search engine.

Shoishab
917 Iqbal Road
Mohammadpur, Dhaka, Bangladesh
Phone: [880] (2) 819 873
Fax: [880] (2) 9122 130
E-mail: shoishab@bangla.net

Shoishab campaigns nationally on the rights of child domestic workers and has demonstrated the abuses suffered by such children through surveys. It also runs classes for children working as domestic servants and other deprived children.

Web site: None

Society for the Protection of the Rights of the Child (SPARC)
No. 14, Fourth Floor
109-West, Sardar Begum Plaza
Blue Area, Islamabad, Pakistan
Phone: [92] (51) 227-9504
Fax: [92] (51) 227-9256
E-mail: isb@sparcpk.org
Web site: www.sparcpk.org

SPARC promotes and protects the rights of children according to international labor standards, while also researching their cause and raising awareness. Often collaborating with other NGOs, the organization works on several issues related to children including juvenile justice, child labor, breastfeeding protection, and corporal punishment.

Publications: The "State of Pakistan's Children" is released by the organization annually analyzing the current state of children's rights and conditions in the country compared to international standards. *Discourse,* an English-language magazine, appears twice yearly focusing on one theme of concern in child rights. Other publications available in Urdu, English, and Sindhi are also provided.

Web site: SPARC's Web site provides access to a wealth of information relating to the core issues of the organization as well as a mission statement, campaign information, and international standards.

South Asian Coalition on Child Servitude (SACCS)
74 Aravali Apartment
DDA Kalkaji
New Dehli 19, India
Phone: [91] (11) 621-0807
Fax: [91] (11) 642-0029
E-mail: mukti@saccs.unv.ernet.in
Web site: www.saccsweb.org

SACCS is a coalition of several organizations that work on child labor–related issues in Southern Asia. The numerous NGOs, human rights organizations, and trade unions that make up SACCS combat bonded labor and child servitude. Since its creation in 1989, SACCS has liberated many bonded children from various industries. One SACCS project is the Mukti Ashram, a rehabilitation center for freed child bonded laborers. See Chapter 5 for a biography of Mukti Ashram's director, Suman.

8

Selected Print
and Nonprint Resources

While the study of contemporary slavery is in its infancy, in recent years, several well-known writers have begun working on it. In spite of that, very few organizations, publishers, researchers, and writers address modern slavery. In turn, this means two things: first, that this cannot be a long chapter—there is simply not a wide-ranging literature on the subject; and second, there are still a lot of unanswered questions about slavery today. Meanwhile, filmmakers have also turned their view to slavery and trafficking, and some award-winning documentaries and one feature film (*Lilya 4-Ever*) are available. This ongoing growth of materials means that it is easier than ever before to learn about contemporary slavery. At the same time, some of the most important and basic questions have yet to be answered about new slavery. What, for example, is the best way to rehabilitate ex-slaves? What is the best way to get governments to take action against slavery? And what are the best actions those governments could take? How many people are actually being caught up in international trafficking? And where are they being sent? How can we explain the demand for enslaved labor in a country like the United States? None of these questions currently have answers. It may be that as you use this book, you will also think of questions that are not yet answered. If you do, try to be adventurous in seeking answers. In the fight to end slavery around the world, the questioning and work of every person is important.

Print Resources

Books

Altink, Sietske. *Stolen Lives: Trading Women into Sex and Slavery.* New York: Harrington Park Press, 1995. ISBN 1-85727-097-5.

Driven by the desire to start a career or escape poverty, women migrate in search of work and a better life for themselves and their families. For some, this search is the beginning of a nightmare experience. From "hotel receptionist" to nightclub "dancer" to "domestic worker," this book exposes how women are hired in their country of origin and then transported, left without money, passports, or permits to become trapped into prostitution or domestic slavery. Branded as illegal aliens and marooned in a culture they don't understand, they have nowhere to go and no one to help them. With personal testimony from women caught in the trafficking web, *Stolen Lives* reveals the violent inner workings of international crime networks, the routes and methods involved, and how the trafficking gangs are able to circumvent the law.

Anderson, Bridget. *Britain's Secret Slaves—An Investigation into the Plight of Overseas Domestic Workers.* London: Anti-Slavery International and Kalayaan, 1993. ISBN 0-90091-829-2.

This book documents the plight of overseas migrant workers in the United Kingdom during a period when returning expatriates and wealthy foreign nationals were allowed to bring domestic staff into the country on a tourist visa. These individuals' lack of independent immigration status tied them to their employer because escape would cause them to lose their right to work at all and be deported. Anderson's investigation uses personal testimony and detailed analysis of the UK concession and wider context of labor migration in a world where economic disparities are increasing. It also looks at the situation of Asian maids plus the situation in Hong Kong and Canada and their attempts to solve the problem.

Anti-Slavery International. *Enslaved Peoples in the 1990s.* London: Anti-Slavery International, 1997. ISBN 0-90091-840-3.

The history of the struggle of indigenous peoples for the recognition of their rights has been intimately connected to the phenomenon of slavery. Throughout the world, indigenous peoples are still subjected to a variety of forms of slavery, and this report charts a cross-section of these terrible experiences in the 1990s, varying from the sexual exploitation of women and children in East Asia to debt bondage and serfdom in the Amazon.

Anti-Slavery International. *This Menace of Bonded Labour: Debt Bondage in Pakistan.* London: Anti-Slavery International, 1996. ISBN 0-900-91835-7.

This book looks at recent evidence of debt bondage in Pakistan and the failure of the Pakistan People's Party government to enforce the law of 1992 that officially outlawed it—despite the commitment by President Benazir Bhutto before winning office to eradicate "this menace of bonded labour." For the use of bonded workers and campaigners on their behalf, the book reproduces in full the text of the 1992 Bonded Labour System (Abolition) Act and the largely disregarded Rules of 1995, which should form the basis for eradicating the bonded system and rehabilitating its victims.

Bales, Kevin. *Disposable People: New Slavery in the Global Economy.* Berkeley: University of California Press, 1999; Revised Edition 2004. ISBN 0-52022-463-9 (PB).

This is an investigation of conditions in Mauritania, Brazil, Thailand, Pakistan, and India, revealing the tragic emergence of a "new slavery," one intricately linked to the global economy. Case studies present actual slaves, slaveholders, and public officials in historical, geographical, and cultural contexts. The author offers suggestions for combating the new slavery and provides examples of positive results from organizations such as Anti-Slavery International, the Pastoral Land Commission in Brazil, and the Human Rights Commission in Pakistan. Archbishop Desmond Tutu called this "a well-researched, scholarly, and deeply disturbing exposé of modern-day slavery with well-thought-out strategies for what to do to combat this scourge." (Also available in Spanish, Portuguese, German, Norwegian, Japanese, Korean, Turkish, Russian, and Italian.)

Black, Maggie. *Child Domestic Workers: A Handbook for Research and Action.* London: Anti-Slavery International, 1997. ISBN 0-90091-841-1.

In many countries, children working as maids, child-minders, garden boys, and general helpers-about-the-house are a familiar sight. Domestic work is, in fact, one of the most common forms of child employment. But it is not known how many children are involved, nor the age range of the workers, what led to their employment, the terms and conditions of their work, and their feelings about it. This book explores ways of finding out about the situation of these children. This practical guide draws on the experiences and views of NGOs and others working with child domestics in Asia, Africa, and Latin America. Examining the reasons why children working as domestic servants deserve attention, the handbook's step-by-step approach focuses on solutions to research and methodological problems.

Brown, Louise. *Sex Slaves: the Trafficking of Women in Asia.* London: Virago Press, 2000. ISBN 1-86049-774-8.

Dispelling myths of the causes of the Asian sex industry, this book explores the process by which young girls are sold or forced into prostitution and allows the voices of the women to be heard through their testimonies and experiences. With a close look into the society in which this captivity and exploitation occur, the author concludes that the strict male domination of the culture is to blame.

Cadet, Jean-Robert. *Restavec: From Haitian Slave Child to Middle-Class American, An Autobiography.* Austin: University of Texas Press, 1998. ISBN 0-29271-202-2.

In his book, Jean-Robert Cadet relates his life in a moving, emotional narrative. As a slave-child to a wealthy mistress in Haiti, Cadet endured both physical and mental torture. From the age of four, his childhood ended, and his life became dictated by the whims of his master. As his story unfolds, the reader learns of Cadet's insatiable desire for knowledge and his determination to attend school. Despite Cadet's slave status, he is allowed to attend the Catholic mission schools, where he takes pride in his natural intelligence. Education carries Cadet throughout life—it is his salvation.

Eventually, Cadet is abandoned by his master, only to be reunited with her in America. At school, his abuse is soon found out by a kind schoolteacher, and Cadet is sent to live with foster parents. The young Cadet must now learn to cope with the demons of the past, and the discrimination of white America. As Cadet climbs through the ranks of the U.S. Army, becomes a successful businessman, marries, and begins to teach school, he must still face racism and intolerance. The reader sees that, although Cadet's lot has improved dramatically since his childhood, his struggle is not yet over. *Restavec* is a gripping tale of slavery, hardship, and determination.

Chang, Grace. *Disposable Domestics: Immigrant Women Workers in the Global Economy.* Cambridge: South End Press, 2000. ISBN 0-89608-617-8.

Chang demonstrates how the women that perform the least desirable jobs in America—as nannies, domestic workers, janitors, nursing aides, and homecare workers—are crucial to our economy and society. In spite of the United States having a long history of immigration, these women workers are often now seen as a potential drain on society. The denigrating attitudes they face can mean official indifference when the workers face serious exploitation.

Colchester, Marcus. *Slave and Enclave: The Political Ecology of Equatorial Africa.* London: World Rainforest Network, 1994. ISBN 9-67999-876-2.

The Equatorial Africa of this study—Gabon, the Congo, and the Central African Republic—has a long, sad history of slavery and the deprivations of foreign forest product extraction. For the forest communities in the region the slave wars, conquest, forced resettlement, and labor in extractive industries and the lumber camps has meant the undermining of their ways of life. Deprived of rights and marginal to national economies built upon oil, timber, coffee, and diamonds, these people still find themselves deprived of a political voice or control of their destinies. Leaked studies carried out for the World Bank and published here for the first time show how the foreign-dominated timber companies act with complete contempt for tentative resurgence of community authority and the reawakening of long-submerged indigenous traditions of equality and justice.

Cotton, Samuel. *Silent Terror: A Journey into Contemporary African Slavery.* New York: Writers and Readers, 1998. ISBN 0-86316-259-2.

This is the disturbing true account of a black American's journey into the horrors of modern-day slavery in Africa. Cotton's odyssey takes him from New York to Mauritania, where he comes face-to-face with the Arab Berbers' centuries-old practice of enslaving black Africans. The book recounts Cotton's month-long trip to Africa, where he conducted ethnographic research and created a film and audio record of contemporary African slavery under the Arabs of Mauritania. The book is also the story of an African-American's struggle to come to grips with the legacy of slavery and the brutal revelation that slavery continues to thrive in Africa today.

DePaul University College of Law. *In Modern Bondage: Sex Trafficking in the Americas.* Chicago: DePaul University College of Law, 2002. ISBN 1-88900-102-3.

Since 1998, the International Human Rights Law Institute of DePaul University has monitored the rapidly growing problem of trafficking of women and children for the purposes of commercial sexual exploitation. This is the report of a project that accomplished a social, economic, political, and legal analysis of trafficking in the Americas.

Ehrenreich, Barbara, and Arlie Russel Hochschild. *Global Woman: Nannies, Maids, and Sex Workers in the New Economy.* New York: Henry Holt, 2002. ISBN 0-80507-509-7.

This book is a collection of fifteen essays covering various areas of the global exploitation of women due to a new global economic system and mass migration. Topics covered include mail-order brides, sex tourism, modern-day slavery, and domestic labor.

Genovese, Eugene D. *Roll Jordan, Roll: The World the Slaves Made.* New York: Vintage Books, 1976. ISBN 0-39471-652-3.

This classic book goes into great detail on the history of slavery in America. The hypocrisy and cruelty of the slaveholder class is documented in painful detail. Genovese quotes extensively from court decisions, slaveholder correspondence, and accounts by former slaves and those who fought for their freedom. This is a good introduction to historical American slavery, and you are unlikely to find a more thoroughly documented account of America's most "peculiar" institution.

Gibson Wilson, Ellen. *Thomas Clarkson: A Biography.* York: William Sessions Limited, 1996. ISBN 1-85072-184-X.

A biography of a man often slighted in the historical record. His was the first large-scale human rights campaign in human history. See also the newer book by Adam Hochschild listed later in this chapter.

Greider, William. *One World Ready or Not: The Manic Logic of Global Capitalism.* New York: Simon and Schuster, 1997. ISBN 0-14026-698-4.

Although not specifically about contemporary slavery, this is one of the best books to explain the transformations in the world economy that are making new slavery possible. It explores the dynamics of the third industrial revolution by describing a story of human struggle: of diverse peoples and nations faced with the same dangers imposed by unregulated global finance, labor, and competition. The resulting picture is bleak, but Greider points the way toward solutions.

Hobbs, Sandy, Jim McKechnie, and Michael Lavalette. *Child Labor: A World History Companion.* Santa Barbara: ABC-CLIO, 1999. ISBN 0-87436-956-8.

A survey of working children from the Industrial Revolution to the present day, this new reference guide goes beyond the usual Third World confines. The authors analyze the problems and psychological and social development of child workers, then present an overview of child labor in specific countries and world regions. They also examine individuals and organizations devoted to improving the welfare of working children and discuss how various governments, private organizations, and courts have dealt with child labor. This reference contains accurate, up-to-date information on a host of subjects, and the alphabetical entries are cross-referenced by category.

Hochschild, Adam. *Bury the Chains: Prophets, Slaves, and Rebels in the First Human Rights Crusade.* New York: Houghton Mifflin, 2005. ISBN 0-61810-469-0.

The campaign to end the slave trade in the British Empire was the first human rights campaign in human history. It may have been one of the most successful as well, but the lessons and the remarkable people who invented human rights campaigning are now all but forgotten. This fascinating book concentrates on Thomas Clarkson, the man who was known as "the Originator" for the way he built up the antislavery movement. (See Chapter 5 of this book for a brief biography of Clarkson.) Starting as a college graduate in 1787, he put slavery on the political agenda and, in time, formed a mass movement that brought legal slavery to an end.

Human Rights Watch. *A Modern Form of Slavery: Trafficking of Burmese Women and Girls into Brothels in Thailand.* New York: Human Rights Watch, 1993. ISBN 1-56432-107-X.

Based on in-depth interviews with Burmese trafficking victims, this book documents the violations of internationally recognized human rights committed against them. It also presents detailed recommendations to the Thai and Burmese (Myanmar) governments and the international community for improving the protection of the thousands of women and girls who are trafficked into Thai brothels each year as well as for ensuring the prosecution of their abusers.

Human Rights Watch. *Owed Justice: Thai Women Trafficked into Debt Bondage in Japan.* New York: Human Rights Watch, 2000. ISBN 1-56432-252-1.

Reporting on the experiences of many Thai women trafficked into Japan working in slave-like conditions to pay back "debts," this book details the dangers experienced by those who escape, the lack of assistance from Japanese officials, and the failings of both Thailand's and Japan's governments in reacting to and preventing the trafficking of women.

Human Rights Watch. *Pakistan: Contemporary Forms of Slavery.* New York: Human Rights Watch, 1995. ISBN 1-56432-154-1.

This book illustrates how, throughout Pakistan, employers forcibly extract labor from adults and children, restrict their freedom of movement, and deny them the right to negotiate the terms of their employment. It blames the government of Pakistan for these abuses, both by the direct involvement of the police and through the state's failure to protect the rights of bonded laborers.

Human Rights Watch. *Rape for Profit: Trafficking of Nepali Girls and Women to India's Brothels.* New York: Human Rights Watch, 1995. ISBN 1-56432-155-X.

This book focuses on the trafficking of girls and women from Nepal to brothels in Bombay, where they compose up to half of the city's estimated 100,000 brothel workers.

Human Rights Watch. *The Small Hands of Slavery: Bonded Child Labor in India.* New York: Human Rights Watch, 1996. ISBN 1-56432-172-X.

Based on interviews with over 100 children during a two-month investigation in India, this report details their plight in the silk, beedi (hand-rolled cigarettes), synthetic gems, silver, leather, agricultural, and carpet industries.

Jok, Jok Madut. *War and Slavery in Sudan.* Philadelphia: University of Pennsylvania Press, 2001. ISBN 0-81221-762-4.

A look back into the history of slavery in Sudan and the regional and religious conflicts that have been under way for centuries, this book refutes popular belief for the cause of current slave practices in the country, and explains the racial motivation behind decades of oppression in the black south.

Kielburger, Craig, with Kevin Major. *Free the Children: A Young Man Fights against Child Labor and Proves that Children Can Change the World.* New York: Harper Collins, 1998. ISBN 0-06093-065-9.

This is the dramatic story of one child's transformation from a normal middle-class kid from the suburbs into an activist fighting against child labor on the world stage of international human rights. Kielburger founded the organization Free the Children with his schoolmates at the age of twelve. This book charts the growing awareness and commitment of these young people and the experiences that propelled them into the public eye as key campaigners against child labor.

Kipiniak, Chris, et al. "Passion Play." *Nightcrawler* V. 2, 1–4. New York: Marvel Comics, February–May 2002.

This four-part comic book series explores the presence of slavery in America. The title character, Nightcrawler, comes to the aid of a Thai woman who has just escaped from her mistress after two years of servitude and eventually defeats an international human trafficker responsible for selling hundreds of desperate people.

Kuklin, Susan. *Iqbal Masih and the Crusaders against Child Slavery.* New York: Henry Holt, 1998. ISBN 0-80505-459-6.

Here is the powerful story of Iqbal Masih's life and death (see his biography in Chapter 5) and of the movement that continues the struggle against child labor today. This book shows how we are all implicated in the global practice of child labor and how we can all work together to end it.

Kyle, David, and Rey Koslowski, eds. *Global Human Smuggling: Comparative Perspectives.* Baltimore: Johns Hopkins University Press, 2001. ISBN 0-80186-590-5.

This book, a collection of pieces, examines case studies of human smuggling in various regions, discusses the legal and social constructions of human smuggling, employment of illegal immigrants and trafficking, and explores the sociohistorical context of these issues.

Lean-Lim, L., ed. *The Sex Sector: The Economic and Social Bases of Prostitution in Southeast Asia.* Geneva: International Labor Organization, 1997. ISBN 9-22109-522-3.

This book focuses on the commercial sex sector and its institutional structures and connections with the national and international economies. It includes case studies of Indonesia, Malaysia, the Philippines, and Thailand, illustrating how vested economic interests and unequal relations between the sexes and between parents and children interact with considerations based on human rights, workers' rights, morality, criminality, and health threats to influence the legal stance adopted by governments and social programs targeting the sex industry. A chapter specifically addresses child prostitution and why it should be treated as a serious problem.

Lebreton, Binka. *Trapped: Modern-Day Slavery in the Brazilian Amazon.* Bloomfield, CT: Kumarian Press, 2003. ISBN 1-56549-155-6.

Documenting the illegal trade in human lives that ends in debt-slavery in the depths of the Brazilian Amazon, this book provides a harrowing view of the lives of slaves, the slaveholders, and the activists working against this injustice.

Lee-Wright, Peter. *Child Slaves.* London: Earthscan Publications, 1990. ISBN 1-85383-044-5.

Based on research done with Anti-Slavery International for a BBC-TV documentary, this book reveals the extent of exploitation of child labor and services throughout the world. It shows how what is eaten, worn, and used every day in Western homes is all too often produced at the expense of poor children's welfare and freedom. It also covers the expansion of the child sex tourism industry as travel to developing countries increases. Includes case studies from India, Bangladesh, Malaysia, Brazil, Thailand, Portugal, Turkey, Philippines, Mexico, and the United States.

Luibhéid, Eithne. *Entry Denied: Controlling Sexuality at the Border.* Minneapolis: University of Minnesota Press, 2002. ISBN 0-81663-804-7.

Women's sexuality has often been a factor in their admission to the United States, in spite of the lack of law. This work explores how the U.S. border became a site for controlling female sexuality. Given that many women who are victims of human trafficking are brought to the U.S. in order to be forced into prostitution, and that many trafficked people are suffering sexual violence, the judgments made at the border can have wide reaching consequences.

McCuen, Gary E. (ed.). *Modern Slavery and the Global Economy.* Hudson, WI: Gary E. McCuen Publications, 1998. ISBN 0-86596-145-X.

Part of the *Ideas in Conflict* series, this book is a collection of short articles by experts that explore and sometimes debate the issues of marginal workers and global slavery, slave labor and child labor, and economic growth and human rights. Blended with the articles are exercises helping the reader to develop reasoning skills, identify editorial bias, and interpret editorial imagery.

McGill, Craig. *Human Traffic: Sex, Slaves, and Immigration.* London: Vision Press, 2003. ISBN 1-90413-217-0.

McGill is a British journalist who has traveled the world to meet and learn from people who have been caught up in human trafficking. He meets Chinese workers desperate to get to Europe, illegal workers in Australia, and women trafficked into Europe and forced into prostitution. Unlike most work on trafficking and human smuggling, he also gets to know the traffickers and smugglers.

Masika, Rachel, ed. *Gender, Trafficking and Slavery.* Oxford: Oxfam, 2004. ISBN 0-85598-478-3.

This book examines the operations of trafficking and other kinds of modern day slavery from a gender perspective. It explores the relationships between gender, poverty, conflict, and globalization that are driving today's slave trade. The authors provide an overview of what trafficking and slavery are, their magnitude, and their complexity.

Meltzer, Milton. *Slavery: A World History.* New York: Da Capo Press, 1993. ISBN 0-30680-536-7.

This is a good introduction to the breadth of slavery's history from ancient times to the present day. It begins with the dawn of civilization and carries the story of slavery forward to the present day. This volume has many illustrations from many cultures and historical periods.

Miers, Suzanne. *Slavery in the Twentieth Century: The Evolution of a Global Problem.* Walnut Creek, CA: Alta Mira Press, 2003. ISBN 0-75910-340-2.

This is the first major historical work covering slavery, and the international efforts to fight it, in the twentieth century. Global in its reach and carefully documented, this book is a central point for any understanding of the evolution of modern slavery. It traces the development of both contemporary slavery and the international antislavery movement, particularly that of Great Britain. The author explains the greater cruelty of newer forms of slavery.

Monzini, Paola. *Il Mercato Delle Donne: Prostituzione, tratta e sfruttamento.* Rome: Donzelli, 2002. ISBN 8-87989-693-8.

Italian-language book on the state of women trafficked into Italy for commercial sexual exploitation. An English version is due out in 2005. Paola Monzini was a researcher with the UN on human trafficking.

Nazer, Mende, and Damien Lewis. *Slave: My True Story.* New York: Public Affairs, 2003. ISBN 1-58648-212-2.

This true story of contemporary slavery of a twelve-year-old girl stolen from her village in Africa, details the abuse and horror experienced among the Nuba, a Sudanese tribe targeted by Arab raiders for slave purposes. Mende, the young girl, is passed from one cruel family of masters to another, beaten repeatedly and allowed no life of her own. After seven years of captivity she escapes.

O'Byrne, Darren. *Human Rights: An Introduction.* Essex: Prentice Hall, 2003. ISBN 0-58243-824-1.

Using case studies and personal testimonies, this textbook provides a cross-disciplinary look at a number of current academic debates within human rights. Topics including torture, the death penalty, slavery, genocide, and refugees are explained in depth and placed within the context of business, globalization, and other areas of human rights concerns. Possibly the best textbook for teaching human rights.

O'Dy, Sylvie. *Esclaves en France.* Paris: Albin Michel, 2001. ISBN 2-22612-259-1.

French-language book. Sylvie O'Dy was one of the founders of the Committee against Modern Slavery in Paris, an organization that has rescued many young women from slavery in that city. This book explores the reality of slavery in the "City of Lights."

Parreñas, Rhacel Salazar. *Servants of Globalization: Women, Migration, and Domestic Work.* Stanford: Stanford University Press, 2001. ISBN 0-80473-922-6.

This is the first cross-national comparative study of Filipina labor migration. The author did extensive fieldwork in Los Angeles and Rome, Italy, finding that Filipina women on both continents were experiencing similar dislocations and exploitation.

Pearson, Elaine. *Human Traffic, Human Rights: Redefining Victim Protection.* London: Anti-Slavery International, 2002. ISBN 0-90091-855-1.

Examining case studies and protection measures in ten different countries across the globe, Anti-Slavery International makes several recommendations regarding various areas of victim protection.

Plant, Roger. *Sugar and Modern Slavery: A Tale of Two Countries.* London: Zed Books, 1987. ISBN 0-86232-572-2.

Explores the link between the enslavement of Haitian workers and the Dominican sugar harvest. The sugar produced then flows into U.S. and European markets. Haitian workers are often enslaved in the Dominican Republic during the annual sugar harvest. Brutally used and paid nothing, they do backbreaking work in terrible conditions. Government and police complicity add to their burden.

Robertson, Adam, and Mishra Shishram. *Forced to Plough: Bonded Labor in Nepal's Agricultural Economy.* London: Anti-Slavery International and INSEC, 1997. ISBN 0-90091-837-3.

Investigates the situation of some of the most exploited groups of rural workers in Nepal and the conditions that have allowed systems of forced and bonded labor to develop and persist despite the official abolition of slavery in 1926. The book concludes with recommendations for government, trade unions, and development agencies, and calls for the introduction of legislation banning bonded labor in Nepal.

Rodriguez, Junius P. *Chronology of World Slavery.* Santa Barbara: ABC-CLIO, 1999. ISBN 0-87436-884-7.

This volume traces the course of events, both great and small, that have defined the meaning of slavery throughout human history. Organized by geographic region and time period, it enables readers to gain a quick understanding of how long slavery has been part of human life and where it has occurred. It combines multiple chronologies, sidebars on specialized topics, primary source documents, and illustrations into a compelling portrayal of slavery from the dawn of civilization to the present.

Rodriguez, Junius P., ed. *The Historical Encyclopedia of World Slavery, Volumes I and II.* Santa Barbara: ABC-CLIO, 1997. ISBN 0-87436-885-5.

Documenting slavery on a global scale, this work is an invaluable resource for anyone wishing to gain an understanding of the history of slavery throughout the world. With illustrations and maps accompanying essays involving specific geographic locations, the encyclopedia delves into the practice of forced labor in successive centuries. Presented in short but comprehensive entries, 700 topics of world slavery are extensively cross-referenced with bibliographical citations for further research.

Rosen, Ellen Israel. *Making Sweatshops: The Globalization of the U.S. Apparel Industry.* Berkeley: University of California Press, 2002. ISBN 0-52023-337-9.

The open trading system of the global economy means that jobs move freely to locations where workers are less expensive. The U.S. clothing industry has seen very large numbers of jobs flow to areas of the developing world. In some of these new factories, the workers are exploited in terrible ways. This book looks carefully at how this loss of U.S. jobs has occurred.

Ruf, Urs Peter. *Ending Slavery: Hierarchy, Dependency and Gender in Central Mauritania.* Bielefeld, Germany: Transcript Verlag, 1999. ISBN 3-93312-749-1.

Offers insights into the "how" of practices of slavery that persist in parts of Mauritania up to the present day. It brings the gendered structures of Moorish slavery to light and examines their impact on strategies and tactics designed to bring this institution to an end. Underlying this study is empirical data gathered during two periods of field research in rural central Mauritania.

Saunders, Kate. *Eighteen Layers of Hell: Stories from the Chinese Gulag* (Foreword by Harry Wu). New York: Cassell Global Issues, 1996. ISBN 0-30433-297-6.

The author shows that millions of people still suffer in *laogai*—forced labor camps—in the People's Republic of China today, and that Western nations participate in slave labor through trading goods produced in the laogai. Among those telling their stories is Harry Wu, a veteran of the laogai who attracted worldwide attention in 1995 when he was arrested by the Chinese authorities while attempting to gather more evidence for his campaign against the laogai.

Sawyer, Roger. *Slavery in the Twentieth Century.* London and New York: Routledge and Kegan Paul, 1986. ISBN 0-71020-475-2.

Though now somewhat dated, this is a good review of the state of slavery in the world in the years prior to the end of the Cold War. Reviews the situation of slavery around the world, looking also at apartheid in South Africa and the case of prison labor in the Soviet Union.

Seabrook, Jeremy. *Children of Other Worlds: Exploitation in the Global Market.* London: Pluto Press, 2001. ISBN 0-74531-391-4.

More than 40,000 children die daily in the developing world from avoidable sickness and disease, and tens of millions of children labor in factories, mines, mills, and sweatshops, or scavenge for a living on city streets and dumps. In the so-called developed world, children's lives are similarly blighted by drugs, alcohol, sexual abuse, and violence. The children in rich countries are tormented by unappeasable market-led hungers, while the children of the poor are wasted by insufficiency. Seabrook argues the global market is responsible for both of these ills.

Smith, Paul J., ed. *Human Smuggling: Chinese Migrant Trafficking and the Challenge to America's Immigration Tradition (Significant Issues Series).* Washington, DC: Center for Strategic and International Studies, 1997. ISBN 0-89206-291-6.

Recent cases of the smuggling of Chinese into the United States have brought this issue very much to the fore. Shipping containers holding trafficked Chinese landed in Seattle, Washington, and Vancouver, Canada, in 1999. The dramatic increase in human smuggling has, in large part, been driven by the significant increase in Chinese citizens being smuggled around the world.

Stearman, Kaye. *Slavery Today (Talking Points Series).* Austin, TX: Steck-Vaughn, 2000. ISBN 0-81725-320-3.

Aimed at young adults, the Talking Points Series looks at some of the most important and controversial current issues. The cause and effects of these subjects are investigated within a global context, with extensive use of illustrations and other evidence. This book highlights the fact that slavery is not a thing of the past and investigates the different circumstances that allow the practice to survive. This is one of the best and easiest-to-use books about contemporary slavery for young people.

Stowe, Harriett Beecher. *Uncle Tom's Cabin.* New York: Harper-Collins (paper), 1987. ISBN 0-06080-618-4.

An international bestseller that sold more than 300,000 copies when it first appeared in 1852, *Uncle Tom's Cabin* was dismissed by some as abolitionist propaganda, yet Leo Tolstoy deemed it a great work of literature. Although "Uncle Tom" has become a pejorative term for a subservient black, the Uncle Tom in the book is a man who, under the most inhumane of circumstances, never loses his human dignity. It is an inspiring book that still has the power to give insights into the mindsets of slavery.

Sutton, Alison. *Slavery in Brazil: A Link in the Chain of Modernization.* London: Anti-Slavery International, 1994. ISBN 0-90091-832-2.

This is a gripping firsthand account of the spread of slavery across Brazilian society based on six months of field research in Amazonia. It includes accounts of debt bondage in forest clearance, charcoal burning, rubber tapping, and mining in the Amazon region, where more than 70 percent of cases denounced in the previous twenty years had occurred and where all thirteen of the indigenous tribes who have been enslaved at one time or another originate. Concludes with recommendations for action.

Taylor, Yuval, ed. *I Was Born a Slave: An Anthology of Classic Slave Narratives* (2 vols., 1770–1849 and 1849–1866). London: Payback Press, 1999. ISBN 0-86241-903-4.

This collection includes narratives from James Albert Gronniosaw, Olaudah Equiano (Gustavus Vassa), William Grimes, Nat Turner, Charles Ball, Moses Roper, Frederick Douglass, Lewis and Milton Clark, William Wells Brown, and Josiah Henson.

Thomas, Hugh. *The Slave Trade: The History of the Atlantic Slave Trade 1440–1870.* London: Macmillan, 1998. ISBN 0-33373-147-6.

This book views New World slavery in its international context. The Portuguese and Spanish who first came to Africa arrived in search of gold. They found it, but they also found social systems in which the ransom, buying, and selling of human beings had long been established. These systems had existed in European antiquity, and now they were revived when, shortly after making contact with Africa, the European nations began to establish colonies on the other side of the Atlantic; the horrible traffic continued well into the nineteenth century. Thomas mines vast archives and previously published histories to make his case. This is one of the best and clearest books about the Atlantic slave trade.

United Nations. *Human Rights: A Compilation of International Instruments.* New York and Geneva: United Nations, 1994. ISBN 9-21154-098-4.

This is a handy reference book for anyone interested in the international conventions and law on human rights. It includes all the major United Nations conventions that concern human rights.

Verney, Peter. *Slavery in Sudan.* London: *Sudan Update* and Anti-Slavery International, 1997. ISBN 0-90091-839-X.

This report gives an outline of the history of slavery in Sudan and its reemergence in the late twentieth century. Peter Verney, editor of *Sudan Update,* puts the slavery issue into context and examines the pitfalls of attributing responsibility solely to the present Sudanese government. He underlines the importance of racial prejudice in Sudan's conflict.

Williams, Phil, ed. *Illegal Immigration and Commercial Sex: The New Slave Trade.* Portland, OR: Frank Cass, 1999. ISBN 0-71464-384-X.

This volume examines the dynamics of the sex slave trade in both Europe and Asia, identifies the role of organized crime, and considers the countermeasures that governments and law enforcement agencies must take to combat this global problem.

Wu, Harry, and Carolyn Wakeman. *Bitter Winds: A Memoir of My Years in China's Gulag.* New York: John Wiley and Sons, 1993. ISBN 0-47155-645-9.

This is the autobiographical account of Harry Wu—arrested as a student and never formally charged or tried—who spent nineteen years in Chinese prison labor camps and returned twice in disguise to document continuing human rights abuses by the Chinese authorities. He succeeded in capturing for the first time on film footage of life in the camps. Forced to work, starved, and tortured, he watched other prisoners buried in unmarked graves as he was reduced from being a member of the elite intelligentsia to an anonymous skeleton.

Articles

Bales, Kevin. **"The Social Psychology of Modern Slavery."** *Scientific American,* April 2002.

In this article, the author explains that, despite popular belief, human slavery still exists. Estimating that about 27 million persons are currently exploited as slaves, this piece seeks to explain the persistence of slavery in modern times. Describing various forms of slavery in real cases and the life circumstances that support its existence, it is made clear that slavery of the past and contemporary slavery are very different. Due to changes in global demographics and economics, human beings have become less valuable and more profitable to their owners.

Cockburn, Andrew. **"21st Century Slaves."** *National Geographic,* September 2003.

Available in the online archive at the *National Geographic* Web site (http://magma.nationalgeographic.com/ngm/0309/feature1/index.html), this article offers an expansive view of international slavery. Beginning in Eastern Europe, a major source of much of the world's trafficking, the author writes of meeting with an infamous slave trafficker from whom more than thirty women were rescued by international police. The women had become debt slaves forced into prostitution in night clubs doubling as brothels. In Mexico, the extreme poverty of peasants driven off their land— in some part due to North American Free Trade Agreement— leads them to move north as trafficked slaves for low-wage jobs in the United States. Some end up as farm slaves on plantations while many women are forced into prostitution.

Colors Magazine, **"Slavery."** V. 53 (December 2002–January 2003). (www.colorsmagazine.com)

This full volume of *Colors Magazine* is devoted to the topic of contemporary slavery. Beginning with modern perceptions of what slavery is, this magazine corrects the prevailing idea that there are no longer slaves and relates the experience of real former-slaves who have managed to escape their torture and exploitation. Sharing individual cases and personal accounts from all regions of the world and all forms of slavery, a human face emerges from interviews with both slaves and masters.

Junger, Sebastian. **"Slaves of the Brothel."** *Vanity Fair*, July 2002.

Investigating the violent underworld of sex trafficking, Junger tells the story of economically backward and, in spots, war-torn Eastern Europe's trouble with corruption and desperation. This article details the process by which many poor and optionless young women are duped by promises of good jobs in the West and then trafficked into foreign countries where they are forced into prostitution. Visiting several clubs and bars where trafficked women are sexually exploited for money they will not receive, Junger interviews several prostitutes who help reveal the corruption rank among the local "businessmen," government officials, and humanitarian personnel.

Landesman, Peter. **"Sex Slaves on Main Street."** *New York Times Sunday Magazine*, January 25, 2004.

Focusing largely on trafficking into the United States and sex slavery carried out there, this article traces the routes taken by traffickers moving their victims illegally across borders and chronicles the stages in a trafficked victim's experience. As the article points out, the key to the success of traffickers is the cooperation of corrupt local officials in Mexico, a country that is both a source of victims and a transit point for women trafficked from Eastern Europe into the United States.

Teaching Packs

A five-part Teaching Pack is available from Free the Slaves. It is aimed at junior high and high school students, but parts can be used with younger children and at the university level. It is an active, hands-on pack that generates lots of enthusiasm. There are role-plays, games, exercises, and plenty of resources for further study. The sections are:

Part 1   Slavery in the 21st Century: A Background Briefing on Slavery and Human Rights

Part 2   Slavery Throughout History (with five learning activities)

Part 3   Slavery and Human Rights (with background information on the Universal Declaration of Human Rights, and six activities, including the "Beware the Slave Trader!" game)

Part 4   Bonded Labor Campaign: Case Studies, Campaigns, and Action Projects

Part 5   Resources and Contacts (with educational resources, useful Web sites, lists of appropriate films, and books)

The Teaching Pack can be downloaded for free in PDF files. It can be printed in color or black and white and reproduction and distribution is encouraged. It can be found under the "Resources" section of www.freetheslaves.net.

Briefings and Reports

Anti-Slavery International. *Children in Bondage—Slaves of the Subcontinent.* London: Anti-Slavery International, 1994. ISBN 0-90091-827-6.

A useful overview of the variety of slavery to which indigenous peoples are still subjected in the 1990s, from the sexual exploitation of women and children in Southeast Asia to debt bondage and serfdom in South America. The report shows how the history of the struggle for the recognition of the rights of the 350 million surviving indigenous peoples is intimately connected to the phenomenon of slavery, and how repercussions of slavery are particularly severe for indigenous people.

Anti-Slavery International. *Debt Bondage.* London: Anti-Slavery International, 1998. ISBN 0-90091-846-2.

A provocative and accessible report that provides an overview of debt bondage around the world. Excellent for use with young people; gives case histories, explanations, and recommendations.

Bequele, A., and W. E. Myers. *First Things First in Child Labor: Eliminating Work Detrimental to Children.* Geneva: ILO, 1995. ISBN 9-22109-197-X.

Uses numerous case studies to discuss the difficulties in defining work that is hazardous to children and the various preventative approaches that have been used.

Black, Maggie. *In the Twilight Zone: Child Workers in the Hotel, Tourism and Catering Industry.* Geneva: ILO, 1995. ISBN 9-22109-194-5.

Children around the world are used and abused in the tourism industry, but this little-studied group of child laborers and their situations are not well known.

Bureau of International Labor Affairs, U.S. Department of Labor. *By the Sweat and Toil of Children: The Use of Child Labor in American Imports—A Report to the Committees on Appropriations, United States Congress (Vols. 1 and 2).* Washington, DC: Government Printing Office, 1994.

The U.S. government conducted this review to identify any foreign industry and their host country using child labor in the export of manufactured products from industry or mining to the United States. It includes regional overviews and an overview of the "abolish or regulate" debate. Common kinds of child labor including bonded labor are included. Also provides country profiles.

Bureau of International Labor Affairs, U.S. Department of Labor. *The Apparel Industry and Codes of Conduct: A Solution to the International Child Labor Problem (Vols. 3 and 4).* Washington, DC: Government Printing Office, 1996.

Examines nine consumer label programs addressing child labor in the hand-knotted carpet, leather footwear, soccer ball, and tea industries together with other efforts by businesses to develop and implement policies prohibiting child labor. An appendix includes the Adidas, Nike, and Reebok codes of conduct.

Bureau of International Labor Affairs, U.S. Department of Labor. *By the Sweat and Toil of Children: Efforts to Eliminate Child Labor (Vol. 5).* Washington, DC: Government Printing Office, 1998.

Reviews the child labor situation in sixteen countries where child labor has been identified as a problem as well as the levels and types of action being undertaken to reduce child exploitation in those countries.

Cross, Peter. *Kashmiri Carpet Children: Exploited Village Weavers.* London: Anti-Slavery International, 1996. ISBN 0-90091-835-7.

Discusses the enslavement of children in the lucrative "Persian" carpet industry.

Effah, Josephine. *Modernized Slavery—Child Trade in Nigeria.* Nigeria: Constitutional Rights Project, 1996. ISBN 9-78294-408-4.

Documents the growing incidence of trafficking in young children sold into domestic, sexual, and economic slavery in Nigeria. Includes analysis of the political economy of Nigeria, the smuggling, kidnapping, and recruitment process, role of parents and middlemen, domestic slavery, and forced prostitution. Published with support from the Ford Foundation.

Forcese, Craig. *Commerce with Conscience? Human Rights and Corporate Codes of Conduct, No. 1, and Putting Conscience into Commerce—Strategies for Making Human Rights Business as Usual, No. 2.* Montreal: International Center for Human Rights and Democratic Development, 1997. ISBN 2-92208-407-8.

This two-part series presents the results of a survey of Canada's largest corporations and their international operations. The survey showed that only one in seven had codes of conduct with minimal human rights standards, and it examines the effectiveness of those that do exist. The second part provides an overview of the kinds of campaigns that work to make corporations more sensitive to human rights abuses in their international operations—strategies for consumers, shareholders, human rights activists, and businesses campaigning for more accountable human rights policies from governments and companies.

International Labor Organization. *Child Labor—Targeting the Intolerable, Report 6 (1). International Labor Conference 86th session, 1996.* Geneva: ILO, 1998. ISBN 9-22110-328-5.

Report submitted to 174 ILO member countries as part of the ILO's campaign against child labor. It surveys international and national law and practice highlighting effective action through new international standards and includes sections on debt bondage, prostitution, and hazardous occupations. For ILO publications in the United States, Canada, and Puerto Rico, contact International Labor Office, 1828 L Street NW, Washington, DC, 20036; phone: (202) 653-7652; fax: (202) 653-7687; e-mail burrylee@ilo.org. (Also published in Arabic, Chinese, French, German, Russian, and Spanish.)

O'Grady, Ron. *The Rape of the Innocent.* London: ECPAT, 1994. ISBN 0-95979-712-2.

From the coordinator of ECPAT, an international campaign to end child prostitution, this booklet focuses on children in Asia who are trapped in the slavery of prostitution. Covers trafficking across borders, sex tourism, pornographers, AIDS, and the need for political change and law enforcement. Includes case studies, statistics, and maps outlining the scale and nature of the problem.

Skrobanek, Siriporn. *Human Capital—International Migration and Traffic in Women.* London: CIIR, 1996. ISBN 1-85287-162-8.

This report shows how the rights of migrant women in Asia are violated. It discusses the definition of trafficking in international conventions and describes the legal and illegal ways in which women are brought from Thailand to work in other countries. Concludes with recommendations for international action to prevent trafficking. The author is coordinator of the Global Alliance Against Traffic in Women.

United States Department of State. *Trafficking in Persons Report, June 2004.* U.S. Department of State Publication.

The fourth annual publication of its kind, this report is a comprehensive account of government efforts to prevent the trafficking of persons. Examining the efforts of their governments, countries are ranked in tiers according to their compliance with the "minimum standards for the elimination of trafficking." Used as a tool of diplomatic dialogue, encouragement and assistance for full compliance is offered by the State Department to listed countries before sanctions for noncompliance are put into effect.

Newsletters and Periodicals

The New Slavery (Special Issue of *Index on Censorship*)

Index on Censorship is a magazine devoted to supporting free journalism and opposing the suppression of the press around the world. For almost thirty years, it has campaigned for imprisoned writers, artists, dramatists, and journalists and published works that have been censored in other parts of the world. Its January 2000 issue was a special issue on new slavery, with contributions from Brian Edwards, Harry Wu, Ali Hassan, and Kevin Bales. Copies of the special issue can be ordered from the magazine's Web site, www.indexoncensorship.org.

World of Work
International Labor Organization
1828 L Street NW
Washington, DC 20036
Phone: (202) 653-7652
Fax: (202) 653-7687
E-mail: burrylee@ilo.org
Web site: www.ilo.org

The Bureau of Public Information of the International Labor Organization provides full text (Adobe Acrobat—PDF—format only) of this magazine at the ILO Web site. Recent issues contain articles about slavery and forced labor; the global unemployment crisis; child labor; the textile, footwear, and clothing industries; and work stress, among other topics. *World of Work* is a quarterly magazine that does not necessarily reflect the views of the ILO. Note that this is a graphically rich magazine, and the files are correspondingly large. It can be ordered from the ILO or down-loaded from the ILO Web site. Back issues are also stored on the Web site and can be read or downloaded there.

Selected Nonprint Resources

Very often the pioneers that open up a new area of human rights are journalists and filmmakers. That has certainly been the case with new slavery. With so much of the public ignorant of the extent of slavery, television plays an important role in raising awareness. Most of the films and videos listed below were not made by the big Hollywood studios or the main TV networks, but they are strong and sometimes shocking to see. One of the best introductions to new slavery is the documentary *Slavery: A Global Investigation,* made by British filmmakers Brian Woods and Kate Blewitt and available from the Free the Slaves Web site (www.freetheslaves.net). This film won a Peabody Award for Best Documentary and two Emmy Awards. You will also find magazines and information here that can be downloaded directly from the Internet. If you are interested in learning more about current slavery issues, it is a good idea to keep an eye on current television listings; news programs are carrying more and more reports on slavery or human trafficking.

CD-ROMs

ILOLEX 1999. Windows, ISBN 9220106043. New customers (first-time buyers): U.S. $200; multiuser license: 50 percent surcharge. Order from www.ilo.org.

Since its creation, the International Labor Organization has developed an extensive body of texts in the field of international labor law. However, these texts are contained in numerous publications that are not easily accessible. This has constituted a serious barrier to their dissemination to ILO constituents and other interested institutions, for which the provisions adopted by the ILO on a particular subject and their application around the world would otherwise provide valuable guidance. ILOLEX is a full-text trilingual database (English/French/Spanish) on international labor standards with sophisticated search-and-retrieval software. A single CD-ROM contains all three language versions. Each language version includes:

- The ILO Constitution
- All the ILO conventions and recommendations
- The Reports of the Committee on Freedom of Association, from 1985
- The Comments of the Committee of Experts on the Application of Conventions and Recommendations, from 1987
- The Annual Report of the Conference Committee on the Application of Standards, from 1987
- The Reports of Committees and Commissions established under Articles 24 and 26 of the ILO Constitution to examine representations and complaints, from 1985
- Ratification lists by convention and by country

In sum, ILOLEX contains about 70,000 full-text documents divided into several chapters. It is possible to search the whole database by subject classification, country, particular convention, or free text query using words or expressions.

Key Indicators of the Labor Market 1999 (KILM). CD-ROM only (single user), U.S. $99.50; ISBN 9-22110-834-1; print and CD-ROM set, U.S. $180; ISBN 9-22111-705-7. Order from www.ilo.org.

A valuable, wide-ranging reference tool, *Key Indicators of the Labor Market (KILM)* provides the general reader, as well as the expert, with concise explanations and analysis of the data on the world's labor markets, including world and regional estimates. Harvesting vast information from international data repositories as well as regional and national statistical sources, this comprehensive reference offers data on a broad range of countries and issues such as labor force, employment, unemployment, underemployment, educational attainment of the workforce, and more for the years 1980 and 1990 and all available subsequent years. *KILM* is available in two formats—standard print version and CD-ROM. The CD-ROM's interactive design allows users to customize their searches by any combination of indicator, country, year, data inputs, and more and makes searching for relevant information quick and simple.

The World Guide 2003/2004

The World Guide is an up-to-date reference opus on the past and present of human societies, offering text, maps, graphics, images, music, and statistics on all the nations of the planet. It provides analysis of main international issues from the human rights, social, and environmental angles. Since 1997, it has been published on the Internet along with *The Guide Weekly*, a weekly update service.

The World Guide is divided into two large sections: The first provides analysis of major international problems and tendencies, and the second offers current information on 217 nations of the world, including some still fighting for their independence, and all the current members of the United Nations.

The first section pursues the problems of population, children, food, health, education, women, work, communications, refugees, indigenous people, debt, aid, trade, arms, transnationals, climate change, international organizations, and so on. Within each subject area, a "themes" subsection is renewed periodically according to how issues have evolved over the two-year period. The 1999/2000 issue carries an overview of the twentieth century on the basis of five thematic areas: the Earth and its peoples, society, science and technology, the economy, and international relations.

In the second section, the main text brings together the history of the country since the times of the first peoples, an element corrected and extended in each edition, and the most relevant events of the past two years. The profile and statistics, giving the latest available figures, complete the update.

The book contains more than 750,000 words, including text and statistical data; more than 250 maps of the countries, with their corresponding regional location; some 650 charts; and 10,000 references. *The World Guide* is researched and published in Montevideo, Uruguay, by the Third World Institute (ITeM) in conjunction with an extensive worldwide network of persons and civil organizations.

The new CD-ROM, which appears with the 1999/2000 edition, incorporates multimedia elements. The text, statistics, and maps of the printed version are accompanied by the flags, national anthems, and a selection of photographs of all the countries on the planet. This version also includes the Amnesty International and Social Watch annual reports. All the data, charts, photographs, maps, and texts can be printed or downloaded to your computer. The CD-ROM or book can be ordered at the Third World Institute Web site at www.guiadelmundo.org.uy or through www.amazon.com. Orders by post can be made to:

Books on Wings
973 Valencia Street
San Francisco, CA 94110
Phone: (415) 285-1145
Fax: (415) 285-3298

The Social Watch Annual Report 2004

Also from the Third World Institute, the Social Watch report keeps track every year of progress and regression in the path toward eradicating poverty and achieving gender equity, a promise made by governments at the UN in 1995 and reaffirmed in the year 2000 at the Millennium Summit. It is published annually in print and CD-ROM format. The electronic version is available to everyone free of charge. Find it at www.socwatch.org.

Exhibitions

The Changing Face of Slavery

This twenty-panel exhibition, available in both A1 (59.4cm × 84.1cm) and A3 (29.7cm × 42cm) sizes, takes the audience on a visual journey through history, from the time of the transatlantic slave trade to slavery in contemporary society. It introduces the idea of rights, both natural and human, and presents the Universal Declaration of Human Rights as the common goal for all peoples of all nations. Children's rights are an important component of the exhibition, which focuses on the worst forms of child labor, including the carpet industry in South Asia and child domestic work in West Africa. It also looks at the exploitation of migrant workers hidden away as domestic slaves in parts of London.

There is a strong emphasis on the both past and present campaigners, from people such as Olaudah Equiano and Mary Prince who fought against the transatlantic slave trade, to present day campaigners working to eradicate such contemporary forms of slavery as exploitative child labor and bonded labor.

The Changing Face of Slavery is ideal for display in school classrooms, libraries, halls, and museums. Available by contacting info@antislavery.org.

Human Traffic

Human Traffic is a sixteen-panel (51 × 41 cm) black and white exhibition, which documents the trafficking of children in Benin and Gabon, West Africa. It is a testament to the extraordinary bravery and courage of children who have been manipulated, deceived, beaten, and raped by the adults who enslave them. It reaches behind the headlines, looking at the people who are fighting for these children's rights and asks what can be done to bring an end to this horrific trade.

Ideal for galleries and creative art spaces, as well as schools and libraries, the exhibition is a powerful and visual educational tool. Available by contacting info@antislavery.org.

Pamphlets, Photographs and Digital Images, Posters, Press Kits, and Other Materials

The International Labor Organization is the part of the UN that is directly concerned with slavery, forced labor, child labor, and trafficking. It produces several kinds of materials in many different languages.

Pamphlets

The ILO provides leaflets that explain its work and address subjects like child labor and slavery. These can be ordered from the ILO or printed directly from its Web site at www.ilo.org. Leaflets include "The ILO: Its Origins and How It Works" and "What We Do: Social Justice and Child Labor."

Photographs and Digital Images

The ILO has photographers around the world documenting the problems of child labor, forced labor, and other work-related issues. Stored on its Web site are thousands of photographs that can be searched and reproduced. The ILO allows anyone to copy and use these photographs as long as the source is credited. A search on the words "forced labor," for example, will generate ten very good pictures.

Historical and contemporary images are now available from Anti-Slavery International in digital form. Where possible, Anti-Slavery will provide the images at a resolution and format to suit individual needs. These are normally sent as e-mail attachments. Fees to reproduction rights are decided on a sliding scale, starting from $65.00; a minimum search fee may be levied on complex image requests. Orders can be made to: info@ antislavery.org.

Posters

New posters focusing on major areas of ILO activities are now available. Employers' and workers' organizations, trade unions, and other organizations active in the promotion of fundamental human rights in the workplace may receive limited quantities (posters are printed in English, French, Spanish, German, Russian, and Arabic). One poster in the series is concerned with slavery. For information, call the Washington, DC, ILO office: (202) 653-7652.

Press Kits

When the International Labor Organization does a large-scale investigation or publishes an international report on a subject, it also provides press kits that break down the information into clear and easily used sections. A good example is the 1996 press kit *Stop! Child Labor,* which deals extensively with child slavery as well as child labor more generally, and consists of three sections: "Child Labor Today: Facts and Figures," "Child Labor: Action Needed at the National Level," and "International Action: Standards Need Reinforcing." The press kits are available in printed form or can be downloaded or printed directly from the ILO's Web site, www.ilo.org.

Other Materials

The director general of the ILO makes regular reports to the UN. These reports are also available from the ILO office or from its Web site. Researchers and officers of the ILO also regularly make speeches to conferences around the world. These speeches are usually available in English, French, and Spanish from the Web site (www.ilo.org) and are cataloged by subject matter.

In the United States, Canada, and Puerto Rico please contact:

International Labor Office
1828 L Street NW
Washington, DC 20036
Phone: (202) 653-7652
Fax: (202) 653-7687
E-mail: burrylee@ilo.org

Videotapes

Agenda 21
Length: 13 episodes of 26 minutes each
Cost: Call or e-mail for details
Date: 1994
Distributor: TVE
Prince Albert Road
London NW1 4RZ
United Kingdom
Phone: [44] (207) 586 5526
Fax: [44] (207) 586 4866
E-mail: tve-uk@tve.org.uk

As the successor to WTN's best-selling Earthfile series, *Agenda 21* offers viewers a popular treatment of topical environment and development issues. The series takes its name from Agenda 21, the agreement signed by over 180 world leaders at the historic Rio Earth Summit in 1992, setting out a blueprint for sustainable development in the twenty-first century. Using this as a framework to explore what sustainable development means in practice, *Agenda 21*'s television magazine format accommodates a mix of topics within each episode and includes episodes with subjects such as slave labor in Burma (Myanmar).

The Amahs of Hong Kong
Length: 11 minutes
Cost: Purchase $95, rental $25 (reduced rates for some groups)
Date: 1995
Distributor: Bullfrog Films
P.O. Box 149
Oley, PA 19547

Phone: (610) 779-8226
Fax: (610) 370-1978

This film explores the lives of Filipina maids, called *amahs,* in Hong Kong. Forced by mass poverty and continuing economic crisis to leave their families and homeland behind, the amahs send 70–85 percent of their earnings back to the Philippines. The women often suffer horrific abuse from their employers, and the sacrifices they make are enormous, but so are the potential rewards: money to educate their children and to improve their own living when retired.

Bonded Labor Campaign
Length: 8 minutes
Cost: $10.00
Date: 1999
Distributor: Anti-Slavery International
Thomas Clarkson House
The Stableyard, Broomgrove Road
London SW9 9TL
United Kingdom
Phone: [44] 020 7501 8920
Fax: [44] 020 7738 4110
E-mail: antislavery@antislavery.org

This video highlights the work of Anti-Slavery Award winners and human rights activists Vivek and Vidyullata Pandit and the plight of those held in debt bondage.

The Carpet Slaves—Stolen Children of India
Length: 47 minutes
Cost: call or e-mail for details
Date: 2001
Distributor: HBO (www.hbo.com)

This documentary follows SACCS, a coalition of human rights organizations and NGOs combating bonded labor and child servitude, as they attempt to find a group of children forced into bonded labor as carpet weavers. Central to the film is the journey made by the father of a boy among the group, whom he hasn't seen since the boy was kidnapped five years earlier. The two are reunited in a surprise raid on a carpet loom worked by child laborers. The charcoal workers in Brazil are also featured in the film.

The Changing Face of Slavery
Length: 30 minutes (plus 60-page booklet)
Cost: $30.00
Date: 1997
Distributor: Anti-Slavery International
Thomas Clarkson House
The Stableyard, Broomgrove Road
London SW9 9TL
United Kingdom
Phone: [44] 020 7501 8920
Fax: [44] 020 7738 4110
E-mail: antislavery@antislavery.org

This is a well-researched video and teaching pack that focuses on slavery past and present for the eleven- to fourteen-year-old age group. Part one concentrates on the transatlantic slave trade and encourages young people to look at why the trade began and its importance for the growth of wealth in Britain. Part two links the growth of that wealth to the Industrial Revolution and the employment of young children. Part three brings the historical roots and contemporary issues concerning child labor together.

The Charcoal People
Length: 70 minutes
Cost: $22.46 (DVD)
Date: 2001
Distributor: World Sales
Zazen Producoes
Rua Perl 251/403
Jardlm Botanico,
Rio de Janeiro, CEP 22460-100
Brazil
Phone: [55] (21) 512-9572
E-mail: zazen@vot.com.brn

This documentary examines the life of the charcoal workers in the rain forests of Brazil. Uneducated, illiterate, and desperately poor, whole families of men work in the hellish business of charcoal making. Interviewing generations of charcoal workers, this film portrays these workers in the midst of misery as beautiful and hopeful.

Children's News 1
Length: 26 minutes
Cost: Call or e-mail for details
Date: 1994
Distributor: TVE
Prince Albert Road
London NW1 4RZ
United Kingdom
Phone: [44] (207) 586 5526
Fax: [44] (207) 586 4866
E-mail: tve-uk@tve.org.uk

This program looks at how the world's governments are responding to UNICEF's call to ratify and implement the Convention on the Rights of the Child. Presented as a "video newspaper," it charts the progress of global ratification since 1990 and focuses on three countries that are taking solid steps to implement the convention: The first is Bolivia, where the government, supported by UNICEF, is undertaking a national drive against infant mortality (one of the highest rates in the world). This is followed by Norway, where the world's first "child ombudsman," or spokesperson for the rights of children, speaks in parliament on behalf of children and campaigns for their rights. The focus next shifts to Thailand, where the government and UNICEF are funding projects to provide young girls with skills and self-confidence through the Daughters Education Program to prevent the exploitation of children, particularly through sex tourism. The program ends with a call for global ratification and implementation of the Convention on the Rights of the Child.

Daughters of Africa: Senegal
Length: 15 minutes
Cost: Call or e-mail for details
Date: 1999
Distributor: TVE
Prince Albert Road
London NW1 4RZ
United Kingdom
Phone: [44] (207) 586 5526
Fax: [44] (207) 586 4866
E-mail: tve-uk@tve.org.uk

Three quarters of Senegal's children don't attend school. Of these, over 60 percent are girls. Child labor is common, and girls as young as nine work as illiterate, domestic servants in the capital city, Dakar. But with support from UNICEF, Tostan—a U.S. NGO—has developed an informal basic education program to provide literacy classes to rural women. Tostan also tries to persuade mothers to attend school with their daughters so they may acquire the basic knowledge that will help them improve their living conditions, and abandon traditional harmful practices like female genital mutilation.

Dying to Leave
Length: 2 × 54 minutes
Date: 2003
Distributor: Film Finance Corporation of
Australia and Thirteen/WNET
New York
Contact: J. Braun
E-mail: braun@thirteen.org
Phone: (212) 560-2715

Originally aired on PBS as part of the Wide Angle series, this two-part program examines the widespread modern phenomenon of illegal migration of persons. Detailing the hardships braved by the desperate number of people escaping economic destitution in their home countries, the video traces the journey made in harrowing means to the goal and employment, often prostitution, slavery, sweatshop labor, or agricultural work. Part One examines the smuggling of persons, while Part Two explores human trafficking.

The Face of Decent Work
Length: 18 minutes
Cost: $12.95
Date: 1996
Distributor: International Labor Organization
In the United States, Canada, and Puerto Rico contact:
Ms. Karen A. Lee
International Labor Office
1828 L Street NW
Washington, DC 20036
Phone: (202) 653-7652

Fax: (202) 653-7687
E-mail: burrylee@ilo.org
Web site: www.ilo.org

This is a riveting exposé of the world's most deadly professions and workplace hazards. By spotlighting mining, agricultural, factory work, and other professions, the video shows how primitive forms of labor have remained unchanged in their methods for nearly a thousand years. It shows the victims of the pressure to produce in an increasingly competitive and global economy—from the world's deepest mine in India, where men still extract coal by hand, to the charcoal fields of Brazil, where families are enslaved in a hellish landscape of smoldering ovens; to the chemical factories of Africa, where innocent children are scarred for life by the fallout of industrial disaster. In their own words and voices, the men, women, and children who endure the most intolerable working conditions on earth tell their stories. Available in English, French, and Spanish.

Going Home Guinea
Length: 31 minutes
Cost: Purchase $150, rental $45 (reduced rates
    for some groups)
Date: 1999
Distributor: Bullfrog Films
P.O. Box 149
Oley, PA 19547
Phone: (610) 779-8226
Fax: (610) 370-1978

Mohammed is just ten years old. For most of 1997, he was forced to act as a young fighter with rebel forces in the jungles of Sierra Leone. His duties included carrying heavy equipment, acting as a personal servant to other soldiers, and torturing and disciplining any of the other child soldiers who stepped out of line. Eventually he escaped to Guinea, where he was one of thousands lining up to register at the Gueckedou refugee camp. In 1997, Guinea was host to an estimated 430,000 refugees: 190,000 Sierra Leoneans and 240,000 Liberians who had escaped the eight-year civil war there. This film evaluates the success of the Guinean government and the UN High Commission for Refugees (UNHCR) in protecting the rights pledged in this huge African refugee population under the OAU Convention.

Haiti's Cinderellas: "They Call Me Dog"
Length: 24 minutes
Cost: Call or e-mail for details
Date: 1994
Distributor: TVE
Prince Albert Road
London NW1 4RZ
United Kingdom
Phone: [44] (207) 586 5526
Fax: [44] (207) 586 4866
E-mail: tve-uk@tve.org.uk

This Danish coproduction focuses on Haiti's population of children from age five to fifteen—three quarters of them girls—who work as domestics in middle-class homes. Forced into unpaid servitude, the majority cannot read or write. Exploring UNICEF's work with such forgotten children, the film shows how—in spite of their bondage—the children find ways to change their lives. Available in English, Spanish, and French.

Holidays for Us
Length: 26 minutes
Cost: Call or e-mail for details
Date: 1997
Distributor: TVE
Prince Albert Road
London NW1 4RZ
United Kingdom
Phone: [44] (207) 586 5526
Fax: [44] (207) 586 4866
E-mail: tve-uk@tve.org.uk

Statistics don't account for the millions of children who live invisible lives as unregistered laborers—their special needs unseen and unmet. But in Bangladesh, Haiti, and India new organizations are investigating their problems, as shown in this video.

Human Traffic
Length: 11.5 minutes
Cost: £6 (VHS)
Date: 2002
Distributor: Anti-Slavery International
Thomas Clarkson House

The Stableyard, Broomgrove Road
London SW9 9TL
United Kingdom
Phone: [44] 020 7501 8922
Fax: [44] 020 7738 4110
E-mail: antislavery@antislavery.org

A video useful for organizational talks and workshops, this short film documents prostitution, child trafficking, and forced labor in West Africa and Europe. Interviews with women trafficked into prostitution in Italy and England, a child slave forced to hawk water on the streets of Ghana, and activists against these injustices all offer a personal view of modern slavery.

I Am a Child
Length: 52 minutes
Cost: $40.50
Date: 1996
Distributor: International Labor Organization
In the United States, Canada, and Puerto Rico contact:
Ms. Karen A. Lee
International Labor Office
1828 L Street NW
Washington, DC 20036
Phone: (202) 653-7652
Fax: (202) 653-7687
E-mail: burrylee@ilo.org
Web site: www.ilo.org

Neither a catalog of horrors nor a fairy tale, *I Am a Child* is a fable of despair and hope. Through compelling images and moving personal stories, the viewer learns about children working in the fields and plantations of Kenya and the streets and workshops of Brazil. They are the innocent victims of poverty and exploitation. To rescue them, to return their childhood to them, is the moral imperative for every humane society. This video is intended as a contribution to that cause. Available in English, French, German, Portuguese, and Spanish.

Inside Burma, Land of Fear
Length: 51 minutes (2 parts for classrooms: 33 min. and 17 min.)
Cost: Purchase $250, rental $85 (reduced rates for some groups)
Date: 1997

Distributor: Bullfrog Films
P.O. Box 149
Oley, PA 19547
Phone: (610) 779-8226
Fax: (610) 370-1978

Inside Burma exposes the history and brutality of one of the world's most repressive regimes. Award-winning filmmakers John Pilger and David Munro go undercover to expose how the former British colony is ruled by a harsh, bloody, and uncompromising military regime. More than a million people have been forced from their homes and untold thousands killed, tortured, and subjected to slavery.

Nobel Peace Prize–winner Aung San Suu Kyi, daughter of the assassinated independence leader Aung San, spent six years under house arrest. In 1990, her party, the National League for Democracy, won 82 percent of the parliamentary seats. The generals, shocked by an election result they never expected, threw two hundred of the newly elected MPs into prison. Suu Kyi's party has never been allowed to take elected office. She warns in the video that far from liberalizing life in Burma, foreign investment and tourism can further entrench the military regime.

It Takes a Child: Craig Kielburger's Story—
A Journey into Child Labor
Length: 56 minutes (2 parts for classrooms, 28 min. each)
Cost: Purchase $250, rental $85 (reduced rates for some groups)
Date: 1998
Distributor: Bullfrog Films
P.O. Box 149
Oley, PA 19547
Phone: (610) 779-8226
Fax: (610) 370-1978

This is the video story of Craig Kielburger (see Chapter 5), who was twelve years old when child labor activist Iqbal Masih was killed in Pakistan. Shortly after, a seven-week trip to South Asia turned him into a passionate, articulate, and effective advocate on behalf of child laborers everywhere. He started a child-run organization called Free the Children, which now has 10,000 members worldwide. It directs lobbying and petition efforts at governments and big business, and has raised over $150,000 to buy children out of bondage and create a school for them, while also raising world awareness.

Jessica: A Saudi Slave
Length: 41 minutes
Cost: Call or e-mail for details
Date: 1996
Distributor: TVE
Prince Albert Road
London NW1 4RZ
United Kingdom
Phone: [44] (207) 586 5526
Fax: [44] (207) 586 4866
E-mail: tve-uk@tve.org.uk

"Saudi nationals believe that if they have hired a Filipino worker, they have bought the whole life of that worker," comments Mustafa, responsible for protecting the rights of Filipino "guest" workers in Saudi Arabia. Jessica Sumanga was just one of 2,000 Filipinos who leave their country every day to work abroad. Her youngest daughter was in need of a heart operation, and so in desperation for money, Jessica left her family two years ago to work in Saudi Arabia. Bruno Sorrentino's horrifying film exposes Jessica's traumatic plight as she runs away from her first employer, who has not only failed to pay her and abused her but has also taken her passport. For the next two years, Jessica is passed from household to household, working as an unpaid maid—she is fundamentally a modern slave. Eventually, she has to turn to illegal means to escape her desperate situation. Winner, Best Television Feature Documentary, Asian TV Film Media Academy Awards (1996); Justice Award, One World Broadcasting Trust Awards (1996, UK); and Bronze Plaque, Columbus International Film Festival.

Life on the Line
Length: 38 minutes
Cost: Call or e-mail for details
Date: 1995
Distributor: TVE
Prince Albert Road
London NW1 4RZ
United Kingdom

Phone: [44] (207) 586 5526
Fax: [44] (207) 586 4866
E-mail: tve-uk@tve.org.uk

In 1988, troops from SLORC—the Burmese military regime's no-
torious State Law and Order Restoration Council—brutally suppressed student demonstrations for democracy in Rangoon (Yan-
gon). In protest, Western governments cut off all aid. Since then,
Burma's military ruler, General Ne Win, has been courting the
West again, seeking finance for new infrastructure and tourist development in the country. Director Damien Lewis and anthropol-
ogist Tom Sheahan spent eight months in Burma (Myanmar) investigating how this is affecting ordinary Burmese citizens.
Traveling through the countryside, they filmed evidence that Ne
Win's government has been forcibly clearing whole villages, rak-
ing the houses with machine guns and rounding up the inhabitants to work—in chain-gangs—on clearing jungle and building
roads for a new pipeline carrying gas from the coast to Rangoon.

Lilya 4-Ever
Length: 109 minutes
Cost: Call or e-mail for details
Date: 2002
Distributor: Memfis Films
33 Charlotte St.
Fifth Floor
London W111R
Phone: [44] (020) 7153 4421
Fax: [44] (020) 7153 4446
Web site: www.metrodomegroup.com

Directed by Swedish filmmaker Lukas Moodysson, *Lilya 4-Ever* is a
fictional representation of the current trend of trafficking Eastern
Europan women to Western Europe to be prostituted as sex slaves.
Lilya is a teenager in a former Soviet country dreaming of life in
America when her mother abandons her, and her aunt, friends,
and school system fail her in the same short span of time. Eventually taken by a boyfriend to Sweden, Lilya finds herself trafficked
and forced to work as a prostitute for her pimp/boyfriend where
her youth makes her particularly attractive to the older Western
men who pay for her. Unable to communicate and without documentation, she has little chance of escape. This film exposes the
desperate circumstances that lead to human trafficking.

Modern Slavery
Length: 10 minutes
Cost: $15
Date: 2001
Distributor: Free the Slaves
1012 14th St. NW
Washington, DC 20005
Phone: (202) 638-1865
E-mail: info@freetheslaves.net
Web site: www.freetheslaves.net

This very short film is an excellent introduction to contemporary slavery. It uses footage from other sources and film shot in India by Free the Slaves. It examines slavery in the United States, India, West Africa, Brazil, and the United Kingdom. The economic underpinning and key actions that governments can take are examined. It is not available for broadcast, but may be used in any other way.

Our News, Our Views
Length: 30 minutes
Cost: $30.00
Date: 1999
Distributor: Anti-Slavery International
Thomas Clarkson House
The Stableyard, Broomgrove Road
London SW9 9TL
United Kingdom
Phone: [44] 020 7501 8920
Fax: [44] 020 7738 4110
E-mail: antislavery@antislavery.org

This video pack examines children's rights, child labor, and the media, and is comprised of eight news reports written, produced, and presented by groups of young people. Designed for fourteen- to eighteen-year-olds, the activities encourage individuals to develop and express their own ideas.

Out of Sight, Out of Mind
Length: 15 minutes
Cost: $15.00
Date: 1999
Distributor: Anti-Slavery International

Thomas Clarkson House
The Stableyard, Broomgrove Road
London SW9 9TL
United Kingdom
Phone: [44] 020 7501 8920
Fax: [44] 020 7738 4110
E-mail: antislavery@antislavery.org

An estimated one million girls under age eighteen work as maids in the Philippines for little or no pay and unlimited hours. Produced with local NGO Visayan Forum, this campaign video was given extensive airing on Philippine television and was also shown in the U.S. Congress. This exposure added to Visayan Forum's work on this issue and has resulted in a new law being proposed to protect child domestic workers.

The Price of Progress
Length: 54 minutes
Cost: Purchase $250, rental $75 (reduced rates for some groups)
Date: 1989
Distributor: Bullfrog Films
P.O. Box 149
Oley, PA 19547
Phone: (610) 779-8226
Fax: (610) 370-1978

This classic film investigates three huge resettlement schemes in India, Indonesia, and Brazil—all sponsored by the World Bank, the world's largest lending institution. Some $30 billion in grants and loans are provided each year by development banks and other institutions to developing countries, frequently for mega projects that involve uprooting indigenous peoples. Using the World Bank's own documents, the film analyzes the social, environmental, and economic costs of some of the bank's lending policies. As one person says, "Next to killing them, the worst thing you can do to a people is to force them to move."

Rights and Wrongs
Length: 3 episodes of 26 minutes each
Cost: Call or e-mail for details
Date: 1995
Distributor: TVE
Prince Albert Road

London NW1 4RZ
United Kingdom
Phone: [44] (207) 586 5526
Fax: [44] (207) 586 4866
E-mail: tve-uk@tve.org.uk

These episodes from the British series *Rights and Wrongs* concern issues of new slavery: "Child Labor" reports from Pakistan and elsewhere on the millions of child workers systematically abused, despite international treaties drawn up to protect their rights; "Human Rights in Asia" marks the sixth anniversary of Tiananmen Square and the twentieth anniversary of the end of the Vietnam War by reviving the debate about human rights in Asia; and "Human Rights Progress in South Africa" examines that country's difficult journey toward its objectives in the year following democratic elections.

Rights, Camera, Action
Length: 30 minutes with booklet
Cost: $30.00
Date: 1999
Distributor: Anti-Slavery International
Thomas Clarkson House
The Stableyard, Broomgrove Road
London SW9 9TL
United Kingdom
Phone: [44] 020 7501 8920
Fax: [44] 020 7738 4110
E-mail: antislavery@antislavery.org

A video and booklet education pack plus evaluation form examining the sensitive subject of the commercial exploitation of children for use with fourteen- to eighteen-year-olds. It covers childhood, the UN Convention of the Rights on the Child, selling children, child prostitution and pornography, and trafficking. It also aims to develop awareness of and take action against this growing global problem, also exploring techniques and issues concerning video production.

Slavery: A Global Investigation
Length: 78 minutes
Cost: $20.00
Date: 2000

Distributor: Free the Slaves
1012 14th St. NW, Suite 600
Washington, DC 20005
Phone: (202) 638-1865
E-mail: info@freetheslaves.net
Web site: www.freetheslaves.net

This is the first major film made about new slavery. It was produced by Home Box Office and the British Network Channel 4, and made by the award-winning filmmakers Brian Woods and Kate Blewitt. Filmed in India, Brazil, West Africa, London, and Washington, DC, it shows real slavery and explains how it fits into the global economy. The filmmakers actually buy slaves in Africa and help to free child slaves in India. This is the most important film made about contemporary slavery.

A Sporting Chance
Length: 9 minutes
Cost: $20.00
Date: 1997
Distributor: Christian Aid (UK)
35 Lower Marsh Waterloo
London SE1 7RT
United Kingdom
Phone: [44] (207) 620 4444
Fax: [44] (207) 620 0719
Web site: http://www.stolenchildhoods.org/webfs.html

About 55 million children work in all kinds of trades in India from sewing sports shoes to serving as domestic servants. Some of these children work long hours making sporting goods that they will never be able to use. The video looks at the work these children do and how local organizations are seeking to improve their lives.

Sudan—The Secret Story
Length: 26 minutes
Cost: Call or e-mail for details
Date: 1998
Distributor: TVE
Prince Albert Road
London NW1 4RZ
United Kingdom

Phone: [44] (207) 586 5526
Fax: [44] (207) 586 4866
E-mail: tve-uk@tve.org.uk

Filmmaker Damien Lewis traveled secretly to an area placed off-limits to UN aid workers to uncover evidence of a deliberate campaign of genocide by the Sudan regime. His film shows that the roots of the problem are manmade and lie in a deliberate policy by the government in the north to clear out the black non-Islamic peoples and impose an Islamic Arabic-speaking state in order to gain control of the south's oil fields.

Tomorrow We Will Finish
Length: 26 minutes
Cost: Call or e-mail for details
Date: 1995
Distributor: TVE
Prince Albert Road
London NW1 4RZ
United Kingdom
Phone: [44] (207) 586 5526
Fax: [44] (207) 586 4866
E-mail: tve-uk@tve.org.uk

Over 150,000 girls between the ages of five and sixteen work in Nepal's 2,000 carpet factories. The stories portrayed in this program are based on cases complied by Child Workers in Nepal, a children's labor organization. They include the history of three girls, Suri, Tama, and Maya, forced by poverty to work in the city's carpet factories for sixteen hours a day and denied their rights as children.

Ujeli: A Child Bride in Nepal
Length: 60 minutes
Cost: Call or e-mail for details
Date: 1992
Distributor: TVE
Prince Albert Road
London NW1 4RZ
United Kingdom
Phone: [44] (207) 586 5526
Fax: [44] (207) 586 4866
E-mail: tve-uk@tve.org.uk

Filmed on location in the Rasuwa district of Nepal, this is the story of ten-year-old Ujeli. Against the advice of her teacher and doctor, who warn of the dangers of early child bearing, Ujeli's parents arrange for her to be married. Excluded from school and forced to work from dusk to dawn, Ujeli rapidly assumes the responsibilities of an adult woman, including motherhood. This tragic tale unfolds in a land where an estimated 40 percent of women get married before they reach age fourteen. As a result, Nepal's maternal mortality rate of 850 per 100,000 live births is among the highest in the world. In Nepali with English subtitles.

Under the Carpet—Bihar's Lost Boys
Length: 15 minutes
Cost: $20.00
Date: 1994
Distributor: Christian Aid (UK)
35 Lower Marsh Waterloo
London SE1 7RT
United Kingdom
Phone: [44] (207) 620 4444
Fax: [44] (207) 620 0719

This documentary takes a look at child labor in the Indian carpet industry and at international campaigning efforts against child labor. For students aged sixteen and older.

Web Sites

There are a few Web sites that exist independently of any other publications or organizations, some of which are the work of students. The ones listed here are excellent introductions to child labor and slave labor.

Free the Slaves
www.freetheslaves.net

This is your first stop for information about modern slavery, current action against slavery around the world, and lots of resources on new slavery. There are fact sheets, the voices and stories of current slaves and ex-slaves, and pictures of slaves and freed slaves from around the world. In the resources section is a complete teaching pack for use with junior high and high school students. A complete linked site (www.activism.freetheslaves.net) is devoted to students and others who want to *do* something about modern slavery. Here you find all the materials needed to launch a campaign against modern slavery. Background documents and links are given in the Resources section. In the Online Store you can buy books and the Emmy Award–winning video *Slavery: A Global Investigation*, as well as all-cotton Free the Slaves t-shirts.

Global March against Child Labor
www.globalmarch.org

The Global March movement began when thousands of people marched together to jointly put forth the message against child labor. The march, which started on January 17, 1998, touched every corner of the globe, built immense awareness, and led to a high level of participation from the masses. This march finally culminated at the ILO Conference in Geneva. The voices of the marchers were heard and reflected in the draft of the ILO Convention against the Worst Forms of Child Labor. The following year, the Convention was unanimously adopted at the ILO Conference in Geneva. The site keeps you up to date with anti-child-labor action around the world.

ILO U.—The Child Labor Web site for High School and College Students
http://www.us.ilo.org/ilokidsnew/ILOU/ilou.html

Sponsored by the Washington, DC, a branch of the International Labor Organization of the United Nations. At this site you can take a crash course in child labor, find out how students can make an impact in the fight against child labor, and join the ILO Student Leader Network to get alerts and updates via e-mail.

Immaculata High School (Somerville, New Jersey) Child Slave Labor News
www.geocities.com/Athens/Styx/7487

The students and faculty of Immaculata High School are very concerned about the problem of child slave labor. Each year, the senior U.S. History II Honors class, taught by Miss Joann Fantina, publishes numerous newsletters covering many aspects of child slave labor. A new group of students takes over the project each year as the previous class graduates. It is a common interest among the students and is continued enthusiastically year after year.

National Underground Railroad Museum Freedom Center
www.freedomcenter.org

The National Underground Railroad Museum Freedom Center opened in Cincinnati, Ohio, in September 2004. This remarkable museum chronicles the history of the Underground Railroad and the fight for freedom of slaves in America before 1865. The museum covers the historical side of the story brilliantly but also hosts several sections on contemporary slavery and on the people, and especially the young people, who are fighting for freedom today. The FreedomStations on the Web site are an interactive learning area where you can do in-depth research on a very large database of photos and documents. This is a great Web site for teachers and students.

Office to Monitor and Combat Trafficking in Persons—U.S. State Department
www.state.gov/g/tip

The U.S. government's main antislavery agency is the Office to Monitor and Combat Trafficking in Persons. Their Web site is a lively introduction to antitrafficking work around the world. The office publishes an annual report on global human trafficking, listing the situation in almost every country. Copies may be downloaded from the site.

Rugmark
www.rugmark.org

Rugmark is a global organization dedicated to taking child and child slave labor out of carpet making and to offering educational opportunities to children in India, Nepal, and Pakistan. Rugmark takes child labor out of carpet making by loom and factory monitoring, as well as consumer labeling. It provides education by running schools for former child workers. Their Web site holds a wealth of information on child labor and the rehabilitation of child workers. It also explains how a certification process works—how carpets with the Rugmark label can be sold in the knowledge that they are free of child and slave labor. You can also find shops that sell Rugmark rugs on this site.

Glossary

Chattel labor   The traditional form of slavery when one person totally owns another.

Child labor   Not all child labor is banned, but sometimes parents pass their child on to another person whether or not money is exchanged, and that person gains control of the child and the child's labor. Children are extremely vulnerable to physical abuse—beatings and sexual—excessively long hours and/or being made to work in dangerous or cramped conditions. Girl domestic servants are especially vulnerable to sexual abuse. Some children are enslaved in debt bondage (see **debt bondage**) where a parent or relative pawns the child, sometimes at a very young age, in return for loans that they can never repay.

Some employers argue they need the "nimble fingers" of children. But they really mean a docile and controllable labor force. A good example would be a ten-year-old boy working fourteen-hour days at a carpet loom. At night he sleeps under the loom with his parents hundreds of miles away in his home village. He may be chained, especially if he has tried to escape.

Convention or covenant   Agreements in international law between sovereign states. A convention is an agreement between states, but one that is less formal than a treaty.

Debt bondage (also called bonded labor)   When an individual works for another indefinitely to pay off a debt. A person becomes a bonded laborer when their labor is demanded as a means of repayment for a loan. The person is then tricked or trapped into working for very little or no pay, often for seven days a week. The value of their work is greater than the original sum of money borrowed. There are in fact two distinct forms of

251

debt bondage, both meeting this criterion but in different ways. In many cases of debt bondage, the labor power (and indeed the very life of the debtor) becomes collateral for the debt. This establishes the trap of bondage since all the labor power of the debtor is the collateral property of the lender until the debt is repaid—the debtor is unable to ever earn enough to repay the debt by their own labor. This arrangement is a hallmark of the debt bondage of the Indian subcontinent. In other areas, the work of the debtor may ostensibly be applied to the debt, but through false accounting or extortionate interest, repayment remains forever out of reach. In the first form, the very nature of the agreement that transforms labor power into collateral practically disqualifies the debtor from ever repaying their debt. In the second form, it is a violation of the agreement, when "the value of those services as reasonably assessed is not applied towards the liquidation of the debt," that traps the debtor (United Nations Supplementary Convention on the Abolition of Slavery, the Slave Trade, and Institutions and Practices Similar to Slavery, 1957). Debt bondage can be inherited from one generation to another, maintaining members of a family in permanent bondage in return for an old loan, the details of which have long been forgotten. In some cases, employers who are owed money sell the debt to a new employer.

Forced labor   Any work or service that a person does not do voluntarily and which is only done because of a threatened punishment or penalty. Forced labor is often a feature of war. There are exceptional circumstances when it is seen as acceptable under international law. A country may make convicted prisoners perform forced labor or compulsory military service. In countries affected by war or civil conflict, such as Burma, those enslaved are often the weak or defenseless such as refugees, members of ethnic minorities, women, or children.

Globalization   That process of social change that is making the world "smaller." Features of globalization are the way that time and distance are no longer seen as barriers to communication, and the way that people all over the world are now exposed to the same products, media, and ideas. One result of globalization is that national governments are less able to control the flow of money, products, information, and people across their borders.

Indigenous (people)   Native or original to an area as in "indigenous culture." Often used to refer to the inhabitants of a territory prior to invasion or colonization as well as to their descendants. Indigenous peoples, such as the native India tribes of the Amazon, are particularly vulnerable to slavery.

Migrant labor   Some domestic workers are subjected to slavery, particularly children and immigrants who work and live in the same house or premises as their employer and are paid little or nothing for their work, often on grounds that they receive food and lodging. They are cut off from families, local society, and possible protection. Cases continue to be uncovered in countries like the United States, where servants are brought in from abroad, either legally or illegally, and then treated as slaves.

Nongovernmental organization (NGO)   NGOs are independent organizations that are not part of any state or interstate agency. They include charities, nonprofit organizations, voluntary groups, professional associations, trades unions, and human rights bodies. NGOs do a great deal of the research and work liberating and rehabilitating slaves around the world.

Serfdom   This is when agricultural workers cannot leave the place where they live and work—often very similar to debt bondage in practice. Where a tenant is bound to live and labor on land belonging to another person and provide them with a service in return, whether for reward or not and is not free to change their status. In many countries, individuals, families, or entire social groups have traditionally been obliged to work for others for little or no reward. This status usually has no basis in law, but the practice persists and is often enforced with violence.

Servile marriage   This is where a young girl or woman has no right to refuse being entered into a marriage. In servile marriage, a young woman is often given in exchange for money or other payment, and she can sometimes be inherited by another person if her husband dies, or even sold to someone else. A typical case is when a twelve-year-old girl is told her family has arranged a marriage with a sixty-year-old man. She has no opportunity to exercise her right to refuse and is unaware that she can do so. "Servile marriage" is listed in the United Nation's conventions as "a practice similar to slavery."

Slave The word "slave" comes from the word *Slav* (as in Slavic peoples), arriving in Middle English from Old French *esclave* and medieval Latin *sclavus, sclava*, meaning "Slavonic" (captive). It descends from Roman times when German tribes supplied the slave markets of the Roman Empire with captured Slavs.

Slavery In the 1956 Supplementary Convention on the Abolition of Slavery, the United Nations defines "slavery" as:

> (a) *Slavery* means, as defined in the Slavery Convention of 1926, the status or condition of a person over whom any or all of the powers attaching to the right of ownership are exercised, and 'slave' means a person in such condition or status:
>
> (b) A *person of servile status* means a person in the condition or status resulting from any of the institutions or practices mentioned in article 1 of this Convention;
>
> (c) *Slave trade* means and includes all acts involved in the capture, acquisition or disposal of a person with intent to reduce him to slavery; all acts involved in the acquisition of a slave with a view to selling or exchanging him; all acts of disposal by sale or exchange of a person acquired with a view to being sold or exchanged; and, in general, every act of trade or transport in slaves by whatever means of conveyance.

And added into that definition are "Institutions and Practices Similar to Slavery" which are:

> (a) *Debt bondage*, or the status or condition arising from a pledge by a debtor of his personal services or of those of a person under his control as security for a debt, if the value of those services as reasonably assessed is not applied towards the liquidation of the debt or the length and nature of those services are not respectively limited and defined
>
> (b) *Serfdom*, or the condition or status of a tenant who is by law, custom or agreement bound to live and labour on land belonging to another person and to render some determinate service to such other person, whether for reward or not, and is not free to change his status
>
> (c) Any institution or practice whereby:

(i) A woman, without the right to refuse, is promised or given in marriage on payment of a consideration in money or in kind to her parents, guardian, family or any other person or group

(ii) The husband of a woman, his family, or his clan, has the right to transfer her to another person for value received or otherwise

(iii) A woman on the death of her husband is liable to be inherited by another person

(d) Any institution or practice whereby a child or young person under the age of eighteen years, is delivered by either or both of his natural parents or by his guardian to another person, whether for reward or not, with a view to the exploitation of the child or young person or of his labor.

However, these definitions do not necessarily serve to define slavery across history. For the purposes of this book, slavery is defined as a social and economic relationship in which a person is controlled through violence or its threat, paid nothing, and economically exploited.

Social clause   *Social clause* is a general term which refers to introducing social standards into trade agreements which have usually been driven by economic considerations only. For example, the North American Free Trade Agreement (NAFTA) now has a social clause making international trade agreements conditional on respect for a number of internationally recognized labor standards. The question of a social clause is one of the areas of controversy in the World Trade Organization. Many people believe that a "social clause" is an important way to prevent goods made with slave labor from being imported to countries like the United States. On the other hand, many developing countries resist a "social clause" because they feel it will only work to keep their imports from being purchased abroad.

State(s) party   In the United Nations Conventions or in international law a *state party* is a country whose government has signed up to a treaty or agreement and is legally bound to follow its provisions.

Untouchables/outcasts   A term used to describe all those in Hindu society, primarily in India, who do not belong to the four major Hindu castes. Untouchables are now designated in India as "scheduled castes." Discrimination against these castes is pervasive in India and Nepal. In Nepal, there are even segregated water fountains in public places for "untouchables." This discrimination is linked to slavery in that most people enslaved in South Asia come from these castes.

Index

About the Author

Kevin Bales is president of Free the Slaves, the U.S. sister organization of Anti-Slavery International (the world's oldest human rights organization), and Professor of Sociology at Roehampton University in London, as well as serving on the board of directors of the International Cocoa Initiative. His book *Disposable People: New Slavery in the Global Economy*, published in 1999, was nominated for the Pulitzer Prize and has now been published in eleven languages. Archbishop Desmond Tutu called it "a well researched, scholarly and deeply disturbing expose of modern slavery." A revised edition was published in 2005. His work won the Premio Viareggio for services to humanity in 2000, while the documentary based on his work won the Peabody Award for 2000 and two Emmy Awards in 2002. He was awarded the Laura Smith Davenport Human Rights Award in 2005; the Judith Sargeant Murray Award for Human Rights in 2004; and the Human Rights Award of the University of Alberta in 2003. He is a Trustee of Anti-Slavery International and was a consultant to the United Nations Global Program on Trafficking of Human Beings. Bales has been invited to advise the U.S., British, Irish, Norwegian, Japanese and Nepali governments, as well as the governments of the Economic Community of West African States, on the formulation of policy on slavery and human trafficking. He recently edited the "Anti-Human Trafficking Toolkit" for the United Nations and published, with the Human Rights Center at the University of California–Berkeley, a report on forced labor in the United States. He is working with the chocolate industry to remove child and slave labor from its product chain and writing on contemporary slavery (see, for example, his feature article in the April 2002 *Scientific American*). His new book *Understanding Global Slavery* will be published in September 2005. He gained his PhD at the London School of Economics.